THE FACTSHEET FIVE ZINE READER

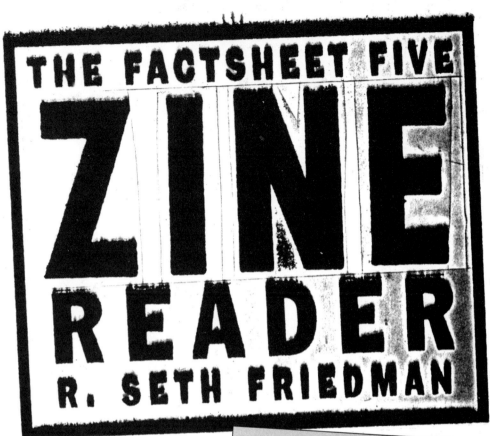

THE FACTSHEET FIVE
ZINE
READER
R. SETH FRIEDMAN

The Best Writing from
the Underground World of
Zines

Three Rivers Press
New York

This book is dedicated to Miriam; without her hard work and masterful editing this book would never have come into being. Without her infinite patience and support *Factsheet Five* would certainly not exist today, either.

I also dedicate this book to all zine publishers, past and present, whose fine work is finally being recognized by the rest of the world.

ABOUT FACTSHEET FIVE

This book is based entirely on zines that have been reviewed in *Factsheet Five* magazines over the past five years. Since 1982 *Factsheet Five* has been documenting the ever-expanding universe of zines. If you enjoy what you read here, you'll probably enjoy reading *Factsheet Five,* too.

Each huge 152-page issue of *Factsheet Five* is packed with reviews of more than 2,000 independent and unusual publications. Every issue catalogs and reviews an abundance of zines—complete with price, critical reviews, and ordering information. Additionally, it includes informative articles on zine culture and tips for budding zine publishers.

Copies are available at better bookstores and directly from the publisher. Send $5 for a sample copy or $20 for a six-issue subscription to: Factsheet Five, P.O. Box 170099, San Francisco, CA 94117.

If you publish a zine and would like to have it considered for review, just send it our way. Please include a letter stating the sample price, the ordering address, if you accept trades for your zine, your email address, and phone number. If you have any other questions, you can always reach us by email at: seth@factsheet5.com or look for our Web page at http://www.factsheet5.com

Copyright © 1997 by R. Seth Friedman

All rights reserved. No part of this book may be reproduced or transmitted in any form or by any means, electronic or mechanical, including photocopying, recording, or by any information storage and retrieval system, without permission in writing from the publisher.

Published by Three Rivers Press, a division of Crown Publishers, Inc., 201 East 50th Street, New York, New York 10022. Member of the Crown Publishing Group.

Random House, Inc., New York, Toronto, London, Sydney, Auckland
http://www.randomhouse.com/

THREE RIVERS PRESS and colophon are trademarks of Crown Publishers, Inc.

Printed in the United States of America

Design by Blond *on* Pond

Library of Congress Cataloging-in-Publication Data
The Factsheet Five zine reader: dispatches from the edge of the zine revolution / [collected] by R. Seth Friedman. — 1st pbk. ed.
    Includes bibliographical references.
      1. American literature—20th century.   2. Popular literature—United States.   3. Underground press publications.
    4. Fanzines. I. Friedman, R. Seth.
    PS536.2.F33   1997
    810.8'0054—dc21
                                                  96-51790
                                                  CIP

JAN 2 8 1998

ISBN 0-609-80001-9

10 9 8 7 6 5 4 3 2 1

First Edition

contents

Work 143

Food 159

Fringe 171

intro-duction

I've read probably fifty thousand zines in the last ten years.

I discovered music fanzines back in the '70s, and just never grew out of them. Five years ago, I restarted *Factsheet Five* magazine, which catalogs and reviews thousands of zines in each issue. Since then, I've become even more fascinated by the strange world of zines and zine makers. It's a world inhabited by the widest assortment of unusual characters and unique stories.

Zines (short for fanzines) contain writing that's unlike anything else in the mainstream: more opinionated than newspaper editorials, more personal than magazine articles, more topical than books. In this volume I've collected the most exciting articles and excerpts that I've come across in zines.

Although zines can be anything from darkly photocopied, handwritten poetry to slickly printed, full-color music magazines, what unites all zine publishers is their passion for communication. Zine makers are driven to publish their ideas purely for the sake of communicating, generally with complete disregard for money, let alone profit.

Anyone can publish a zine—all it takes is the desire to write and publish ideas. Although many zines come from people in their twenties, there are zines from people of almost every age and background. Most people publish zines just for the joy of it, but occasionally professional writers start up zines as an outlet for their more creative impulses. Publishing zines allows these talented writers to print articles that their daytime editors would have a fit over. Zines aren't restricted to "objective" news reporting or informative magazine articles; they give writers the freedom to write from a more opinionated perspective.

This quirky personal writing is what draws people to zines. Open up one zine and you'll find someone waxing eloquent about his collection of beer-bottle openers; while in another someone will be writing about her abusive husband and recent divorce; and in a third you might find a hateful rant about Howard Stern and his legions of fans.

Until quite recently, zines were an exclusively underground phenomenon, bartered and traded (generally by mail) through a network of zine aficionados who operated beneath the mainstream's radar. But in the past few years, publications from

Details to the *New York Times* have attempted to document the zine phenomenon, spurring interest in a whole new wave of both zine readers and zine makers.

Some zine publishers have a passion for computer desktop publishing and design. Their publications may easily blend in with other magazines on the newsstand. Other publishers experiment with type and images to make their zine boldly stand out from the crowd. At your local Tower Records or independent bookstore, you'll probably discover several of the slicker zines for sale. Through the power of independent magazine distributors, these slick-looking zines have been able to reach a national audience. While nowhere near as ubiquitous as *Rolling Stone,* these independent, music-oriented publications are the success stories in the zine world.

However, these publications are more the exception than the rule. More commonly, a zine publisher struggles with an outdated computer system (or an old typewriter or just pen and paper), creating a publication in which readability often takes a backseat to passion. The most typical format for zines is a small, digest-sized booklet, created by folding several sheets of standard-size writing paper. This convenient booklet format allows the publisher to produce a publication that's compact and easily carried around or sent through the mail. Most zines print maybe a hundred copies at the local Kinko's. The zine publisher then gives out a few copies to friends and fans—and ends up with several dozen to "distribute."

This is where the power of the U.S. mail comes in. Zine publishers make use of a sprawling network of publishers and readers, all connected through the U.S. postal system. Sending their zine off to another zine publisher, they might be lucky enough to receive a copy in trade or even better, be reviewed in that publisher's zine. This network of mutual reviews and trades is the lifeblood of the zine community. It's through this network that the unsuspecting reader might pick up a single innocuous-looking zine and then be exposed to an entire world of bustling activity.

This book is a gateway to the incredibly varied world of zines. More than just a simple introduction, this book features a broad overview of virtually everything that's happening in zines. After poring over the aforementioned fifty thousand zines, I've compiled this anthology of the best articles and essays that zines have offered in the last decade (while avoiding the temptation to compile a twenty-volume encyclopedia of zine writing).

So dive right in to this underground sea of zines. Start at the beginning or head straight to the sections that appeal to you the most. Are you interested in music, travel, food, politics, or sex? If you come across something that is uniquely appealing, check the appendix in the back. I've included the zine publishers' addresses so you can contact them directly. Write them a letter, order a back issue, subscribe to their zine. This isn't just an anthology of writing, it's a written invitation for you to join this incredible community.

A Brief History of Zines

Zines are looking so professional these days that sometimes it's difficult to tell the underground zines from the mainstream magazines. In alternative bookstores all across the country you'll find zines with slick covers, color printing, tight binding, and sharp design. A quick look might lead one to think that the modern-day zine is just an offspring of mainstream magazines like *Details* and *Newsweek.*

Nothing could be further from the truth.

The origin of the modern zine is much more humble than that. The term *zine* evolved not from the word *magazine,* but from *fanzine,* a term that originated with science fiction magazines of the '30s and '40s.

In 1926, Hugo Gernsback launched *Amazing Stories,*

the first magazine devoted exclusively to publishing original stories of science-based fiction. This magazine featured a special letters section where readers could discuss the scientific basis of the published stories. Hugo made a minor decision that changed the face of science fiction forever—he printed the full addresses of the letter writers so they could contact each other directly.

Within a few years, associations and discussion groups formed, where readers of science fiction talk about the stories they had read. One such group, the Science Correspondence Club, started up an amateur publication allowing members to easily keep in touch with one another. When its first issue was published in 1930, *The Comet* (later renamed *Cosmology*) went down in history as the world's first fanzine.

Over the years, the popularity of science fiction grew by leaps and bounds, and fan societies and fan magazines grew along with it. In 1940, the term *fanzine* became the recognized abbreviation of "fan magazine," and, on January 17, 1949, the always-good-natured *New Republic* picked up on this hot, new trend:

Readers of science-and-fantasy, like readers of detective fiction, come from all classes and occupations. But unlike the whodunit fans, they seem to be infected with a virus. They read, reread and analyze stories with the zeal of scholars tracking down the key word in a Shakespearean play. They correspond with other sufferers, sometimes in letters running to twelve pages. They snip favorite stories out of magazines and bind them into their own private anthologies.

They publish magazines—fanzines, as someone (someone who reads Time, *no doubt) has called them. One bibliography of fan magazines currently listed more than a hundred titles, adding apologetically that several more may have since come into being.*

The '30s, '40s, and '50s were a golden era for the science fiction fan. Fueled by the popularity of the mimeograph duplicating machine, hundreds (maybe thousands) of people caught the bug and took on the call to publish their own fanzine.

The mimeograph machine was developed by both Thomas Edison and Albert Blake Dick at roughly the same time. Always the go-getter, Edison beat Dick to the punch and landed his patent in 1880. It lay idle for several years until A. B. Dick discovered it while searching out his own patent. The two joined forces, and several years later they were ready to take America by a storm. Dick's most brilliant idea was not the invention itself, but his plan to use Edison's name on the label. In the 1880s, the Edison name had true star quality. Dick coupled it with an intriguing brand name taken from the Greek, and in 1887 the Edison "Mimeograph" duplicator was born.

The mimeograph was hardly the first printing machine, however. Johannes Gutenberg is of course the father of the modern printing press. It was in the fifteenth century that Gutenberg developed movable type printing, but it wasn't until Colonial America that folks like Ben Franklin finally brought the printed word to the common man.

Ben Franklin believed in the power of the press, and he founded America's first circulating library. In 1734 he published the first edition of *Poor Richard's Almanack*. His self-published annual pamphlets mixed folklore, humor, news, history, political commentary, and discussions about his personal life. Sounds very much like our modern-day zines. In 1776, Thomas Paine published his opinionated political tract *Common Sense* as a call to arms to end the British monarchy. The published works of Paine and other patriots influenced the Colonial settlers to rebel against their oppressive ruler. It may not be that easy anymore to get everybody to rebel, but reading modern-day political zines you get the impression that these contemporary self-publishers have political convictions that are just as strong.

Jumping ahead to 1865, the end of the Civil War led to a birth of the middle class with more leisure time and the pursuit of hobbies. A wide variety of educational toy printing presses were made available to people of all ages. In 1876 the National Amateur Press Association was founded, which laid the groundwork for the modern form of collective publishing still thriving today, known as apas.

It was artists and writers who took up the call of self-publishing in the early part of the twentieth century. Classic letterpress printers and A. B. Dick's mimeograph duplicators churned out Dadaist manifestos, surrealist journals, anarchist broadsheets, and "little magazines" of serious literary intent. Publications from Dada artists like Hugo Ball, Hans Arp, Francis Picabia, Tristan Tzara, and Richard Huelsenbeck were short-lived but highly influential. The direct influence these had on the modern zine might be hard to trace, but the similarities are easy to find.

Dada, as an art movement, was nihilistic in character and was the last word on cultural rebellion. The publications reflected that nihilistic, rebellious nature—with its chaotic design and cutting-edge writing, they threw all established conventions to the wind. Dada's artist-publishers viewed the literary establishment as the enemy and aimed their publications' attacks directly at the cultural elite. Today's zine publishers feel the same animosity toward the mainstream media, corporate magazines, and monopolistic record companies. They, too, are attempting to shatter the norms of society by attacking the elite.

The '30s, '40s, and '50s were a vibrant time for self-publishing. Fanzines of all sorts covering science fiction, fantasy literature, mysteries, and comic books were published by people of all ages. Jerome Siegel and Joe Schuster published five issues of their fanzine, *Science Fiction,* in 1932. In the third issue they created the character Superman, which ended up on the cover of DC's *Action Comics* six years later. Noted underground cartoonist Robert Crumb also got his start in fanzines. Robert, along with his brother Charles, created *Foo* in 1958. Robert also contributed strips to several other fanzines throughout the late '50s before moving to San Francisco and starting up the legendary *Zap* comic.

The mid-1960s saw the birth of a revolution in alternative publishing. Fueled by growing political unrest and the availability of inexpensive offset printing, thousands of people tried their hand at starting up alternative newspapers across the country. Most notable are the papers that formed the UPS (Underground Press Syndicate) in 1967. Founding members included the *Los Angeles Free Press,* the *East Village Other,* the *Berkeley Barb,* San Francisco's *Oracle,* Detroit's *Fifth Estate,* Chicago's *Seed,* and Austin's *Rag,* and the UPS soon grew to include hundreds of regularly published alternative newspapers.

The *Fifth Estate* was started by Harvey Ovshinsky in 1965. Ovshinsky got his start by publishing a fanzine while he was still attending high school in Detroit. After spending a summer working on the *Los Angeles Free Press,* he returned to Detroit to start a similar effort there. The *Fifth Estate* grew by leaps and bounds, and by 1969 it was printing 20,000 copies every week. Now, thirty years later, the *Fifth Estate* has returned to its once humble beginnings. Publishing about four times a year, with its outspoken political nature and unassuming character, it now seems more like a zine then ever before.

Paul Williams also spent his high school years publishing a science fiction fanzine. Then, in 1966, he figured that if he could publish a fanzine about science fiction, why not publish a fanzine about rock and roll. At that time, there were business magazines for the music industry, pin-up picture magazines for teenage girls, and magazines for the

folk music community, but no publications by and for fans of rock music. Williams took the plunge (though it wasn't that big of a plunge—500 mimeographed copies of a 10-page fanzine) and published the first issue of *Crawdaddy*.

By the third issue Williams had switched to offset printing, and by the fourth sold a full-page ad to Elektra Records. The publication continued to grow, featuring a full wrap-around cover on the sixth issue and a photograph of Paul McCartney on the cover of the eleventh (taken by Linda Eastman on the occasion of their first meeting). By 1968, circulation had grown to 25,000, but Paul decided to leave the magazine. He had started *Crawdaddy* to encourage people to take rock and roll seriously, but by that time people were taking it much too seriously.

Crawdaddy continued on, covering music and underground culture—it was published in various forms with different editors until 1979. Then, in 1993, Paul started up *Crawdaddy* once again. Looking very much like his original fanzine (or any music zine you might come across these days)—it's simply designed, filled with in-depth discussions about music, and has a uniquely personal character. The original music zine lives again.

The late '60s saw a synergy between outspoken political commentary, literary experimentation, and heartfelt critiques of rock and roll music. But an unusual thing happened in the mid-1970s. What had once been the rebellious voice of a generation, turned into the boring ol' establishment. The excitement of rock and roll turned into the oppressive doldrums of overblown stadium rock. To counter this trend, a new genre of music evolved, and with it, a new genre of music fanzines. Punk rock had finally arrived.

In 1976, fresh out of SVA (the School of Visual Arts, where he studied cartooning with Harvey Kurtzman and Will Eisner) John Holmstrom, along with "Legs" McNeil and Ged Dunne, published the small-

circulation magazine *Punk*. This publication had the heart of a music fanzine but the character of an underground comic.

On the other side of the pond, *Sniffin' Glue* made its appearance as the leading British punk music fanzine. While Holmstrom's *Punk* featured slick printing and an appealing comic-book design, *Sniffin' Glue* featured sloppy hand-lettering, uneven typewritten interviews, and darkly reproduced pictures. *Punk* magazine has gone down in history as a chronicler of New York's CBGB's scene, but the character and style of *Sniffin' Glue* still lives on in the punk rock fanzines published today.

These two were by no means the only punk rock fanzines being published in the late '70s. There were probably untold hundreds published in the United States and Great Britain, but, like the music itself, most punk rock fanzines rejected history and ended up lost to time.

If the Zine Publishers' Hall of Fame were to erect a statue, my vote goes to a neglected hero, Chester Carlson. As a teenager in the 1920s, he published a little magazine for amateur chemists, but it wasn't until he got his dull job retyping technical manuscripts for an electronics company that he thought of bigger, better things. He dreamed of a machine that could duplicate a printed page at the touch of a button. He developed his idea and secured a patent for it in 1939, but it took him five more years to convince a company of the usefulness of an instant, dry duplicating machine.

The first commercial Xerox machine was released in 1959, but it was another ten years or so before they became common in most large offices. It took a few more years for the nascent fanzine publishers/office slaves to gain access to the sacred machines. By the time the '80s rolled around, Xerox machines had made their impact on American society and the zine publishers were on their way to create a revolution.

In the early '80s, Mike Gunderloy spent a lot of time reading and writing for science fiction fanzines. After a while, he started noticing quite a few other types of zines, including punk rock fanzines, political newsletters, humorous pamphlets, and publications from fringe societies. Mike was an avid letter writer and wanted to tell all his friends about the unusual publications he'd come across. Instead of writing the same information over and over, he tried to simplify his life by producing a short mimeographed list, which he dubbed *Factsheet Five*.

Unfortunately, this newsletter did anything *but* simplify Mike's life. Within a few short years, word of *Factsheet Five* spread far and wide. Before he knew it, that simply mimeographed newsletter had turned into a thick 124-page magazine that proceeded to consume his entire life.

As the '80s rolled on, Kinko's copy shops started appearing on every corner and copies of *Factsheet Five* were being sold in the newsstand right next door. Thousands of people picked up on the idea that they, too, could publish their own zine. Thousands did.

Computer equipment took the production of zines to a whole new level. Soon, people were able to design their simple zines using the latest computer desktop publishing systems. The resulting flood of zines proved to be too much for Mike's humble little project—and in a rash decision, he decided to give it all up after forty-four issues. The magazine was quickly sold to Hundson Luce, who also found the project too massive. By the end of 1991, it seemed like *Factsheet Five* was gone for good.

When I heard of *Factsheet Five*'s demise, I thought a vital resource like that was too important to lose. I poured everything I had into restarting the magazine, and by January '93, issue #46 of *Factsheet Five* was on the shelves. It proved to be as popular as I'd hoped. As long as people continue

to make zines, *Factsheet Five* will continue documenting all that's happening with them.

To many people, the Internet and the World Wide Web offer the same promise as the network of zines. Through the power of the Internet, they can meet like-minded individuals, engage in discussions on topics of similar interest, and create virtual communities. The most surprising development has been the growth of electronic zines, or *ezines*. Created on computers but never quite making it to the laser printer or Xerox machine, these ezines exist primarily on network servers, computer disks, and on-line systems. Some of these ezines are extensions of their paper cousins, while others exist solely in virtual space.

While paper-based, photocopied zines are quick and easy to publish, ezines are even easier. Costing virtually nothing to produce, an ezine can have an audience of thousands, with a potential audience reaching into the millions. Because they're so easy to produce and distribute, ezines are growing by astronomical proportions, with virtually no end in sight.

Some soothsayers are predicting the demise of paper-based print and the demise of paper zines along with them. However, I see the future in a slightly different light. Finding it cheaper to publish on CD-ROMs and computer on-line systems, corporate magazines may stop printing on paper altogether. If this occurs, paper-based publishing will most likely be viewed more like an art form. A similar transformation occurred when the birth of photography helped shift portrait painting from a skilled craft to a fine art. Zine publishing will prosper in this new realm of aesthetic expression, and zine publishers will be appreciated for their mastery of the art. People enjoy reading printed pages and will always find pleasure in the texture of paper. So while corporate magazine and book publishers abandon paper, zine publishers will find a ready audience, hungry for the publications they produce.

miscellanea

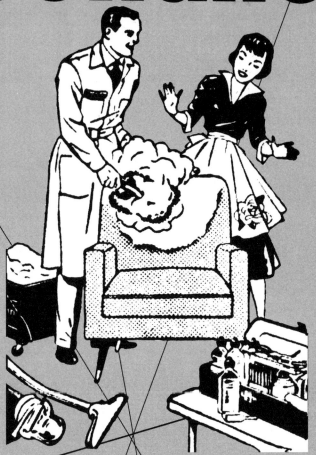

S ome zines are easy to classify—it's not hard to tell when you've found a sex zine or a music zine or a political zine or a food zine. But much of the writing that you come across in zines is impossible to classify. Maybe a bit personal, maybe a bit off-the-wall, the writing in many zines is unlike anything you'll find anywhere else.

The pieces in this opening section provide an excellent introduction to zines. My selections in the first group just don't fit into the classifications I've set up to organize this book. They range from the intensely serious to the ridiculous—just like zines themselves. It's a good place to get your feet wet in this bizarre, new world.

Some of these are my all-time favorites. I hope you enjoy them as much as I have. Feel free to jump around. This isn't a novel, or a scientific textbook—it's a lively collection of some unique writing that's truly on the cutting edge.

TALES FROM THE OLD-SCHOOL ZINE YEARS

By **Candi Strecker** *from*

Sidney Suppey's Quarterly and Confused Pet Monthly

Years ago, back before *Factsheet Five,* back before zine shops like See Hear or Quimby's, there were a few brave souls who found a forum for their creativity in self-publishing. Without any strong guidance or models to work from, these early pioneers patched together ideas borrowed from science fiction fandom, '60s alternative newspapers, underground comix, and the punk rock revolution. This synergy, bringing disparate elements of early forms of self-publishing together, is what makes the modern-day zine revolution so vibrant.

Nowadays, you can tell your *grandmother* that you do a zine and she'll most likely know what you're talking about. Zines are an accepted form of self-expression with demonstrated models, how-to books, support groups, and established forms of critical analyses.

Candi Strecker was one of those early pioneers. The first issue of her zine, *Sidney Suppey's Quarterly and Confused Pet Monthly,* was published back in 1979. Since she didn't even have a word for the product of her self-publishing labors, she presented it to her friends as "Here's my . . . my . . . *this thing I'm doing."*

This essay was written in 1996 and chronicles her early days of publishing. It kicked off the twenty-third issue of her zine, which was a special compendium of highlights from the first sixteen issues of *Sidney Suppey's Quarterly and Confused Pet Monthly.*

If you want to know about the early days of zines, Candi would certainly be a good person to ask. Thankfully, she beat us to the punch and presented this story of what it was like.

It's early 1979. I'm twenty-three years old, living in Ann Arbor, Michigan, three months out of college with a master's degree in library science. I'm working my first full-time job, double-checking citations that would appear in *Mathematical Reviews,* a monthly index of every book and article published in that formidable field. Today it sounds like a dream job: incredibly low-stress toil, in the service of Higher Knowledge, in a pleasant university-town setting. But at the time I thought I was suffocating. Even the serene classical music playing in the background all day long was torture when I wanted to be twitching along to punk rock music. My coworkers, though only a few years older than me, were comfortably resigned to the situation, and kept reminding me how lucky I was to have a library-related job at all, during a recession in the Rust Belt.

But I was young, I was jumpy, I felt I was marking time in a backwater while the world passed me by. My school friends had graduated and moved away, and office friendships didn't have the same urgent intimacy. I missed those intense late-night conversations about the big things in life, about dreams and goals and sitcom theme songs. As they moved out of my life, I wanted to keep track of everyone with whom I'd shared those magical bonding moments, everyone I'd met who had that crucial sense of the absurd.

Most of all, I was bursting with things to say, but I didn't have the least idea how to make myself heard. I had a terrific love of magazines of all kinds, from glossy trend-spotting trash to the engineering journals *Math Reviews* received from India that seemed to be printed on brown paper towels. But my vague notion of working for or writing for a magazine seemed about as absurd as the moonings of a cowtown girl who wants to "go to Hollywood and be a star." I didn't live in New York City, I hadn't gone to elite universities where I could make connections with the right people. I was just a nobody from nowhere, with the wrong degree from a second-string state university, so I told myself to be realistic and quit wishing for things that couldn't possibly happen. (Also, I had spent a miserable year in journalism school, until it became clear to me that I was too bashful to do any kind of writing that required asking other human beings questions.)

But my egomania grappled with my timidity, climbed up onto its shoulders, and yelled in my ear: "They" could close the gates of New York publishing against me, but they couldn't keep my words out of print *if I had my own magazine.*

This audacity still amazes me: that when the logical approach seemed impossibly difficult, I came up with an alternative path so absurd that no competent person would have even thought of it. But self-publishing let me start small and take low-risk baby steps, until finally last year I became what I'd always wanted to be, a paid, published writer. So what if it took me fifteen years to get where a confident person could have in two or three? If I hadn't taken this indirect path, I wouldn't have gotten there at all.

The world has changed since 1979. Back then, I couldn't even tell my hippest best friends what I was trying to do, because the idea of a self-published zine wasn't out there as a frame of reference; all I could do was sheepishly hand them my stapled sheets and say, "Here's my . . . my . . . *this thing I'm doing.*" Today, zines are so well covered in the media that my stockbroker sends me every article he sees in the major papers about them. To picture my position as I stood on the threshold of publishing my first issue, you have to imagine a world without *Factsheet Five* (let alone alt.zines!). There was nothing to suggest a community existed that would be receptive to my ramblings, there were no lists of addresses to send trade copies to, there was nothing to model my product on, and no idea of what a zine "should look like." Conversely, this gave me infinite freedom to do whatever I wanted. There were no clichéd zine ideas to worry about avoiding, no daunting

in-crowd of successful zinesters to try to impress. In particular, I didn't feel the need to specialize, the way people do in today's crowded zine field. I was free to be general and personal and inconsistent, until I struck upon my own style and set of continuing interests.

It's tempting to say that I sat down with rubber cement and typewriter and invented the zine, but even at my most egotistical I know that's not true. I invented *my* zine, by taking the elements of my life and shaping them into a vehicle. But the modern zine, like television, was the simultaneous co-invention of many independent tinkerers. And we didn't pull the idea of self-publishing completely out of thin air; there were some rough models to follow.

I was dabbling in science fiction fandom then, meeting a few people and attending conventions. There, I saw my first science fiction "fanzines." This subculture has a tradition of self-publishing dating back to the 1930s, but I wasn't impressed with the random examples I saw. Their graphic sensibility was minimal, they were pointlessly printed via mimeo instead of photocopy, and they were usually filled with page after page with of nattering "lettercols" (interlaced letters and editorial responses). But I came away with the revolutionary notion that *anybody can publish something.* It was a great idea, even if I didn't like where they were taking it.

Another parallel universe I'd glimpsed was the hippie-underground-free-papers that sprouted up in many major cities in the 1960s. I was especially impressed by a 1969 paperback anthology I'd found called *How Old Will You Be in 1984? Expressions of Student Outrage from the High School Free Press* (Diane Divoky, ed., New York: Discus Books), which spread the fabulous rumor that some *high schoolers* were publishing their own "free papers." Also inspirational were the sarcastic political flyers I was finding posted around the University of Michigan campus, signed "The Last International." The sheer boldness (and the anonymity!) of this method of putting ideas out before the world made a big impression on me. As it turned out, I was attending the U of M at the same time as their creator, the infamous Bob Black, though I wasn't to meet him for another two or three years.

Underground comix were another source of inspiration. The whole genre came from outside the publishing mainstream, but the king of outsiders was Harvey Pekar, whose autobiographical *American Splendor* was audaciously self-published from the most unlikely metropolis in the world, that joke of cities, nearby Cleveland. This comic book's very existence proclaimed that life *anywhere* could be worth writing about.

Punk rock's do-it-yourself ethos was also in the air, the

idea that instead of waiting for big record labels to discover them, bands should issue their own cheap 45's with self-scribbled sleeve art. One of my biggest life-changing moments was the day in 1977 when I saw the not-yet-famous, not-yet-recorded band DEVO play a free gig on the Kent State University campus. It was one of those moments that you realize you've unknowingly been waiting for all your life. They were nobodies from the biggest nowhere of all, from blue-collar Kent and Akron, Ohio, *just like me*—and they'd found a way to make meaningful art out of that.

Or maybe my entire inspiration was the famous phrase spray-painted on a freeway overpass somewhere between Kent and Cleveland, known and cherished by all cool people in northern Ohio, a phrase we repeated among ourselves like a secret mantra: "IGNORE ALIEN ORDERS."

Besides having all these rough models in mind, in early 1979 I encountered the self-publishing prototype that finally propelled me into print. Back in the late '70s, my favorite reading matter was the *CoEvolution Quarterly*, a magazine spin-off of the *Whole Earth Catalog*. Despite its roots in the hippie migration back to the land, *CQ* had evolved into a daring and serious magazine, an unfailing source of startling and contrarian ideas, with a solidly pro-science attitude that promoted not only solar power but early personal computers and orbiting space colonies. *CQ* wasn't just a magazine to me; it was a way of looking at the world, like an inclusive paper Internet. In early 1979 (issue number 20) they published a feature unlike anything I'd seen before. Anne Herbert, one of the magazine's editors, had begun self-publishing a little Xeroxed handout for her friends called *The Rising Sun Neighborhood Newsletter*, and this issue contained several pages' worth of excerpts from it.

I recognized immediately what these anecdotes and observations were: carefully edited journal cullings! Well, I had years' worth of journals to cull from, too. The word *neighborhood* in the title suggested that this kind of publication could be more than just a one-way letter-substitute; it could link strangers into a virtual community. Another encouraging factor was that Herbert seemed to be a parallel version of myself, another bookish gal from a churchy background in rural Ohio. While I really don't remember a turning-point moment of decision when I said, "I'm going to do something like that, too," it's clear that shortly after I saw the *CoEvolution Quarterly*'s reprints from the *RSNN*, I produced the first *Sidney Suppey's Quarterly*.

There's only one dry remark in my 1979 notebooks about this whole ambitious undertaking, dated 5/31/79: "I think the *SSQ* is the only project I've ever begun without reading a how-to book first." Of course, discovering how-to was half the fun. I'd never known, until that first office job, what miracles could be wrought with the combination of rubber cement and white-out and Xeroxing. Nobody told me about situationism and *détournement* and appropriating, but it was obviously cool as hell how one could carefully reword headlines with cut-and-paste trickery. The results weren't just funny, they were revealing, as if secret messages had been lurking in these banal grocery ads and TV listings all along. I loved even the most tedious work, like hunting for a letter "e" of exactly the same size and typeface as the "a" I wanted to replace, then trimming it to fit and pushing it into place with a toothpick. I reveled in the painstaking monotony of creating titles with press-type, burnishing down letter after letter so it looked "real," indistinguishable from something typeset. And I loved every tricky triumph of ingenuity over expense. If I needed a dotted line or dingbat, I'd pore over old magazines to find one instead of buying a few bucks' worth of press-down borders.

I really feel like an old-timer when I remember how difficult it was to get those early issues copied double-sided. The copy machines could do it, but the copyshop employees got all bent out of shape by the request, because it was something no one ever asked for. People thought of photocopying as a way of making copies of existing things, not as a way of publishing new stuff. Unassertive and shy as I was, it was torture to speak up and say, "I want *this* side on the back of *that* side . . ." all the while in utter dread of being asked the unanswerable question, "But what *is* this?"

Self-publishing taught me a great deal about writing. I learned to write tersely, because one bloated paragraph could force me to add another page to an issue, and its cost would come directly out of my pocket. Individually knowing so many of my readers taught me to write clearly, because I knew which readers would miss certain references unless I inobtrusively slipped in some background information. In theory my zine was a fun, casual project, but I chose each word with an eye toward its exact impact.

"Looking real" was another goal I took seriously. Beginning with the first issue, I tried to put together all the elements of a real magazine, including logo, volume numbering, and an editorial. That issue's colophon proudly asserts, "All rights reserved © 1979" with the c-in-a-circle penned in by hand. Later I learned to cannibalize this character from the manufacturer's name on the borders of sheets of press-type letters. When Macintosh computers came along, I finally had the realness tool I'd dreamed of—one that could print out my "©" with just a set of keystrokes!

LARRY-BOB'S GUIDE TO SELLING OUT

•

By **Larry-bob** *from*

Holy Titclamps

I think a common event in the next few years will be a "selling-out" in the zine world similar to that which has happened with "alternative" music. With alternative music, major labels figured out that they could package and sell "hipness" by releasing records by bands that already had a healthy underground following. Face it, you can't manufacture Nirvana like the Monkees (Rage Against The Machine and Stone Temple Pilots notwithstanding). A similar thing will happen with zines. Zine editors will be hired by media conglomerates to give magazines a hipness cachet. But just as with alternative music, which is punk stripped of its political message, zines will be stripped of their political content, made safe for advertisers. Because the medium is the message. The message of a mainstream record is "sell out to a big corporation." The message of an underground record is "put out your own record." The message of a zine is "do your own zine." The message of a glossy magazine is, "buy this magazine and don't think for yourself."

Since zine people are going to sell out anyway, they might as well do it right. Lisa Palac (aka LaBia) started out doing the zine *Magnet School* in Minneapolis, wrote occasionally for *Your Flesh,* moved to San Francisco and worked for *On Our Backs* for a while, then "edited" the piece of crap porn/cybersploitation magazine *Future Sex.* Considering how good Lisa's past efforts were, one got the feeling that its editorial content was actually controlled by the straight white male financiers. That's a good example of how not to sell out.

So here's some guidelines to selling out:

1. Demand artistic control. The record label/publisher is interested in using your hipness to attract the dollars of hip people. It's in their best interests not to water you down too much, but it's also in their best interests not to alienate advertisers. Fuck 'em. If advertisers pull out, get hipper advertisers. Why aren't there Ben & Jerry's ads in *The Advocate,* instead of Absolut Vodka? (I know, I know, B&J's are cow-exploiting hippies.)

2. Don't be afraid to speak out in criticism of anything, including your boss or advertisers.

3. Don't deny that you've sold out.

Selling out is only an option for a tiny minority of people. Only a few of the kids who idolize sports stars can escape their lives by becoming athletes. We're not interested only in getting success for ourselves, but in liberating everyone. Everyone can do a zine, but not everyone can work as a magazine editor. I think all artists should work, and do their art in their spare time. Nobody should struggle to get these stupid grants.

One commonly asked question (both friends and interviewers have asked me) is, if you could, would you make *Holy Titclamps* your full-time job; would you make it big and glossy? It's sort of like the question "would you become straight if there was a pill?" The question assumes that being glossy is a desirable thing.

If you spend all your time and money on the underground publications and music, you shouldn't have any time or money left to waste on mainstream media.

When you see an article about one of your underground heroes in a mainstream publication, for heaven's sake, don't BUY the glossy mag. By all means, read the article on the stands. (This is a library, not a store!) But

holy titclamps

moby dicks and torsos: is that all there is to gay art?

file under "queer"

$2

issue no. 10   summer 1992

the reason why these people agreed to participate was so that mainstream people would learn about and hopefully join the underground, not so that underground folks would put money into the pockets of publishing magnates. Frequently I do mainstream media stuff as a favor to friends of mine who are writers. I help them to get some money out of the magazine or newspaper. Not to say that I have not benefited from mainstream media exposure. If the article actually prints my address (make sure to demand your address be printed when cooperating with the enemy), I get plenty of mail, from people who have never seen a zine before.

In 1994, the British music press featured "queercore," as they call it, as flavor of the month. As usual, the writer asked leading questions and wrote the article to fit with his preconceived ideas. The danger is of mainstream media shaping movements rather than things evolving organically. People get distorted ideas based on mainstream media interpretations rather than hearing directly from the source. Even if addresses appear, many more people read the mainstream article than actually send away for the zine.

The press also tried to feature the band Huggy Bear and the Riot Grrrl movement. They refused to talk to the press. I think that's a good strategy; another one is to demand that magazines only publish unedited manifestos. Everyone always thinks that they will be the exception when dealing with the media, but you almost always get screwed over. Eventually, the British press had a backlash against HB and RG, as they always do. The thing is, we zinesters are different than any other colonized group, in that we have the means to speak back. Not that the press is all that worthwhile to spend a lot of time fighting

against, instead of the things we're really interested in. I'm just saying, don't be fooled into wasting your money on their rags when you should be investing money in the underground.

It's like the question of whether to shop at the big corporate discount store or your friendly neighborhood store. When you spend at the corporate store, your money gets sucked into the corporation. When you shop at the local store, your money stays in the community. It's the same thing with spending on mainstream and underground media. Who would you rather give your money to?

Here's a parallel: Food co-ops and punk culture. Food co-ops started to bring people kinds of food that weren't available at supermarkets. For years they had the market to themselves—but slowly, the number of people eating organic/natural food grew. Eventually, supermarkets got hip to the fact that there was a sizable market which they were missing out on. They started selling tofu and brown rice, and even started having bulk food sections. Today you can buy food in corporate supermarkets that ten years ago you could only get in food co-ops. But food co-ops had two facets: the food was natural, and they were run cooperatively. Grocery stores may have changed the food they sell, but they have not changed the way they are run. Meanwhile, co-ops are forced out of business, while grocery stores make millions on natural foods.

The parallel is that punk has two characteristics: the sound of the music, and the way it is produced—Do It Yourself (DIY). The sound of punk is to natural food as the DIY ethic is to worker-run cooperatives. Corporate grunge (TM) takes the sound, but not the DIY. Corporate bulk food takes the taste but not the cooperative management. The solution: only shop at worker-run co-ops (there are yuppie co-ops that are not worker-run, but are governed by boards of stock-owning yuppies). Only buy music done by DIY bands and labels (there are labels that are nominally independent, but are really corporate). Shoplift from grocery stores, and buy used corporate records. Yeah, it's probably not going to bring capitalism/consumerism to its knees, but it's a start.

WHAT I WAS TAUGHT

•

By **John Kehoe** *from*
Gulp

Many people have experimented with the "mini" format of zine design. Most successful have been the self-published cartoonists who print small runs of their *minicomics* using Xerox machines. Created by twice folding over a standard 8½ × 11 sheet of paper, the resulting small-size zine is easy to print, send through the mail, and carry in your back pocket. Andy Stevens has had great successes with his mini-size zine, *Gulp.* He mixes wacky comics, single-page fiction, never-dull poems, and his patented three-word reviews. This short essay from John Kehoe fits perfectly on two small pages in *Gulp.* Like the zine itself, this essay is ultra-condensed an overview of everything John has learned in twelve years of schooling.

1. Mathematics

Let X equal Y. Y has six apples. Each apple is worth 30 cents. X has 7,530 apples. Each apple is worth 13 cents. How long will it take Y to grow an equal number of apples, if the weather is good? Show your work.

2. History

Columbus discovered America, or maybe a Viking did first but didn't tell anybody. And there were people living here when Columbus got here, and the reason we took the land away from them was because there were more of us than them, and they never got around to inventing the wheel. Later there was a war between the states, which got started over slavery. Miss Jane Pittman helped Harriet Tubman guide escaped slaves to freedom in the North, finding her way by feeling for moss on tree trunks, because the moss grew on the north side of the tree. The North won the war. There was a world war after that, and then another, and we dropped an atomic bomb on Japan.

3. English

Grammar is important. There are verbs, nouns, pronouns, adverbs, adjectives, and punctuation in grammar. A comma is a form of punctuation, and so is a period. Neatness counts.

4. Science

Gas burns, if it is the right kind of gas. Cells divide and receive nutrients through the process of osmosis. Frogs can have their brains fucked up so that they can be cut open and we can watch their hearts beat. If you are too much of a pussy to cut open a frog and watch its heart beat, you fail science, even if you are a girl.

5. Foreign Languages

Un crayon est gris. The pencil is gray. *Le cahier est bleu.* The notebook is blue. *Je t'aime.* I love you. *Garçon!* Waiter! *Voulez-vous couchez avec moi, ce soir?* Would you like to sleep with me tonight? *Putain.* Whore.

6. Social Studies

There are three branches of government. The executive, the judicial, and the legislative. They check and balance each other. We have a constitutional right to say unpopular things, to do unpopular things, and to be unpopular, although this right is not absolute and is sometimes taken away from us. We also have a constitutional right to buy, sell, and discharge firearms at each other, at targets, and at wild animals.

7. Industrial Arts

Wear safety glasses. Don't put your fingers in the machinery; don't let loose clothing get tangled in the machinery; don't breathe solvents on purpose; don't let solder drip onto your pants leg; establish a point of perspective in your shop drawings; don't forget to wear safety glasses; when the going gets tough, the tough get going; excuses are like noses—everybody has one.

8. Fine Arts

Music is a joyous expression of man's emotions. Classical music is the highest art form there is, and black people invented jazz. Ballet may seem really stupid, but it isn't. White is the absence of color and black is the presence of all colors. Museums are interesting places and the repositories of our cultural heritage. Sometimes artists go too far. Art has something to do with beauty and truth.

9. Life Studies

Don't drink; don't do drugs; don't smoke cigarettes; don't have sex unless you know what all the consequences of having sex are, which includes having babies. There's nothing wrong with being a homosexual, although some people think there is something wrong with it, so maybe there is.

10. Independent Study

Working in a fast-food place, a grocery store, or a discount department store is worth a credit toward graduation.

THE REAL FREAKIES
•
By **Jackie End** *from*
The Freakie Magnet

I love collector-oriented zines. These publications, created by folks who are completely obsessed with unique types of objects, are targeted to people who are similarly obsessed. Collectors of nostalgic pop-cultural flotsam seem to have the most fun, but unfortunately they can often go overboard. I *loved* my old Matchbox cars and probably still have a few floating around, but it's my understanding that the current wave of collectors are only interested in "mint" cars. This obsession with pristine condition and resale value seems to take all the fun out of it.

The Freakie Magnet covers, but doesn't fall prey to, the speculator market that seems to be overtaking cereal box collecting; instead it focuses on the fun of it all. In each issue you'll find discussions about such memorable childhood cereals as Quisp, Quake, Count Chocula, Boo Berry, and of course Freakies. It covers every aspect of cereal obsession, from the packaging to the premiums, and even the cereal itself. Freakies cereal was hugely popular in the '70s. Seven lovable little monsters who never had their own TV show but nonetheless became immortalized in the most wonderful toy premiums. Jackie End describes how she designed the characters while working at an advertising agency and based the characters on several of her coworkers and even her boss.

This is the true story of the Freakies as presented by Jackie End, their creator, to the New Haven Ad Club on February 11, 1975. Jackie, who was in her early 20s at the time, created the Freakies for Ralston Purina at the advertising firm of Wells, Rich, Greene in 1971.

The Freakies were born about four years ago. Ralston came to us and said, "We want to try to crack the children's cereal market. Don't worry about what goes into the box. We'll make something the kids like and that's good for them, but what we need is a concept." Since no one really took the project seriously, the assignment was given to me. But what no one knew was that I actually watched Bugs Bunny and Daffy Duck every morning (and Rocky and Bullwinkle on Sunday). At any rate, since I knew kids love monsters and since I love monsters, I thought it would be smart to do a cereal on monsters.

I knew I had to create characters the kids would respond to, because when you're selling a children's cereal you're not really selling the product—most kids' cereals taste about the same—you're really selling "fun." You see, children have difficulty differentiating their attitude about the "spokesman" from their attitude about the cereal.

So the creative format actually becomes the product.

Now, since I didn't think Ralston was really serious, either, I decided to base all the Freakies on people in the agency. And now, I'd like to explain to you who the Freakies really are!

I guess the best place to start is at the top: BossMoss, the leader of the Freakies, in other words, their Boss. BossMoss is really Charlie Moss who is the president of Wells, Rich, Greene.

BossMoss is a very intelligent leader. And whenever the Freakies have a problem they go to BossMoss. He never solves the problem, but they go to him anyway because he's kind and understanding. BossMoss has one unfortunate habit: he's always reminding people he's the boss! And sometimes you can hear him from miles away shouting, "I'm the Boss. I'm the Boss! And never spell my name wrong!" It seems that every time Charlie goes to any kind of formal luncheon or dinner, the place card always spelled his name wrong. (As I said before, I never expected this stuff to get on the air!)

As for BossMoss being an understanding leader, all I can say is, the fact that I am still working at Wells, Rich, Greene absolutely proves he is!

The next Freakie, Snorkeldorf, is based on Stan Dragoti, who was the co-creative director of WRG at the time. Snorkeldorf is in love with himself. He thinks he is the most beautiful Freakie there is. And he carries mirrors with him wherever he goes. He also writes love poems to himself like:

Mirror mirror on my dresser
Compared to me everyone is lesser.

If the Freakies were fighting for their independence, Snorkeldorf would be at the tailor getting his epaulets made bigger. Snorkeldorf's character came from the fact that Stan Dragoti is probably one of the best-looking, best-dressed men I've ever seen. And I've seen a few!

The third Freakie, Gargle, is based on a writer who used to be at WRG. He was very British and after seventeen years in this country, he still sounded like Ronald Coleman. At any rate Gargle is your pseudo-intellectual. He has read the entire encyclopedia from cover to cover and he's given to pontificating. If the Freakies were fighting for their independence, Gargle would be at the front lines arguing the futility of war with the enemy.

Next we have Goody-Goody. Goody-Goody is based on Grace Feldman, who is our head of personnel. I think at the time I was angry at Grace for not getting me a chair for my office or maybe a phone extension or something. I got my revenge through Goody-Goody, who is a compulsively neat person and who is always complimenting Boss-Moss. Goody-Goody is possibly the greatest noodge of the Western World.

Next is Grumble. I fashioned him after someone who used to work at the agency. Grumble is somebody's hard-headed Jewish Grandfather with foot trouble. Grumble is always saying things like: "When is this commercial gonna end, my feet are killing me!"

Next is Hamhose. Hamhose is the only Freakie who isn't based on someone at WRG. Hamhose is based on a cat I used to have named Pigpen (if you can follow that). Hamhose is very shy. He's so shy he spends all of his time in a garden hose. Hamhose says it's very comforting to be in a garden hose all day because you can take long walks all by yourself.

The last Freakie is Cowmumble. Cowmumble is based on me (four years ago). Cowmumble is very insecure and is always reading self-improvement books like *The Power of Positive Thinking*, and mumbling things like: "Every day, in every way, I am getting better and better." And let me tell you, it works.

As I said before, I never expected Freakies cereal to go but when Ralston concept-tested the Freakies characters, the kids loved them. The test consisted of showing an illustration of each Freakie and describing each Freakie's personality. Some of the kids' comments were really cute. One little girl said that there was a girl like Goody-Goody in her class at school. A little boy said that he likes to be alone, too, and he wished he was small enough to stay in a garden hose all day. And another boy said, "I like Snorkeldorf the best, because I'm great, too. And it's hard when you're great."

Another thing the kids responded to was the look of the Freakies. An art director named Alex Tsao designed them, and they are probably the most charming monsters you'll ever see.

The Freakies scored higher in that test than Cap'n Crunch had in his first concept test. And at that time Cap'n Crunch had been the only really successful introduction into the kids' cereal market in five years. Although a lot of other cereals tried.

The next step was a test market. A test market consists of doing just what you would do if you were advertising across the country: you get the cereal on the shelves, you run the commercials, and then you wait and see what happens.

What happened was, Freakies cereal got a 65 percent higher trial than the pre-sweet norms. We also got a 75 percent higher repeat purchase than the norms. And when we looked, we found we had a 98 percent awareness, which means that 98 percent of the households in the test market cities knew about the Freakies. In other words, it was a good idea to go national. So Ralston Purina built a factory and in September 1974, the Freakies became a reality for the rest of the country.

Since then I've had some very gratifying experiences. For instance, Freakies fan clubs have been springing up all over the country. Not just among the five- to twelve-year-olds but among college students as well.

We keep getting requests for T-shirts from fraternities and sororities. We also got a letter from a little boy in the Midwest who said he had organized a Freakies club and that there were seven members, each with the name of one of the Freakies. He, of course, was called BossMoss. But, he said, since there were only seven Freakies, and since he had another twenty kids who wanted to join, couldn't we create twenty more Freakies so that he could let the other kids in the club, too. I told our client that I would be happy

to write to him suggesting that he start going into Boss-Moss No. 2 and Snorkeldorf No. 3, and so on. I was not really up to making another twenty enemies!

Today the Freakies are doing very well. I think this is because with seven different characters there is a Freakie for every kid to relate to. Also, I think the fact that Freakies is the only cereal concept without a straight good guy/bad guy conflict situation makes it that much more interesting to the kids.

I really don't mind that it took four years for the Freakies to go national. When a company is investing the kind of money you've got to invest to launch a new product, you want to be as sure as you can be about the results. But I must tell you that when I saw the first Freakies commercial on my own television set, I toasted them with a glass of champagne, even though it was nine A.M. on a Saturday morning!

YORINATE IN KUP

•

By **Fran Pelzman Liscio** *from*

Hip-Hop Housewife

Lots of people have precocious children who say cute things. Not all those people, however, have the wit it takes to make those cute things interesting to anyone besides the kid's immediate relatives. But Fran Pelzman Liscio does. Her zine, *Hip-Hop Housewife,* is a laugh-out-loud funny mishmash of short pieces. Each issue includes parenting tips, observations about current events, film criticism, and "The Testosterone Index," a compendium of the cute and/or sexy men in the media. Besides being totally entertaining, *Hip-Hop Housewife* (like another zine in this book, *Hip Mama*) is part of a trend in parenting and family-oriented zines that just goes to show not *all* zines are made by slackers for slackers. Besides, *Hip-Hop Housewife* makes staying home with your kids seem like a laugh riot. In these pieces, we get to see the evil side of her grade-school-age daughter, Laura.

I guess a "knock-knock" joke would be too bourgeois

Laura wanted to entertain a friend and her brother, Gregory. So she took a Mickey Mouse cup off the counter and urinated into it. I hustled her off to the stair landing to holler in private. "Laura! What were you thinking! That was a disgrace!" "But MOM!" Laura laughed glibly, waving in the direction of the kitchen. *"Those kids thought it was hilarious!"*

H3 Guide to Kids' Birthday Parties: Go Off-Site!

Why does spring always bring a fresh crop of kids' parties with it? Well, here's a quick guide:

RULE #1: Like the headline says, go off-site. This can be as important to your survival as the off-site playdate. Why? Simple. A roomful of children—any roomful, any time, anywhere—wants to trash your house and frighten your dog. They need to. It's what they live for. "Ah," you say. "I'm having the party in my Pierre Deux living room, but it will work out. I've invited all the parents to stay during the party, so they can each control their own child. It will be a snap. I'll really have nothing to do." Forget it. You'll find yourself racing across the room screaming, "Stop! Stop! Stop! For the love of God, put that Baccarat cachepot back on the mantel!" to a three-year-old whose parents are casually cramming guacamole and tacos into their mouths less than two feet away. In fact, the only reason they came was for the bagels and a chance to see their kid demolish someone else's crystal for a change.

RULE #2: There is no rule #2. The only rule that matters is rule #1. After that, it's a crapshoot.

You forgot "yorinate in kup"

I decided that Laura and Greg were watching too much TV. "Here's a pad and pen, Laura. Why don't you write a list of all the things that you and Greg could enjoy doing instead of watching TV. You could put down going to the park, or playing on the swings." Twenty minutes later I came across this list lying on the couch:

Mess up house!
Swings! Park!
Throw couwch ocross room!
Be crasy!
Brake window!
torcher mom!
torcher House!
Wach TV!!!

Call Allstrallia!!
Call China!
Steell candy!
Throw chers ocross room!
Driving Mom crazy
Desurt first!
Poop Don't flush!

LES PENNICK'S SMART COMPUTER SHOPPER TIPS

•

By **Ken Davis** *from*

Hitch

Hitch is filled with pointed (and sometimes vicious) satire aimed at annoying people in the film industry, American politics, and anywhere else editor Rod Lott can find a target. If this sounds a bit like *Spy* magazine, you're right on course—the main difference being *Hitch* is consistently funny and entertaining, where *Spy* is . . . well, you know. With its tightly written articles, sharp design, and regular publishing schedule, *Hitch* is always on the top of my reading pile.

It's hard to find the one or two best pieces from the many issues of *Hitch,* only because every one has been so great. Rod writes much of it himself, but he's also good at coaxing great writing from his friends.

Ken Davis' Les Pennick has the unfortunate occupation of selling computers for the local Radio Shack store. He's not quite down there with car salesmen (though a heck of a lot more honest), and his typical customer is someone who will most likely use his computer for playing action/adventure video games. In our first selection, Les offers advice to those who are considering buying a new computer—not for advanced spreadsheet analysis, not for desktop publishing, but to play a really rad game of *Doom II*.

In the second piece from *Hitch,* Ryun Patterson explores the seamier side of life. He relates a true tale of donating blood plasma for fun and profit, probably the *last* thing that anyone would do for money. Ryun describes the *careful* screening process, the painful procedure, and the resulting cash bonus (fifteen bucks).

Some call me a computer connoisseur, and I am not humble enough to disagree. I mean, selling computers at Radio Shack for almost eight months has given me a certain degree of expertise in the field of technological paraphernalia. People are always asking me for advice on what to look for when buying a computer. It's similar to when a doctor goes to a party and is asked by the celebrants to look at their bum ankles, rashes, and other miscellaneous ailments.

Why, just last weekend, I was on my lunch break in the food court and had just begun to enjoy a candied apple when a passerby noticed my Radio Shack nametag. He pulled up a chair and picked my brain for almost twenty

minutes! I am usually not bothered when people want my advice, but I was trying to enjoy a candied apple, for crying out loud! But I am a tree and I can bend. I graciously gave the man a few nuggets of wisdom, and this seemed to please him.

It gave me such a good feeling that I thought it would be a great idea to share this information with the readers of *Hitch*. Heed my advice! Use the tips that I have given you or you will end up with some crappy machine that won't even play *Doom II* without locking up.

When looking for a new computer, consumers would be wise to go with a high-end Pentium system. Make sure you get one of the new Pentiums that doesn't have the floating point division flaw. Chances of the flaw affecting the average user are remote, but when you are about to attack a Former Human Commando with your plasma rifle in *Doom II,* you don't want a division error to ruin your aim.

When it comes to choosing your monitor, do so carefully and don't get some cheap, 15-inch job. One of the best monitors I've seen is the ViewSonic 21G. It has a 21-inch, flat square screen, .25-dot pitch and 1600 × 1280 non-interlaced resolution. At $1,700 it isn't cheap, but play *Doom II* on it for a few minutes, and you'll appreciate the difference a few extra dollars can make.

One of the biggest rules of thumb when shopping for a computer is to buy the most RAM and biggest hard drive you can afford. I completely concur. The more RAM the better. *Doom II* runs sluggish with 4MB, decent with 8MB, good with 12MB, but great with 16MB! If you can afford more RAM than that, then I would not try to stop you. Can you imagine *Doom II* running on 32MB of RAM? Man, that would be a hoot!

Most people wonder what size hard drive to get. The 170 MB hard drive used to be the standard. Today, the standard is at least 500MB. However, I would highly recommend at least a gig. *Doom II* only takes up about 15MB of precious hard-drive real estate. But take my word for it: when you start collecting *Doom II* add-on wad files and editors, you will be glad you have the extra storage space.

Sound is also important. Honestly, as long as your sound card is Sound Blaster–compatible, you will be fine. It's the speakers you want to ensure are of the highest quality. Don't settle for the cheap speakers provided with most computer systems today, unless you like the thought of a Fire Imp's scream sounding like it's coming out of a tin can. On my computer, I have Yamaha YST-MSW10 Powered Stereo Subwoofers. With these babies, the Barons of Hell in *Doom II* don't just grunt when I blast them with my Rocket Launcher, they *howl!*

One mustn't forget the importance of a modem. When you consider the fact that the modem will be your vehicle on the way to alt.games.doom on the Internet and will also be your means of playing DeathMatch *Doom II* with friends over the phone lines, I'm sure we can agree that only the fastest modem will do. One can also buy modems that are voice-compatible. For most people, this is just an unnecessary frill, unless you plan to use your computer as an answering machine or voice-mail system. Since you will spend many hours on the Internet playing DeathMatch, I would advise against it.

Many people are interested in buying a printer with their new computer system. Again, this is one of those bells-and-whistles deals most people can do without. Many people will argue that they need a printer to produce reports for their business or papers for school and other such foolishness. To them, I say, "What are your priorities?" If you feel it is a "must-have" and want to waste the money, go ahead. I'm just saying don't spend a lot of money frivolously on peripherals you don't need, and whatever you do, don't buy a Tandy, because they are crap.

Hopefully, with these tips, you are better informed on what to look for when buying a new computer system. If you're ever at Bannister Mall in Kansas City, feel free to stop by for a visit. If I'm not working at the Shack, look for me in the food court or hanging around Le Mans Arcade.

PLASMA DONATION: LAZY MAN'S DREAM OR NEEDLE-RIDDEN NIGHTMARE?

●

By **Ryun Patterson** *from*

Hitch

Are you tired of eating macaroni-and-cheese dinners for months on end?

Are the roaches in your apartment getting too forward now that they have realized you're too poor to buy another can of Raid?

Not to fear. There's a way any healthy person can grab a couple extra bucks with minimal effort while keeping all of his material possessions.

This miracle of capitalism is called plasma donation, and it's fun and easy. How fun and easy, you ask? Well, let my experience guide you toward a fulfilling experience full of needles, interesting people, and exhilarating light-headedness.

The first step to plasma donation is finding a place where plasma is accepted. Imagine your surprise and embarrassment if you show up at McDonald's with a gallon bag of plasma, and they say you have to pay money! You can usually find the nearest plasma center in the newspaper within ads that say, "Do you need X-tra cash for X-mas?" or something of that ilk.

Myself, being knowledgeable of the nearest plasma donation center, headed straight for the offices of Norman, Okla.'s own NABI Biomedical Inc. I walked into the brightly lit facility with joy in my soul and a renewed faith in America's capitalist system. What I left with, though, is a different story.

Mary, with whom I checked in, was thrilled at my choice to forgo a job and live solely off the sale of my bodily fluids. She gave me several pamphlets to look over, including "The Facts About Plasma Donation." This tract outlined the process in which I would donate my plasma, the portion of my blood (and yours, too) that contains water and proteins. It also is the material that makes up the corona of the sun, so I can see why it is valuable.

I learned that they would extract my blood via plastic tube and run it through a centrifuge, thereby separating the plasma from the red blood cells. These happy crimson globules then return to my body while the plasma is collected in a bag underneath the machine.

I returned to Mary's desk, satisfied with my knowledge in the arcana of plasma sales. She then proceeded to hand me 123 different waivers that shielded NABI from responsibility in the event of accidental death, deformity, bruises, and overextraction of bodily fluids resulting in mummification.

After I signed these, she asked me a list of questions, including, "Have you had any piercings or tattoos in the last 12 months?" and the ever-popular "Since 1979, have you taken money or drugs for sex?" I answered "no" to both of these, thankful for the fact that I went into rehab for my heroin-for-sex addiction in '78.

Following this little Q&A, I sat down and waited for my name to be called. When it was, I got ushered into a tiny booth where my blood pressure and temperature were taken.

I asked Denise, my friendly booth technician, if anyone had ever failed these tests, and she replied, "You'd have to be comatose or dead not to pass these ridiculous requirements. One guy came in here, and he had pneumonia. He was coughing green stuff everywhere." After my stats were taken and she took some blood from my finger, Denise pronounced me "well above requirements," which meant, basically, that I was physically fit enough to have my lifeblood siphoned.

I waited in the entrance room for a bit more, and eventually I was called back to the donation area, or, as I call it, the Temple of Doom. It was a cheery place, with posters

on the wall proclaiming me a hero for helping all sorts of hemophiliac kids and burn victims with my plasma, a fluid I almost never use anyway.

I was given a plastic bottle and told to recline in a nifty, vinyl-upholstered couchlike thing with an interchangeable armrest. Once I got comfortable, a guy in a white coat came up to me and announced, "Hi, I'm Vincent, and I'm going to stick you."

This is where the horror began.

My new buddy Vince, I found, was a licensed phlebotomist (from the Latin *phlebos,* which, loosely translated, means "copious amounts of blood," and *tomus,* meaning "to extract through lengthy and often torturous means"). I didn't know whether he actually trained for this title, or if he just sent away for it with several proofs-of-purchase from Count Chocula. He didn't look all too menacing, though, so I didn't jump up and run away.

Although I figured they were going to have to be tricky in getting a rubber tube in my vein, I didn't know that the utensil for this project would be a FIVE-INCH NEEDLE!

"This may sting a little," Vincent told me, as he prepared to ram the piece of metal into my fragile body. I grinned and tried to bear the intrusion as best as I could. I hardly screamed at all.

Once that was over, I thought it would be smooth sailing. Pumping my hand on a foam bike-handle thing, my blood went flowing from my body into the ungodly vampire machine. I laid back and noticed a TV positioned in my line of view, with a movie just starting.

"This is going to be a piece of cake," I thought. "I'll just lie here and watch some goofy movie like *Slap Shot* or *Strange Brew* and I'll be done in no time."

As the credits rolled, I realized it was worse than that. Much worse. The movie they had decided to screen was *Alive,* the heartwarming true story of a bunch of South American soccer players whose plane crashes in snowy mountains where they discover the many ways of preparing human buttocks. So, just to clarify, I was lying there listening to some actor named Antonio-something say, "I always thought Ricardo had a nice ass, but this is delicious!" while some hell-spawned satanic device drained me of my only current possession. Then my plasma machine starting beeping. Thinking I had somehow doomed myself to a low sperm count, chronic halitosis, or some other handicap, I yelled for Vincent at the top of my lungs.

In about five minutes, Vince came over and told me it was beeping because I was finished. My Stokeresque nightmare was over.

My $15 reward didn't go far that week, so I had to keep giving plasma, which I do to this day. I now have a scar on my left arm the size of Idaho, and I'm beginning to look a little pale. But don't let me dissuade you from going down and donating right now.

It may be painful, scary, and a little weird, but hey, you get free money, a free movie, and free grape Kool-Aid, and that's what America is all about.

Isn't it?

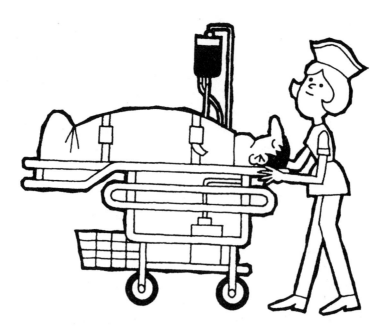

Mike McGonigal has gone through the most incredible up-and-down cycles during his years publishing *Chemical Imbalance*. An incredible music fanzine, *Chemical Imbalance* mixes writings about some of the most exciting music ever made with cutting-edge literature and avant-garde art. Started back in 1984, it was published regularly until 1992, when drugs, violence, and the pressures of urban living proved to be too much for Mike.

He vanished off the face of the earth until quite recently, when he reappeared in Tennessee. While none of the back issues are available, he's back on track and has started publishing this eclectic collection once again.

Bob Flanagan's life was also like a roller-coaster ride. The difference is that Bob's life was headed in one direction—only I'm not sure which direction it was. Born with the genetic disorder cystic fibrosis, Bob's childhood was a struggle and fight against death. Cystic fibrosis is a tragic disorder that requires constant medical attention and induces very premature death. The repeated hospital visits and internal pain led to Bob's early predilection for masochistic fantasies. Over the years, his experiments with S/M became more open and public, leading to some groundbreaking performance art that explored disease, modern primitive rituals, and the extremes of sexuality.

While his doctors never expected him to live to see his tenth birthday, Bob just recently passed away, at the miraculous age of forty-three. He left behind a memorable body of work, including several books, videos, and performances. This poem was first published in *Chemical Imbalance,* but Bob originally wrote it to accompany his performance "Nailed," in which he attached fifty clothespins to his nude body, sewed up his scrotum with a needle and thread, and then nailed it to a wooden board using a hammer.

WHY

●

By **Bob Flanagan** *from*
Chemical Imbalance

Why:

Because it feels good; because it gives me an erection; because it makes me come; because I'm sick; because there was so much sickness; because I say FUCK THE SICKNESS; because I like the attention; because I was alone a lot; because I was different; because kids beat me up on the way to school; because I was humiliated by nuns; because of Christ and the crucifixion; because of Porky Pig in bondage, force-fed by some sinister creep in a black cape; because of stories about children hung by their wrists, burned on the stove, scalded in tubs; because of "Mutiny on the Bounty"; because of cowboys and indians; because of Houdini; because of my cousin Cliff; because of the forts we built and the things we did inside them; because of what's inside me; because of my genes; because of my parents; because of doctors and nurses; because they tied me to the crib so I wouldn't hurt myself; because I had time to think; because I had time to hold my penis; because I had awful stomach aches and holding my penis made it feel better; because I felt like I was going to die; because it makes me feel invincible; because it makes me feel triumphant; because I'm a Catholic; because I still love Lent, and I still love my penis, and in spite of it all I have no guilt; because my parents said BE WHAT YOU WANT TO BE, and this is what I want to be; because I'm nothing but a big baby and I want to stay that way, and I want a mommy forever, even a mean one, especially a mean one; because of all the fairy tale witches, and the wicked step mother, and the stepsisters, and how sexy Cinderella was, smudged with soot, doomed to a life of servitude; because of Hansel, locked in the witch's cage until he was fat enough to eat; because of "O" and how desperately I wanted to be with her; because of my dreams; because of the games we played; because I've got an active imagination; because my mother bought me tinker toys; because hardware stores give me hard-ons; because of hammers, nails, clothespins, wood, padlocks, pullies, eyebolts, thumbtacks, staple-guns, sewing needles, wooden spoons, fishing tackle, chains, metal rulers, rubber tubing, spatulas, rope, twine, C-clamps, S-hooks, razor blades, scissors, tweezers, knives, push-pins, two-by-fours, ping-pong paddles, alligator clips, duct tape, broom sticks, barbecue skewers, bungee cords, sawhorses, soldering irons; because of tool sheds; because of garages; because of basements; because of dungeons; because of "The Pit and the Pendulum"; because of the Tower of London; because of the Inquisition; because of the rack; because of the cross; because of the Addams Family playroom; because of Morticia Addams and her black dress with its octopus legs; because of motherhood; because of Amazons; because of the Goddess; because of the moon; because it's in my nature; because it's against nature; because it's nasty; because it's fun; because it flies in the face of all that's normal (whatever that is); because I'm not normal; because I used to think that I was part of some vast experiment and that there was this implant in my penis that made me do these things and allowed THEM (whoever THEY were) to monitor my activities; because I had to take my clothes off and lie inside this

giant plastic bag so the doctors could collect my sweat; because once upon a time I had such a high fever my parents had to strip me naked and wrap me in wet sheets to stop the convulsions; because my parents loved me even more when I was suffering; because I was born into a world of suffering; because surrender is sweet; because I'm attracted to it; because I'm addicted to it; because endorphins in the brain are like a natural kind of heroin; because I learned to take my medicine; because I was a big boy for taking it; because I can take it like a man; because, as somebody once said, HE'S GOT MORE BALLS THAN I DO; because it is an act of courage; because it does take guts; because I'm proud of it; because I can't climb mountains; because I'm terrible at sports; because NO PAIN, NO GAIN; because SPARE THE ROD AND SPOIL THE CHILD; BECAUSE YOU ALWAYS HURT THE ONE YOU LOVE.

Another person who has seen some serious ups and downs over the years has got to be Rollen Stewart, a.k.a. the Rainbow Man, a.k.a. John 3:16. Completely obsessed with TV since childhood, Rollen made it his life's work to be seen on TV as often as possible. It was in 1977 that the idea he was waiting for dawned on him: he realized that by simply donning a wild-looking rainbow-colored Afro wig and clowning around at national sports events, TV cameras would put him on the air.

Then, in 1980, the TV camera's interest in his rainbow antics seemed to fizzle out. He turned to religion and changed the focus of his brief TV appearances to Bible scriptures, holding up a sign reading "John 3:16." Stewart eventually succumbed to insanity and earned himself three prison life sentences.

Sam Green's tale of Stewart's rise and fall is certainly one of the most fascinating accounts of his life. This essay originally appeared in Jeremy Braddock's *Verbivore*. Jeremy has an uncanny knack for compiling and assembling the finest writing. One of the most compelling zines out there, *Verbivore* features well-researched, well-written reports from the darker side of reality.

THE UNBEARABLE MELANCHOLY SAGA OF THE RAINBOW MAN

•

By **Sam Green** *from*

Verbivore

A lonely white guy crying out in the wilderness

 buzz swept through the press pack outside the Los Angeles International Airport Hyatt Hotel. TV reporters phoned their assignment desks, asking for more airtime on the 6 o'clock. Newspaper

reporters made a case for page one. Hell, this was a lead story: the nut barricaded in room 718 holding a hotel maid hostage wasn't just any nut. It was that guy who used to show up at televised sporting events wearing a rainbow-colored Afro wig or holding up a sign that said JOHN 3:16. The Rainbow Man, they called him. Rock'n Rollen. What a weird story.

Inside the Hyatt an LAPD hostage negotiator spent most of the day speaking with the Rainbow Man—a.k.a. Rollen Frederick Stewart—on the phone. Stewart said he had a .45 and if he wasn't given access to the media below, he'd start shooting at passing jets. The plan was to stage a live televised three-hour press conference. As Stewart told the negotiator, he'd done his homework and now had the police in a corner.

ROLLEN STEWART: *I've watched* Cops, *you know, the cop shows, to try to get an idea of what you will do and what you won't do.*

LAPD: Rollen, with all due respect, maybe you watch a little too much TV.

RS: *I watch a lot of it.*

LAPD: Well, you shouldn't look at it so much.

RS: *It's a good learning tool. I watch all reality television.*

LAPD: There's not too much reality on TV.

RS: *No, I mean all real-life situations—reality television, shows like* 9-1-1, Current Affair, Sally Jesse Raphael—*anything where it's live. I don't watch anything that's not a real talk show or a real-live show. There's a lot of reality TV shows on right now.*

LAPD: If that's the case, and you say you watch a lot of those real-time TV shows, then you ought to know that no one ever wins in a situation like this. OK, unless you do exactly what the police tell you to do.

Several minutes later:

LAPD: Rollen, you want some sandwiches?

RS: *I've watched way too many cop shows to fall for that.*

Sitting in the evidence room of the Los Angeles Superior Court last year, I glance over the exhibits from *People v Rollen Frederick Stewart:* a greasy and forlorn rainbow wig in a brown paper bag, a cheap .45 caliber pistol, a worn Bible. It was a sordid end for a man who had flown high.

In his day, Rollen Stewart had "appeared" on TV during the Masters golf championship, the Kentucky Derby, the World Series, the Superbowl, and hundreds of other events. The Rainbow Man character was so well known it made *St. Elsewhere, Beavis and Butthead,* and *Peanuts.* It was Rollen Stewart's life. He spent almost a decade barnstorming the country on a ceaseless publicity tour for the Rainbow Man and later for John 3:16. He forsook marriage, a roof over his head, and any semblance of a normal life to make the world *see* him.

But in the end, it was this very passion and intensity that consumed Stewart. I was drawn to the barely visible ripple he had made in the river of history. Like the Watts tower, it seemed like a monument to both the absurdity of life and the nobility of trying anyway.

There's not much left of the Rainbow Man today. Stewart had almost no possessions by the time he ran amok. His ex-wife—a schoolteacher in Los Angeles—gave me a paper bag full of newspaper clippings that chronicled his "career." Reading through them, I was able to piece together this story.

VERBIVORE
THE INDUSTRY LEADER
Verbivore / issue 3 $3.95
SECURITY WATCH
Conspiracy: The New Religion
Bridget Brown on alien fashion
Slavoj Žižek on conspiracy theory

Born in 1948, Stewart grew up in Spokane, Washington. He describes his childhood as unhappy: his father, a car salesman, died of cancer when he was ten. His mother became an alcoholic and recluse; Stewart became a self-professed television addict, finding refuge in *American Bandstand* and the *Ed Sullivan Show.*

People who knew Rollen remember him as a morose, insecure guy eager to make friends. In high school, he was the one who'd steal beer from the grocery store where he worked and offer it to the cool kids so they'd hang out with him.

After high school, Stewart's life was a series of false starts: he studied business briefly at Yakima Junior College; he worked at Boeing, and then in retail. He went through a quick marriage. In 1968 his mother was killed in a house fire and his only sister was strangled to death by her boyfriend. Friends say Stewart never recovered.

By the mid-1970s, Stewart was "retired," living on a small ranch near the tiny town of Cle Elum, Washington. He was married for the third time and "sailing around the world on his waterbed," as he told friends. He made money selling gravel from his land to the state highway department, so he had plenty of time for drag racing, snowmobiling, smoking dope, going for the world's record with his foot-long Cossack mustache and watching TV.

Life was good, but Stewart wanted more—especially more *attention.* He studied a book called *How You Can Appear in TV Commercials.* But it was while watching TV in 1977 that the proverbial lightbulb went on over his head. "I realized that if I could be seen at nationally televised events I could create a personality that would be internationally known using the satellite dish," Stewart remem-

bers. "Instead of going to Hollywood and waiting in casting lines for years, I would be world-famous overnight and do TV commercials, get paid for having fun, see the sports, get world attention and have complete control of my life."

The problem was Stewart needed a hook. He was thin, balding, wore Coke-bottle glasses, and, aside from the big mustache, he was the dictionary definition of forgettable.

And then, on New Year's Eve 1976, Stewart and his wife were driving to Seattle to celebrate. On a whim she put on a rainbow-colored Afro wig. Everyone they passed laughed, honked, and waved. Suddenly, Stewart had his angle.

Excerpt from Stewart's Autobiography:

1977 NBA finals, game 5: Portland Trailblazers vs. Philadelphia 76ers. Went into the stadium and at half-time I walked around the bottom aisle. A cameraman grabbed me and said, "Stop, I'm going to make you world famous." I started jumping and dancing. He said, "hold on, wait till you see the red light." Seconds later, on it came and for seven seconds I did what was to be known as my traditional dance for the red eye: shaking my face, curling my long mustache, tossing my hair about, giving positive hand signs—V for victory, num-

ber one, thumbs up and A-OK—while dancing wildly about. Once I saw the red light, I was hooked. I'm a very quiet, shy sort of person, but when I put on the rainbow and saw the red eye, I became the most outgoing person in the world. After the game, went out to the hamburger stand wearing the hair and a young boy and his father who had seen me on TV came running over and started telling me that they had just seen me and making quite a fuss. At that time I began to see how people identify with someone they had seen on TV and what a great, positive loving relationship it created.

In the late 1970s, a time when a man could capture the country's imagination by riding a rocket engine into the Snake River Canyon, or a guy could get famous by putting a bag over his head and telling dumb jokes—an era when the currency of fame in America was trading at all-time lows—the Rainbow Man was at the right place at the right time.

More accurately, he seemed to be every place all the time. After his third wife left him, Stewart took the wig on the road, flying each year to the World Series, NBA finals, and NCAA finals. Every Christmas he made a heroic circuit, driving and flying to 14 different college bowl games scattered around the country in just 12 days.

At each game the objective was the same: get in front of a cameraperson and jump about wildly. During a lull in play a director often needs "color" shots; what better image than the clown with the rainbow wig? Stewart estimates that his plan worked at 90 percent of the games he attended. After a year or two of popping up on TV week after week the Rainbow Man was a full-fledged TV personality.

Telephone calls for interviews were now coming in hot and heavy. The world was starting to notice the Rainbow Man everywhere and it was really great. Far beyond my initial expectations. Then a big call came from Anheuser-Busch. They wanted me for a national commercial—just what I wanted to do. They flew me to LA to shoot it at the Coliseum. It was a football commercial showing a game and me doing my stick [sic] in the stands. I joined the Screen Actors Guild and got paid every time it was on TV. Some days it was on 4 or 5 times. It ran for 2 years and paid my expenses for 1978–9.

Like the stars he watched on *Dick Clark*, Stewart got an agent. He embarked on an ill-fated singing career (someone wrote him a disco song called "Free Dancin'," but no record label was interested). He appeared on talk shows in the Seattle area, partied a lot. And, of course, he continued to show up at sporting events.

The Rainbow Man had Made It. But something was missing. "I began to see how shallow and unhappy the Hollywood high was by talking to different stars on talk shows and seeing the fickle way the public would build you up and tear you down on the next Friday," Stewart says. "I became somewhat disillusioned. Still enjoyed the attention, but was searching for what my calling would be."

"He thought that when he got rich and famous, he'd be happy," said William King, a friend. "But instead, he was rich and famous and still feeling like that same lonely kid he was in Spokane."

It was at the 1980 Superbowl in Los Angeles where Stewart bottomed out. Lately, he had been augmenting the rainbow wig with crazy outfits to keep the cameras focused on him. For the Superbowl he wore a fur loincloth, with nothing on underneath. During the game, women stuck their hands under the loincloth and felt Stewart up.

Perhaps the sexual objectification was a final straw: Stewart returned to his hotel room depressed, and turned on the television to an obscure religious show called *This Week in Bible Prophecy*, with Dr. Charles Taylor. It was a show that tracked current events looking for, and usually finding, warnings of a coming apocalypse. Stewart was immediately born again.

"It wasn't like a bolt of thunder of anything," Stewart says. "But it hit me as 'This is the calling, this is the reality, what you've been looking for, this is what you're to do for the rest of eternity, to call the Lord through the secular airwaves.'"

Stewart was a man with renewed purpose. It was now clear that God had created the Rainbow Man to give him a pulpit once he was saved. Within six months he had sold his ranch and the rest of his possessions, hopped in his pickup truck, and set off on a peripatetic mission to get the Word on TV—a journey that would last almost a decade.

Once saved, Stewart's routine changed. He still showed up at televised events wearing the rainbow wig, only now he sported a "Jesus Saves" shirt, too. And while the Rainbow Man had once been merely a hobby for Stewart, it was now a full-time job. He lived out of his car. Slept in rest stops. Bought a *TV Guide* each week and followed the cameras. There was football, baseball, and basketball. Golf, game shows, and beauty pageants. But *any* live, televised event would do.

When Mt. St. Helens erupted in Washington State, as soon as the first ash started to fall on my pickup I drove right around the ash storm and was on the mountain prophesying. There were the shuttle launches, the full eclipse of the sun. I used to love to stand outside of the Senate and the White House—Sam Donaldson and the other reporters would close out the news or do a live report and I could stand behind the different newscasters and be seen in the background.

Stewart lived frugally. He ate one meal a day, usually at McDonald's. He still smoked pot every day. In 1984 he married for the fourth time, this time to a schoolteacher he met at a Christian singles mixer in Virginia. They continued his "ministry" together, sleeping in the back of a Toyota minivan and living off the money from the sale of Stewart's ranch. When an interviewer asked what he'd do when the money ran out, Stewart said that the apocalypse would solve that problem: "All signs point toward World War III. Christ will come back before my money runs out—we're living at the end of the age."

As The End grew nearer, Stewart's message began to change. In the mid-1980s, he got rid of the rainbow wig completely and began carrying a sign or banner bearing a phrase that would become his new trademark: John 3:16. The verse states: "For God so loved the world that He gave His only begotten son, that whosoever believeth in Him should not perish, but have everlasting life." Stewart's goal was for writers and TV reporters to recite the verse to the fans at home (as I have just done) thereby spreading the Word for him. Two points, Stewart.

While TV directors had seen the Rainbow Man as a goofy crowd shot, John 3:16 was a nuisance, and Stewart was forced to adjust his M.O. accordingly. He began using a battery powered monitor during events so he could see exactly what the director was shooting and crash the shot. Stewart's ex-wife has a stack of VHS tapes that show a JOHN 3:16 sign unfolding in the stands behind home plate at a Dodgers game, popping up next to the bobsled run at the 1990 Winter Olympics, and appearing from behind a tree at the Masters golf tournament.

These guerrilla tactics pissed off directors. Most just did their best to frame Stewart out of the shot, but a director for NBC took him out on the back nine in a golf cart and threatened to break his legs if he showed up on the course again. Like a fickle lover, television had had enough.

By the end of the 1980s, Stewart could see that the John 3:16 ministry was coming to the end of the road. His money was gone, and Jesus was still not back yet. He wrote an autobiography, but no publisher would touch it. His wife left him, claiming he once choked her for standing in the wrong spot with her sign at the World Series. The final blow came when a drunk driver totaled his car in Los Angeles. Stewart was stuck. The End was right around the corner and a hundred million Americans were still unsaved!

Hard Copy, June 11, 1991:

> *It's one of the strangest real-life stories television has given us. For years millions saw him on television, carrying his message of Christian love and faith. Everyone thought he was just a harmless kook. But now the Rainbow Man is a fugitive, considered armed and dangerous by the FBI, and no one wants to bet where he'll strike next!*

Marooned and frustrated in Los Angeles, Stewart put aside John 3:16, much as he had put aside the Rainbow Man almost ten years before, and created a new character: the "Backslidden Christian." With the Backslidden Christian, Stewart proved the old adage that genius rarely strikes twice. He began leaving high-powered stink bombs around Los Angeles; he hit the Crystal Cathedral in Garden Grove (one of the world's only drive-in churches), the Trinity Broadcasting Network offices, and the *Orange County Register* offices. Along with the stink bombs, he'd leave a note describing himself not as the Rainbow Man or John 3:16 but as a hater of Christianity—the Backslidden Christian. He'd sometimes sign the notes "The Anti-Christ."

The idea was *almost* brilliant. Unfortunately, *Hard Copy* and the L.A. TV stations framed the story a bit differently, focusing instead on Stewart himself, whom police fingered immediately, and the kook angle. It was a juicy story, full of irony and a postmodern fusion of TV and reality ("one of the strangest real-life stories television has given us"). Stewart's prophecy teachers received nary a mention.

While the media had fun with the story, police took Stewart's antics seriously. The Santa Ana D.A. charged him with four felonies, and in the spring of 1991 Rollen Stewart became a fugitive.

"The idea was to run with the Backslidden Christian until they found out it was me and then I knew I had to get a fake green card and live in these skid row hotels," Stewart said.

For Stewart it was easy to go underground: no one recognized him without the rainbow wig. For more than a year he floated around the Bladerunner-meets-Dickens world of downtown Los Angeles, living in SRO hotels—an existence that would bring out the Travis Bickle in almost anyone.

Stewart spent most of his time "hooked into the media" —his euphemism for a hard-core television addiction with a heavy emphasis on reality programming. He still smoked pot every day, saying, "It takes the edge off to where I can just barely tolerate the insanity of the world."

When he wasn't watching TV, Stewart spent his time navigating the city, planning his next move. One afternoon he took a bus out to Disneyland, on another he went to Los Angeles International Airport. He was location scouting, looking for a place to stage another act in the fifteen-year performance piece he now referred to as "the final presentation."

"I knew I had to be out a little bit more, before I would end the presentation," Stewart said. "I walked everywhere, took mass transit to get all the places I was checking out for my final presentation, when I would turn myself in and try to get worldwide attention in a press conference."

In the spring of 1992, while a fugitive in Los Angeles, Stewart wrote the following tract which now sits in a file at the Los Angeles County Superior Courthouse:

> *Jesus is going to rapture the church soon. Perhaps even on Sept. 16, 1992. After the rapture, Juan Carlos of Spain, who will be revealed as the anti-Christ, eventually will sign a peace treaty with Israel and lead the European Common Market in a one-world government with Roman Catholicism as the false prophet. They chop off your head if you refuse to take the mark 666—the universal product code—on your hand or forehead. So Jesus chose me to alert you. My actions are justified in the fifth amendment, time of war, defensive necessity, a crime to prevent greater harm.*

On September 22, 1992, Los Angeles police got a call from a maid at the LAX Hyatt. A man with a gun had forced his way into room 718 while she was cleaning. Luckily, she had managed to dash to the bathroom, lock the door, and was able to use the phone next to the toilet.

Within minutes, firefighters arrived at the hotel and evacuated more than five hundred guests. The bomb squad came. Sharpshooters ringed the place and trained high-powered rifles at Stewart's window, which he had plastered with signs citing Mark 8:36, John 3:16, and other Bible verses.

Stewart told the LAPD that the world was going to end in six days. He needed to hold the three-hour press conference to explain what was going to happen and urge people to repent.

But the LAPD's *Hostage Negotiations Handbook* probably doesn't include "Provide suspect with satellite uplink to the networks" among the acceptable ways to end a stand-off. So for nine hours the LAPD negotiator made vague promises; he stalled, he flattered Stewart, he tried the ol' sandwich trick—anything to wear Stewart down. He risked the maid's life rather than give some nut free airtime (imagine the precedent it would set).

Outside the Hyatt, the media had no idea what Stewart was trying to do. The "final presentation" had spun out of control. Despondent, Stewart smoked a joint and wept. At 6 P.M. a SWAT team kicked down the door and took him into custody. He got a lot of airtime on the news that night, but the story was not about the End of the World, which was only days away, it was about a clown who'd gone off the deep end. It was, as one anchor quipped, "the end of the rainbow." In the summer of 1993, Stewart was offered a twelve-year sentence to plead guilty. Instead, he went to trial. Finally, it would be his moment to speak, to warn the world that The End was still right around the corner. As his defense, Stewart read the Bible, crying during the passage where God turns Lot's wife into a pillar of salt. The jury, however, was unmoved and found him guilty of kidnapping and making terrorist threats.

At the sentencing, the prosecutor called Stewart a "David Koresh waiting to happen" and told the judge to throw the book at him. As his fate became clear, Stewart tried to make a final, passionate appeal, but the judge wouldn't let him speak. In a panic, Stewart began to yell. Nearly a dozen bailiffs wrestled him to the floor and carried him out of the courtroom like a battering ram. An angry judge then sentenced Stewart to *three* life terms in prison. That evening, another TV news anchor remarked that it was "the end of the rainbow."

And so it was the end of the road for Rollen Stewart. There would be no last-minute leniency from a judge struck by the naive passion of his dream. There would be no *Oprah* on Stewart and the dangers of too much TV or the loneliness of modern American existence or the fact that celebrity and the media have become soma for a nation of alienated and miserable fucks. Stewart wouldn't even make *People*'s 1994 "Whatever Happened To?" issue.

I filmed an interview with Rollen Stewart last year at the California Men's Colony, a minimum security prison outside San Luis Obispo. My first reaction to the grizzled senior citizen across from me was that the guard had brought the wrong inmate. This guy looked more like Burgess Meredith than the happy clown I'd seen for years

on TV. As Stewart grimaced and shifted in his seat, he radiated an overpowering sense of anguish.

As he faced life in prison, I wondered if Stewart had finally realized that the Faustian bargain he'd struck with the media all those years ago, his "dance for the red eye," had been a giant rip-off. I asked was he bitter, did he feel that the media, myself included, had exploited him?

"No," Stewart replied gruffly. And then, for the first time that afternoon, he smiled; he even chuckled. "Actually, I'm exploiting you. Who else in this prison is having an interview today?"

Sure he had regrets: "In terms of the LAX Hyatt, who knew that the maid would lock herself in the bathroom and there'd be a *phone in there?* I should have checked." Sure, he'd also been premature, Stewart admitted, but 1994 *was definitely the year.*

I ran through the rest of my questions, mainly about his childhood and years as the Rainbow Man, but Stewart kept bringing the conversation back to the rapture and his "presentation."

"This story would be of interest to *Inside Edition, 20/20, Dateline, 60 Minutes*—your twelve-to-fifteen-minute format," he pointed out between questions. "Also, it would be of interest to *Donahue* and *Oprah* where they could send a camera and have me on live.

"I think it would pay off for you to write all the talk shows and news shows and tell them what you have here," he continued. "It would better your career, get you into the mainstream where you'd be a correspondent with Sam Donaldson tomorrow night. Because this isn't football or World Cup Soccer . . . this is the most important story in the world."

THE BAD BOYS OF THE VATICAN

•

By **Jeff Schweers** *from*

DIS

While *DIS* is no longer being published, in its three exciting issues it compiled some of the sharpest political commentary, unique illustrations, and obscure histories in zinedom. Well-balanced, enjoyable zines like this one are a rare find.

While I loved *DIS*'s ongoing feature on celebrity temper tantrums (e.g., Buddy Rich and Orson Welles), my favorite piece was Jeff Schweer's overview of the baddest of the bad popes. Until I read this summary, I simply assumed that throughout history, all the Catholic popes have been the noblest of men. It's not like this information has been wiped from the history books— just do a bit of digging and you'll find it, too. It's just that mainstream magazines would rarely print an article like this, for fear of offending their readers. Zine publishers just don't care *who* they piss off, which is what makes zines so exciting to read.

hy are people so sensitive about a movie title like *The Pope Must Die?* Imagine those words spoken by the dignified members of the Cardinal College after realizing too late that they elected an inept, incestuous bumbler to the Church's highest office, not once but again and again and again, and it becomes amusing. To some people, anyway. To others, well, one man's joke is another man's blasphemy.

> It is now a thousand years since these territories and cities have been given to the priests, and ever since then the most violent wars have been waged on their account. . . . How is it possible there has never been a good pope to remedy such evils?
>
> Giovanni De' Mussi,
> Chronicle of Piacenza, c. 1350

There were many popes over the years that the Church would probably rather leave buried among the other unsavory skeletons in the catacombs. Some of the occupants of the most sanctified seat in the Catholic Church stooped to some of the lowest, most treacherous and even bizarre types of behavior, and their actions are neither unique nor typical in the vast context of papal history. Just for fun, let's dig up a few of these fusty symbols of all that was holy and wise on earth, and see how these bad popes met their fates.

STEPHEN VI. More bizarre than bad, Stephen presided over the grisly trial of his predecessor. He had the body of Pope Formosus, which had been lying in state for eight months, exhumed and propped up on the papal throne to stand trial in what became known as the Synod Horrenda. After Stephen finished spitting insults at the corpse, he stripped it of its robes, hacked off the three fingers of the right hand used for blessings, and threw Formosus's remains into the Tiber to sleep with the fishes. Stephen's popularity didn't last long after that, and he was strangled without ceremony.

POPE JOHN XII. The original wild one, the Caligula of the papacy. He was 16 when he was named Pope John XII, a year after his father died. John had a real knack for sacrilege. He consecrated a 10-year-old boy as bishop, ordained a deacon in his stables, and had another cardinal-deacon castrated. He pilfered the church coffers to pay for his vices and prayed to pagan gods to help him at dice. Once he and his buddies raped women pilgrims in the basilica of St. Peter, and then stole the small offerings they left on the altar. John's reign was cut short when an angry cuckold caught him in the act and hit him so hard on the head that he died three days later.

BONIFACE VII. A strange little priest named Boniface Franco strangled the reigning pope and got himself elected. He was soon despised, and fled Rome. Boniface bribed his way back to Rome under the guise of a Byzantine agent, murdered the current occupant of the chair, and installed himself again as pope. The Romans could not stomach a pope who killed his two predecessors, so they slaughtered Boniface and dragged his body through the streets.

BONIFACE VIII. Benedict Gaetani was a wily old fellow, a member of the Sacred College and a skilled lawyer, who secured the Chair of St. Peter and the name Boniface VIII through all sorts of duplicity. He was so corrupt that he appears in all three books of Dante's *Divine Comedy*. He was also responsible for the conditions in Florence that led to Dante's exile. Dante loathed Boniface so much that he drags him through hell, purgatory, and paradise to appear before St. Peter, who says, Boniface has "made of my cemetery a sewer."

CLEMENT VI. He bought Avignon outright from the Queen of Naples for 80,000 gold florins, which was at least one-fourth of the papacy's annual expenditures. He then hired artists to gussy up the papal palace, where he held lavish banquets for all of his friends. Clement carried on an

incestuous relationship with his niece, Cecile de Turenne. Petrarch ridiculed Clement, calling him "this ecclesiastical Dionysus with his obscene and infamous artifices and his Semirami, soiled with incestuous embrace."

URBAN VI. Picture a dull, mid-level bureaucrat working for the Internal Revenue Service who suddenly becomes President of the United States and turns rabid. That's pretty much the story of Urban VI, who ruled off and on from 1378–1389. Mockingly called the "little bishop," he was a churlish bureaucrat who turned into a raving tyrant when the crown was thrust upon his head. He abused the cardinals during his opening address, hurling insults and yelling at them to shut up. His violence toward the cardinals and his subsequent actions led to the Great Schism.

ALEXANDER VI. Rodrigo Borgia was elected Pope Alexander VI in 1492, the same year Columbus set sail for the New World. Borgia was the baddest of bad popes, the king bee of maliciousness, the sultan of sin. And his brood was no better. They did it all: incest, fratricide, adultery, simony and nepotism, to name some of their favorite hobbies. The Borgia family had an insatiable lust for power that nearly destroyed the papacy.

Borgia took up with Vannozza Catenei around 1470, and she gave him four children—Giovanni, Cesare, Lucrezia, and Joffre—while she was married to two other men in succession. Even after Vannozza lost her looks, Borgia took good care of her. As pope, he seduced the soon-to-be-married sixteen-year-old Giulia Farnese, whom the wits of Rome dubbed "Christ's bride." As much as he loved women, Alexander was not particular about his bedmates. One historian says he was "most sensual toward both sexes." His real taste, however, was for power. After becoming pope, Alexander VI married off his daughter Lucrezia to the kinsman of a powerful cardinal, and made his son Cesare a cardinal at eighteen. His son Giovanni was already a duke.

It would take too long to detail all of Alexander's political maneuverings, but it's enough to say that Machiavelli was a big admirer of the pope's strategies and wrote glowing analyses of both Alexander's and Cesare's statecraft. The Borgias used every trick in the book to acquire as much land as they could. But Cesare was feared more than his father because of one crucial difference: While Alexander murdered for political reasons, Cesare took things more personally. A drunken reveler lost his hand and tongue for mocking Cesare. A Venetian accused of circulating a hostile pamphlet was drowned in the Tiber.

LEO X. Pope Leo X's words following his election were, "God has given us the papacy—let us enjoy it." And

enjoy it he did. While the Medicis were more civilized than the bloodlusting Borgias, they found new ways to siphon church money into their coffers and they turned the Vatican into a pleasure palace. The cost of maintaining the Medici lifestyle, however, tapped out the Church completely. Although Pope Leo X brought artists and scholars to Rome, he was considered a write-off because of the large debts he amassed.

CLEMENT VII. A total disaster. During his reign, Rome was brutally attacked by imperial troops that should have been its protectors; the English broke away from the Church; and the Protestant movement flourished. By the time Clement died, the office of the pope was no longer a seat of temporal power—just the figurehead of a church that was no longer seen as the absolute dispensation of God on Earth.

The pope is dead. Long live the pope.

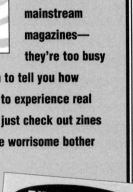

SIDE EFFECTS OF LIVING: 25 REASONS TO DRINK

•

By **Michael Gorgei** *from*
Pinch Point

There's a certain style of writing that's found only in zines. You never find extreme anger or brutal satire in mainstream magazines— they're too busy trying to sell you booze than to tell you how they really feel. If you want to experience real emotions or stinging satire, just check out zines like *Pinch Point*. Without the worrisome bother of keeping advertisers happy or avoiding offense, the contributors to *Pinch Point* just let it rip. Past issues have included sharp satires that target their least favorite celebrities. But to avoid a lengthy, tangled lawsuit I didn't choose anything from the eviller side of *Pinch Point*'s celebrity bashing. Instead, I selected this simple piece that lists the real reasons people drink—to get drunk.

We Make David Letterman Cry

Because someday I'll be dead.

My family hates me.

I don't know what's good for me.

There's so much I want to forget.

It helps me sleep.

I'm having a real tough time with the modern world.

It enhances my personality.

I was never good at sports.

It's the one thing that separates us from animals.

It gives me the courage to do great things, like ask a girl for her phone number or lose twenty dollars to an obvious pool hustler.

It's _____ night.

It just feels right.

It's a great way to meet people.

Because of what we did to the Indians.

It beats working.

Although I have a job now, I'm going to lose it sometime.

My parents did it.

My parents didn't do it.

Would you rather I shoot dope?

It's not a sin, is it?

Just fucking look at me.

It makes the voices go away.

There's nothing on TV tonight.

Because someday every person I've ever looked at, kissed, passed on the freeway, taken change from, stood in line for tickets with, worked eight hours a day next to, borrowed a ballpoint pen from, *drank with*, made fun of, loved, hated, watched on TV, played Coleco Mr. Quarterback with, smiled at, will be dead.

Thanks to the growing cult of cocktail/lounge culture, drinking is coming back in style. Sure it's elegant to dress up in smart clothing and drink impeccably prepared martinis, but heavy drinking will always have its down side. Alcoholism, drunk driving, job loss, depression, killing hangovers, vomiting, and random violence are dark spots in the equation that may just as well be better left unmentioned.

SURVIVING THE LOW LIFE: BETTER LIVING THROUGH CRANK

•

By **Jeff Koyen** *from*

Crank

Crank is certainly one of my favorite zines. It's tightly written, creatively designed, and never fails to impress me with its coarse tales of hard living. Editor Jeff Koyen is one pissed-off dude. But instead of just mouthing off at whatever flickers up on his TV set, he goes out and *finds* fucked-up shit, and tells you what's wrong with it. Reading his zine you realize he just doesn't care how many enemies he makes by presenting his views with brutal honesty.

After reading several issues of any zine you start to form a picture of what its editor is like. After reading several issues of *Crank* I get the impression that Jeff is a smart, creative individual who isn't shy about his passion for drinking and living on the edge. Since it was written several years ago, I'm not sure if the lifestyle portrayed in this essay still accurately describes Jeff's, but it's a compelling portrait of excess. You may want to heed his advice—it comes from experience.

L ots o' kids dream of living that crazy, down-trodden lifestyle that all the great ones lived. Sure, baby: wake up at noon, slug down a couple pints to settle that stomach, shower, shit, and hit the nearest bar by two. Well, you know what? I've been there, friends, and it ain't that easy. It works well for a few weeks. In fact, it's very refreshing to binge for a month or two when your job has you in a deep rut. But then you find that extra twenty pounds hanging on your pasty, fat face; your boss is walking the line between pity and anger; and one evening you realize that a lot of things in your apartment are broken . . . things like all the lightbulbs, more than half the dishes, and your intestines. You need a fixin' up, pal. And you SWEAR that next time, you'll be ready for that glass all over the floor that keeps sticking in your feet when you try to walk to the fucking bathroom. But you know what? You won't be ready, because you'll just pluck out the glass, empty your bladder, and go back to bed, drunk and happy.

Believe me when I tell you that I've hit lower than most of you. No, no, I've never killed anyone, or beaten up my girl in a drunken rage; none of those bullshit stories. You want a true anecdote from one man's bottoming out? OK, one Thursday morning, sitting with my boots up on my desk at work, I noticed what looked like splotches of white paint on the tops of my shoes. Huh? I took a closer look and wracked my brain for an explanation. Had I painted recently? Spackled? Walked through cement? Nope. Aaahh, it finally hit me: the last time I'd worn those boots, I'd gotten so drunk I wound up vomiting in the gutter outside my apartment. The white spots were the last of the turkey sandwich I'd eaten earlier that evening. At least it didn't smell—not that I could notice, anyway. That was a turning point—I knew I had to start being a tad more responsible in this ridiculous life I was leading. Even if it only meant washing my boots before I was sober enough to be ashamed.

So, for all you guys and girls stuck in the same sinking, stinking boat, it's time to take the rational approach to this overly rewarding lifestyle. The MBA phrase-boys call it "Proactivity." I call it "Living Smart."

HERE ARE THE THINGS YOU SHOULD OWN IF YOU PLAN TO LIVE THE LOW LIFE:

Some are intended for cleaning up the inevitable damage;

Some are intended as diversion against the boredom that inevitably leads to violent, drunken binges;

Some are just meant to make your life seem more respectable, which (if you believe the 12-step programs) is important to keeping your impulses under control.

As with all things *Crank*, I take no responsibility for YOUR actions, but, please, do send photos of the damage, especially if it involves flesh.

Wet/Dry Shop-Vacuum

Though it's primarily viewed as a masculine toy, a good shop-vac can serve both sexes equally. Much like a pair of ViceGrips, a wet/dry shop-vac can do anything and everything your clumsy little hearts desire.

The vac that saves our apartment just about every weekend is a Sears Craftsman, 6.0 gallon, 2.0 horsepower powerhouse. This particular model costs $40, which seems a little steep, but you've got to understand—it was NECESSARY after a bad night of cheap beer and mad dog. The glass was 2 inches deep, no shit, and our new friend chewed it up without choking.

But let's forget the OBVIOUS industrial applications for a moment. We also have a recurring problem with mice. And the runt cat that Tom picked up—much to our surprise—has turned into a formidable mouser. Now, a mouse hunt is fun to watch in your living room, but when that last bit of squealing life is squeezed from Mickey's head, it's your job to dispose of the remains. Should you scoop 'em up in a wad of paper towel? Wrap 'em in the morning paper? Fuck, no. Get your shop-vac out and suck little Jerry straight up to mousy heaven. Come to think of it, I think those three little mice corpses are still rotting in the bottom of the vac. I wouldn't lie to you.

Electric Heater & Microwave & Toaster Oven & TV w/ Antenna

Months ago, in one of the local newspapers, I read an excerpt from the latest "GenX" handbook. The excerpt concerned the multicolored envelopes from utility companies stamped URGENT that pile up on the author's coffee table; a relentless stream of unpaid bills marking her Generation X lifestyle. It angered me to near-violence.

What an obnoxious load of self-glorifying bullshit. What a stupid fuck that author must be. Who the fuck glorifies unpaid bills? Who the fuck wants unpaid bills? Unpaid bills have left my credit rating so bad that I can't get a fucking gas card. I can only DREAM of a Sears charge card. I'd probably have to get a fucking co-signer to borrow ten bucks from a friend.

I do have trouble paying my bills on time. But I can only

speak for myself: I never have enough money to cover all my bills every month. So, every month, I pay one bill's balance from the previous month. Maybe when that NEA grant comes through with a few grand, I'll pay everyone off. In the meantime, I DON'T LIKE HAVING MY FUCKING UTILITIES SHUT OFF BECAUSE OF UNPAID BILLS. And I'm sure as fuck not going to use my unpaid bills as a badge of honor for induction into the Generation X Club.

Right now, there is no heat and no cooking gas in the apartment. Surprisingly, this time it's not our fault—it's our cocksucker landlords, who accrued a $6,000 bill with the gas company and then stopped paying the mortgage on the property. So the bank foreclosed and doesn't want to pay the $6,000 to get everything turned back on. THIS IS TRUE. And it's decidedly NOT hip and GenX. It's cold, just plain fucking cold.

- I cook everything in the microwave now that the stove and oven are useless.
- I WISH I had a toaster oven; if the gas isn't turned on yet, then I'm looking for a used one this weekend.
- I have a space heater next to my bed for the 4 A.M. chill that tears through the paper-thin windowpanes.
- The cable is still on, because I consider that bill a priority. (I can't seem to live without the Food Network, which is odd, considering I didn't cook that much even when the gas was on.) Still, the TV antenna is in easy reach.

Get these items if you're planning to fuck up your bills because you're either too much of an asshole to pay them on time and/or you're too broke. You'll be happy you own them, believe me.

Good Bottle of Red/Good Bottle of White

It doesn't matter which you prefer. Just go out and blow twenty bucks on a couple decent bottles of wine. Oh, just shut the fuck up—I know that $10 ain't gonna buy you something you can serve the president, but we're down at my standards, OK? Don't know shit about wine? Neither do I, so do what I do—Mondavi. It looks nice on a cheap wine rack, and makes a great gift if you get roped into a dinner or something at the last minute.

Spackle

And a spackling knife, trough, and wall-repair patches (for small jobs, they work wonders).

So, yes, we've put some holes in our walls. (Fuck you, it's better than picking barfights. Boys will be boys, right?) We found that you should also know the location of the nearest hardware store, naturally, for those things you never think you'll need, like tile grout.

Ice Pops

My secret for surviving particularly nasty mornings. Better than drinking water, because they've got some sugar to get your belly into shape. They're not too solid, so that you can still keep them down (or IN, if your bowels are the problem).

Ice pops are also fine treats to give to neighborhood kids (so long as you don't look the type to stick razors in apples). They, in turn, will put in a good word with the folks who, in turn, will give you one last chance to turn down that Big Black before calling in the law at 3 A.M.

A Good Sense of Humor

Because you're either going to laugh at your shitty life, or do yourself in as soon as one bad month comes to a spirit-crushing end. If you choose the latter, I'm sure there are at least three dozen little zines out there with kooky advice for potential suicides. Go consult them.

No suicide tips here, kids. I advocate squeezing every drop of indulgent experience out of this mundane life some people call "sacred." I'd like to think that I've helped you achieve that goal.

I WAS A MANIC-DEPRESSIVE, DOPE-SHOOTING, SUICIDAL HOMOSEXUAL TEENAGER

•

By **LMNOP** *from*

babysue

Some zine publishers internalize their anger and churn out bitter rants about what's wrong with the world. LMNOP channels his bitter feelings into hilarious satires that explore a myriad of subjects. His zine, *babysue*, combines silly, light-hearted comic strips and satire that bites so hard it verges on being offensive. Like the best satirists, he captures the essence of reality and then twists it around so we're laughing at ourselves. Very disturbing is this true-life story of his teenage years engaging in gay sex and drug abuse. Many people experiment with drugs in their teens but probably not to this extent. I've often talked to LMNOP, and I'm happy to report that while he does have a very dark sense of humor, he's alive and well and living in Atlanta.

I was a Manic-Depressive, Dope-Shooting, Suicidal, Homosexual **TEENAGER** in Atlanta in the Seventies — LMNOP

As a kid, I was squeaky clean. I never drank, smoked pot, or did drugs. Except for the fact that I was heavily into bizarre music, I was relatively normal.

The first drug I ever took was LSD. I was 14 at the time. The experience was frightening but interesting.

My family was highly dysfunctional. I couldn't relate to my parents or my siblings. As a result, I turned to outside friends for support.

Workaholic Father / Goodie Goodie Mom / Socially Retarded Brother / Neurotic Sister

My two closest friends in high school were Jon and Lewis. Jon was a drug dealer. Lewis was a male prostitute. They were both heavily into drugs and the gay scene.

WANNA buy some drugs? / Wanna buy me? / JON / LEWIS

I was in awe of these fellows because they were doing things that I could never DREAM of doing. After several months of hearing about all of the excitement, I decided to take the plunge.

WHOLESOME FAMILY LIFE / THE QUEER SCENE

Lewis took me to a gay bar for the first time when I was 15. I felt I was physically grotesque at the time, so the experience was a mental FREAK OUT. I was a nervous wreck.

I'M SO UGLY! NO ONE COULD LIKE ME! I'M RETARDED!

The second time I "went out" with Lewis, I ended up going home with an older man. We did lots of drugs and had WILD sex. I was hooked.

WANNA GO TO MY PLACE? / SURE / THIS CAN'T BE HAPPENING!!!

As time went by, I began taking more and more drugs. I smoked marijuana almost continuously. I started taking tranquilizers to make high school somewhat bearable.

EQUANIL

At one point, I was taking about 30 tranquilizers a day. I used to wake up and not be able to remember large chunks of time or how I had acquired different items.

NAZZ / WHERE DID THESE RECORDS COME FROM?! / YOU BOUGHT THEM YESTERDAY, SILLY!

I found out eventually that Jon and Lewis were shooting drugs. I was shocked. At first, I didn't believe them. My own friends...INJECTING DRUGS into their VEINS?!? No way!

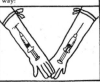

The good part about all of this is that even though I was royally fucked up, I was somehow better able to deal with my family and my sexuality.

I'M LEAVING! / GO TO HELL! / FUCK EM!

Jon, Lewis, and I used to boast about who we'd had sex with the night before. The most important information in our little group was who we had FUCKED last and who had screwed the most guys!

I FINALLY GOT BEN! / BILL IS TAKING ME TO KEY WEST. / I HAVE A DATE WITH FRED! / I'M IN LOVE WITH JOE! / ED CALLED! / JIM FUCKED ME!

About that same time my sister was getting married. I didn't want to go to the wedding but my parents forced me...so I decided to shoot up ACID beforehand.

MARRYING 'CAUSE SHE'S PREGNANT

After adjusting to the "news," I decided to try it for myself. After all, my friends seemed to be having a GREAT time!

By now, casual sex had become a way of life. In the seventies, there wasn't really any reason NOT to have sex with strangers.

LET'S DO IT!!!

By age 16, my situation at home was much worse. I had grown to hate my family. In a fit of depression, I accidentally overdosed on valium and had to be rushed to the hospital.

EMERGENCY EMERGENCY EMERGENCY EMERGENCY EMERGENCY

I looked everywhere but couldn't find any insulin syringes. I finally gave up and opted for using a large syringe intended for use on animals (my father was a veterinarian).

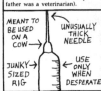
MEANT TO BE USED ON A COW / UNUSUALLY THICK NEEDLE / JUNKY SIZED RIG / USE ONLY WHEN DESPERATE

Shooting up drugs made me feel WONDERFUL. Lemme tell you, there's no better way to get the full effect of the drug!

After all, the worst thing you could get was syphilis or crabs...and those were both curable.

YOU GAVE ME THE CLAP, YOU ASSHOLE! / SO GO TO THE DOCTOR, WIMP!

I was unconscious for 3 days. When I awoke, I had no idea of what was going on.

IT CAN'T BE THURSDAY. WHAT HAPPENED TO TUESDAY AND WEDNESDAY?

I shot up 2 hits of blotter LSD. When I removed the needle, my arm began bleeding profusely...just as I started tripping BIG TIME.

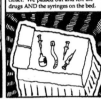

THE SLEAZIEST THEATER IN AMERICA

•

By **Jack Stevenson** *from*

Celluloid All

With the ubiquitousness of home video cameras, 8mm home movies have been nearly wiped off the face of the earth. While new fathers might be ecstatic about the ease and convenience of shooting home videos of their kids, underground filmmakers are less enthusiastic about this change. Because of the reduced demand for traditional home movies, it's become nearly impossible to buy and develop super-8 and other amateur-grade film.

For a while, Timoleon Wilkins published this informative zine for film students, experimental filmmakers, and fans of underground film. Sadly it's no more, but while it was published, each issue featured discussions on various film stock grades, reviews of artist films, and advice on touring your film around the country. One of the most useful features was the resource guide to small film-processing labs, describing the types of film each lab develops and how good a job they do.

One of the columnists, Jack Stevenson, spent a lot of time touring America, showing his films and checking out the local film scenes. While living in San Francisco, he came across this unique movie house. I'm not sure if it's still in business, but it certainly sounds as if it earns its description as "The Sleaziest Theater in America."

I lived in many cities in America during the last ten years, and being a film freak I immediately familiarized myself with the local movie scenes—pornos, art house, rep, museum, and university archive cinemas as well as the cinema clubs, Chinese action theaters, and free library-screenings circuit. From the sleaziest XXX-porno dives where you can tell the regular customers because they bring their own flashlights, to the highbrow, rarefied aestheticism of holy chapels of "cinema" like the Harvard Film Archives in Cambridge and the mortuarylike sanctum of the Pacific Film Archives in Berkeley, California (where they don't even permit the sounds of human breathing—let alone chewing on a bag of candy or popcorn—as reverent cineastes gather 'round to witness the mummified cadaver of cinema).

The difference between the lowest of the porno dives and the highest of the university archive cinemas is striking in its simplicity: in the porn cinemas people are LIVING, engaged in every biological activity you can think of, while in the archive cinemas the people are DEAD, or pretending to be dead, while the films they watch are almost equally as close to death. It's like listening to the sound of the respirator.

I choose life over death, and therefore I dedicate this column to a brief survey of the gutter-elite of America's porn theaters where a naked enthusiasm for life gushes forth like cheap malt liquor from a just-opened bottle that's been shaken vigorously.

I'm talking here only about *film-projected theaters* because to me, video projection is a life-negation that saps the force and spirit from a movie theater and, even worse, video projection is deprived of the elemental life force that originates from the mechanical process of film projection, as any scientist can tell you. The basic 24-frames-per-second flicker of light is replaced by an electronic image that lacks the power to entrance the subconscious. Anyway, when you cross off video-projected theaters from your travel plans, that leaves you with only a handful of theaters to visit in America. Most major cities have at least one remaining film-projected

porno theater where you can be fairly sure to be subjected to the most appalling conditions imaginable. In Baltimore, be sure to visit the Apex Theater in the Fells Point district—the same neighborhood that gave John Waters his start and where several landmarks from the Waters milieu still remain. Next, visit the Apple Theater in Seattle at the corner of Pike and Boren Streets. And in San Francisco be sure to wrap up your dream vacation with an afternoon at the Mini Adult Theater in the grisliest part of San Francisco's hairiest neighborhood, the Tenderloin, at the corner of Jones and Golden Gate. Pick a pleasant, sunny day to visit the Mini Adult to add to the jarring contrast of the vile darkness into which you are about to be plunged.

You enter the small ticket lobby. A couple of movie posters are crudely taped into old poster cases long ago smashed out and battered almost off the wall. These posters consist of maybe one simple image and crude lettering advertising a film that you can be sure isn't playing inside—the posters often feature cutouts pasted on the paper in a style that comes strangely close to the European Art-Brut where insane or retarded patients assembled collages seemingly at random—except these posters lack any spark.

You approach the ticket window streaked with greasy desperate fingerprints and the suds of dried whiskey. An Oriental guy takes your $3 with dirty hands as you see over his shoulder that he's repairing one of the two Bell & Howell 16mm projectors used in the cinema. These are junky classroom projectors they never clean and gobs of hair and crud often jam into the gate clouding the movie with giant hairy bobbing insect shapes. The ticket booth in fact doubles as a projection booth. To say this guy is "in charge" is surely a leap of logic since he never leaves this barricaded little room and likely the last thing on earth he wants to know about is what exactly is going on inside his little theater.

You push aside the moldy curtain over the doorway entrance and enter into total darkness . . . bumping into an immobile cluster of men gathered in the aisle just beyond the curtain. No one says anything. Words, even words of surprise or anger when you step on someone's foot, are never uttered here. Nobody has a voice *or* face in the Mini Adult.

You find a seat, carefully feeling in the darkness so that you don't end up sitting on someone's lap. After a while your eyes adjust to the darkness and you realize that a theater that was almost full when you entered is now almost empty —the density and deployment of the audience changes rapidly here and without any apparent connection to the movie that's playing. A lot of men wander about in confusion as well, as if they are completely oblivious they are in a movie theater—even though the beam of the projector is shining directly into their blank faces, creating a brief, hairy silouette on the screen that no one ever complains about.

The dim projection beam of the Bell & Howell slices the fetid, smoky darkness to shine an image on the "screen" up front, which is not a screen at all but merely a wood wall painted white. A wall with a few bashes in it and a loose board hanging here and there. The place is not big, maybe fifty people at most could sit down in the old, hard, uncomfortable rows of movie seats, bare wood. But there is plenty of open floor space and the joint has the feel and atmosphere of an auto garage or a forgotten storage room for sacks of rice and lard. The sound of the movie is too low and distorted to hear what's going on; the speakers sound as if somebody put their foot through them or somebody had their head jammed into one of them. Enhanced by the vague echo in the room, it sounds like you're listening to the film underwater. The films are all grade Z ultra-low budget XXX films from the 1970–72 era that had muddy sound quality to begin with, and used a lot of generic easy-listening music. So, largely you get distorted, wobbling, echoey easy-listening music, recorded in a bathtub, while on screen, grainy images in lurid reddish colors of greasy-bearded-with-long-sideburns guys are screwing skinny hippie chicks in unappetizing close-up. The films have been run a million times through projectors and they don't rent them; they just have piles of reels sitting in the back room and throw them on the projectors at random. Often you'll be waiting for the second half of a movie to come on and they just start up another reel of a different movie and you realize it doesn't matter at all. They keep projectors running AT ALL TIMES because the last thing anybody ever wants to happen is for the lights to come on at the Mini Adult Theater!

The films are all of heterosexual pornographic activity, although you never see a woman in the place. Even the most drugged-out junkie prostitute wouldn't go in the place, and the sex acts that occur here are of the other variety. For some reason a lot of very old and almost blind men frequent the Mini Adult, tenants of the many fleabag residential hotels nearby for which the Tenderloin has been known for decades. Just now one of these nearly blind old geezers is feeling his way down a row of seats for a place to sit while several patrons deftly dodge out of the way of his groping advance. In addition to the sense of ghostlike anonymity people have there, it's impossible in many cases to figure out if some of these very straight and respectable (or very old and oblivious) duffers are here looking for something specific, or if they truly did just wander in unknowing. They don't have a face and they don't have a clue, and there are no clues about them. It's impossible to "read" a lot of these folks.

As I said in the beginning, people LIVE here, they drink beer and smoke marijuana and engage in sex acts, and SLEEP . . . and take drugs in the lavatory located up front to the right. And they piss . . . somewhere. The lavatory, however, is reserved for assembly line dispensing of quick hits of crack cocaine—the kind of thing that hits you like the wallop of a baseball bat to the back of your skull 15 seconds after you snort or smoke a hit. Many times somebody will stumble out of the lavatory directly into the glare of the projection beam with nose twitching and eyeballs rolling in bloodshot ecstasy only to falter clumsily into the front row of patrons who remain uncannily silent as they skillfully slip out of his slippery, epileptic, involuntary embrace.

Often a guy will emerge from the bathroom sucking on

a can of beer, finishing it and throwing it on the floor where it hits with a bang. The only person I ever saw who appeared to be in some fashion WORKING there or in some position of authority in the Mini Adult, was a black guy who was dragging around a plastic garbage bag full of empty cans he was picking out from between the seats. He then noisily crushed them and dropped them into the bag. Two indistinct forms were sitting in the next row over, engaged in an unprintable and unconcealed sex act when the "can man" came up to them, looked around them for empty cans and continued on without a word.

The most notorious of the sleazy sex theaters, clubs, and hotels in New York and California were closed in the mid-1980s in reaction to the emergence of AIDS, but the Mini Adult remains one of those little joints so low down below the cops' radar that they don't even bother with it. The only people who know about the Mini Adult are the people who go to it. In a city where decadent punk, gay, and lesbian performance artists covered in piercings and tattoos seek to achieve new levels of shock, the wildest, "free-est," most utterly permissive and anarchistic little joint remains completely unknown. Sleaze is in style in S.F. but the Mini Adult continues to spin its own orbit.

The only time I heard a spoken word in the Mini Adult, the sound of a human voice, was when I had treated two friends from Detroit to an afternoon at the Mini Adult and we were leaving. "Goodbye, Officers!" rang out in sarcastic salutation as we passed through the tattered curtain over the exit door and into the blinding, brutal sunlight of the "real world."

24 HOURS IN HELL'S PANTRY

By **Sam Pratt** *from*

Ersatz

One of the more obscure neighborhoods in New York City is Hell's Pantry. It's not as hip as the East Village, certainly not as upscale as the Upper East Side, and not as glamorously dangerous as the South Bronx. Like its slightly more uptown neighbor, Hell's Kitchen, the Pantry is full of history, and full of a sort of disreputable kind of life force as well. The neighborhood abuts 42nd Street, so if you think of Times Square as the Magic Kingdom of New York City, Hell's Pantry is what goes on behind the scenery at that amusement park. From hookers to wholesalers, terrific food markets to open-air drug markets, the neighborhood has it all.

Sam Pratt, editor and publisher of *Ersatz,* one of the most appealingly designed and nicely written palm-sized zines out there, lives in Hell's Pantry, and produced this diary of the sights, sounds, and smells of the West Side, from early Sunday morning to early Monday morning.

Raise a dome over Hell's Pantry, and you'd have an instant Quentin Tarantino theme park—the buildings are even likely to fall over. Swaggering pimps in purple shirts, dive bars that haven't been mopped in years, couples crowding into dark doorways to exchange blow jobs for drugs . . . Some of the more pathetic and peculiar sights available to the naked eye in Manhattan can be found here, in the quadrangle bounded by 8th and 11th Avenues to the east and west, 34th and 42nd streets to the north and south. This downtown end of the notorious Kitchen is distinguished on the one hand by glistening vats of olives in the terrific wholesale food markets, but on the other by the glistening byproducts of crack dealing and prostitution. Here's a day in the life of the New York City's least trendy nabe . . .

SUNDAY, 9 A.M. A rusty, dented van marked "Elmhart Scrap" pulls up to the corner of 37th and 9th. The driver opens the back door to set up a sidewalk shop, buying scrap metal and copper wire from scavengers. Homeless men come and go at a brisk pace, burdened with all manner of old pipes, hubcaps, and coils; they leave counting handfuls of singles.

SUNDAY, 2 P.M. Jackies—one of several bargain stores on 8th Avenue—catches a shoplifter with a three-pack of sweat socks, value $1.07, under her raincoat. (It's a sunny day.) The crime doesn't merit a call to the cops. Besides, Jackies administers a deliberately cruel and certainly unusual punishment. The Polaroid comes out from behind the counter, and the thief is forced to pose with the purloined items. The photo then gets taped up with the others in a tawdry tableau by the front counter, titled "Photos of Thieves."

SUNDAY, 4 P.M. An ancient broom serves as a prop for the corner drug lookout. If the broom had more than a half-dozen bristles, this would easily be the cleanest corner west of Park Avenue. Just a stone's throw away, policemen guard a building on the corner of 38th Street that collapsed months ago, pitching a workman to his death on the Lincoln Tunnel access road below. The demolition of this site generated so much dust that firemen had to hose down the wreckage to maintain visibility along the avenue.

SUNDAY, 5 P.M. At the Javits Convention Center on 11th Avenue, a gift fair is wrapping up, so to speak. The neighborhood parking lots jack their daily rates up to $17 per day from the usual $7. Overdressed exhibitors bark instructions at assistants unloading wares from their luxury cars. A man with a shiny hook in place of his left hand minds a 10th Avenue lot. The hook spears a stack of punched index cards, and proves useful when his all-news radio station gets staticky: reception clears up with a touch of the hook to the transistor aerial.

SUNDAY, 8 P.M. Three off-duty cabs are parked in front of a Pakistani restaurant. Cabbies stop for a quick meal, a bit of gossip, and perhaps a look at *Taxi Talk,* a free newspaper jam-packed with useful information such as how to get from 110th-and-Amsterdam to Ludlow-and-East Houston without stopping for a red light. Contrary to popular myth, it isn't in a driver's interest to take passengers for a longer ride. The only profit margin comes in that initial $1.50 automatic charge. A long string of very short trips makes for a good day of hacking.

SUNDAY, 9 P.M. A young couple bickers on the steps of 434 West 37th Street, oblivious to the fact that the handsome (but boarded up) edifice which now serves as their backdrop was an Alimony Prison during the first half of this century.

SUNDAY, 10 P.M. The author arrives home from dinner with his father at The Supreme Macaroni Company to find no fewer than six men crammed into the entrance of his loft above Dragon Auto Repair, smoking crack. It's a nightmare version of the '50s telephone booth prank, only not very funny—especially to a parent. The first few times this happened, Yours Truly waited fearfully across the street until they finished. Now he makes a businesslike beeline for the door, saying, "Sorry guys, I gotta get in there." Apologetic, even affable, the crackheads disappear in search of a more hassle-free spot.

MONDAY, 1 A.M. The sound of a horse's hooves echoes off the building in the (finally) quiet street. A Central Park carriage driver is calling it quits for the night, taking his steed to one of several former tenement buildings near 11th Avenue. In warmer weather, horses crane their necks out of the open windows of six-story walkup apartments converted into stables.

MONDAY, 3 A.M. Apart from Moe's Deli (serving an oddly chlorine-flavored brand of rotgut coffee), only one neighborhood business stays open around the clock: the XXX video parlor, advertising All Male, All Female, Foreign, Bondage, and Amateur pleasures ("Buddy Booths" also available). It's a favorite location for independent movie makers looking for local color. When not obscured by vans and production assistants, the parlor's flashing neon bathes the corrugated metal roll-down doors of the shops across the street in multicolored holiday light.

MONDAY, 8 A.M. A motionless clutch of men and women stand on the curb, all staring silently in the same direction. Only their eyes betray any movement: They are scanning the wall in front of them, which is bare except for 12 to 15 small signs. Handwritten in Chinese and Spanish, these advertise work available that day for garment workers and carters. Another week begins in Hell's Pantry.

SURVEILLANCE
•
By **Gregory Hischak** *from*
Farm Pulp

When graphic designers look for leading-edge publications they often think of *Emigre,* but when asked where they get their ideas from, many admit to looking for inspiration in zines. The more insightful would probably turn to *Farm Pulp,* with its wonderful design—integrating inserts, fold-outs, and found graphics—that's more nostalgic in feel than modern and cold. Backing up that playful design, Greg Hischak compiles plenty of enjoyable writing, tackling each subject with gusto—mixing his own original pieces with lots of appropriate reprints.

She was a whore. I knew that. Everybody there knew that. You don't have to tell me that. Shit, I know that. I wasn't blind. I wasn't born yesterday. Do you think I got a job with bank security because I had fucking *Oblivious* written all over my face?

I knew what she was. I mean I saw her out there every day. I watched her every night. I knew.

At first it was just voyeurism, I suppose. I almost liked watching her get fucked like that, and then . . . well, and then.

Somewhere in there it became infatuation. Her surveillance became what I lived and breathed and then I didn't like watching her get fucked like that anymore. I couldn't stand it. I wanted to see all those shits dead.

But me, what could I do?

It was my job. My job was to watch. Keep focused on that door, all day, all night.

"Just watch the door, pay no fucking mind to her out there." That's what Russ, my boss, says. Pay her no mind.

A thousand bodies moving through that door all day. I have to check every one of them out, and every time I look up she's standing right there.

Eight o'clock in the morning and she's there already with a line forming. People lining up just waiting to fuck her. There wasn't a gimp on the block who hadn't smudged her or cracked her across the face. She didn't have a slot that wasn't used in some way. There isn't a button on her hasn't been pushed to its limit and I never saw a time where she didn't take it.

So I watched her take it a thousand times a day and in the morning she's still there taking it all over again. And there wasn't a fucking thing I did except watch.

At nights I'm hidden in the windows, watching the door. Watching her outside in this circle of light. It's like a tiny concrete stage with characters emerging into the light one at a time. A quick pump at the slot and a grabbing of cash. One after another, all night she's pumped and handing out stinking money like they were doing her some kind of favor.

Man, that torched me.

Being fucked like that and handing off those sweet, oily bills. Snatched up by shits and carried off to the end of the light. There on the lip of that tiny stage they smack lips and count out their fucking twenties, exiting before the next john emerges.

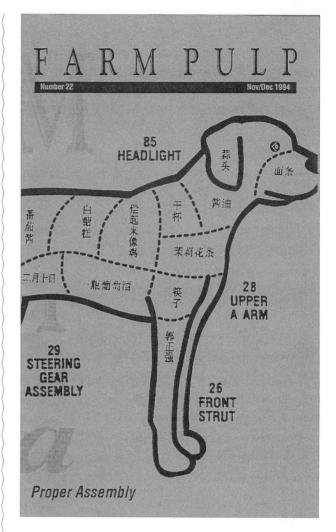

My job was to watch the door and my job got repetitive real fast.

I guess I would have fallen for a fucking Coke machine if they had put one of those outside.

To be honest, there was this time I had it hard for this newspaper box. Real sweet-like, dark red newspaper box. Sold the dailies. I got a little peak every time someone pulled out the *Times*. Nothing really came of that though. She was stolen within the week and I forgot about her.

Now that newspaper box wasn't like *her*. She never had to do *her job*.

I had really begun to feel for her and her job. Somewhere in there infatuation became . . . feelings, compassion. It was like love. Not a real love, as though I was capable of any real love, but something that hurt more than just an infatuation. Like love, something that manifested a compassion.

. . . Huh.

(A flashback)

I was watching them cut this recess into the wall. I'm security, OK? So I'm watching them cut this recess into the wall. Then they wheeled her up. Man was she pretty then. She was slid real snug-like into that recess. Her power came on. Right there I saw her power come on just like that. Flashy back-lighting and brushed aluminum, a pert little keypad and little upturned screen that had Fuck Me For Money written all over it.

And what kind of job is that writing Fuck Me For Money all over someone's face? Who does that job?

She had that little slot. Tapered little slot that whispered Stick it right here, mister. Hey, mister. Fuck me with your big card, mister. Stick it in there fast and hot until I scream your name and shit out your twenty bucks. Take it quick and cram your receipts and soiled tissues into this hole here.

Russ is shaking me hard. "Keep your eyes on the door, right?" Russ is spitting in my face and wiping me off with a towel. "That ATM ain't no business of yours, right? You got a job and your job is to keep focused on that door. Keep it focused on that door and not some little cash machine parading her thing, or you're fuckin' history. You got it?"

Russ is OK, really. He can't be expected to understand these things. Russ set me up here at the bank. He's got a woman to go home to at night. He doesn't see the things that I have to see. If he did see them he would have the choice to close his eyes. Not like me. Even if I could.

I hate having you see me in this state. Man, I hate it. Naked and dissed across a table. Yeah, it's cold. You better believe this table is cold. There's cold air running all through me here. I'm all over this table and there's cold air all inside me, between me, through me. Fuck, I hate having you see me this way, man.

Russ?

Is that you Russ?

I can't see of course. They've taken out my eye. But here's the last thing I remember seeing: I was watching her. My gaze fixed on her standing there. I didn't look at anything else anymore. I was thinking I could say something. I only needed to say a word. All I needed to decide was which word . . .

Suddenly Russ's face is real big right in front of me. Right in my face he's yelling and I could see that he's shaking. Russ is screaming awful shit at me and I notice there's blood trickling across the floor. Blood running down under those doors and I wondered how long it had been there. All that blood on the floor.

They brought in stretchers and carried out bodies.

Two guys, fucking desperate types like, killing those tellers for money. What kind of job is that anyway? Who does that? And what the hell is this? People fucking for money, people killing for money, people working all the time for money and I'm supposed to keep an eye on all of them?

I know they watched the tape right away. Russ's face is real big and mean in front of me and I know they've been watching the tape. Now even I could tell them desperate guys all look the same, but they've just got to see the two desperate guys on the bank video. Like it was important to them.

I know for a fact they saw nothing but that little cash machine. Nothing but my little cash machine being fucked by all those pigs thirty frames a second. That's all they're seeing because that's all I'm showing them.

That door was my job. I should have been watching that door, I know that, you don't have to tell me that. You think I don't know that?

Russ turned me off that afternoon. It was black. You want to ask what it's like to be turned off?

It's black.

Russ unscrewed me from the ceiling, stuck me in a bag and carried me out those doors.

I was probably within feet of her, but I was turned off. All I could see was nothing. All I could say was nothing and she had nothing to say back.

Did you even know I was there? The whole time, watching you the whole fucking time? That was me. That's what I was hoping to say.

I was there and I found you so beautiful. Though blind, I could still see what no one else could. And I saw you as beautiful.

Me? I'm nobody. You don't know me from Adam.

I am a camera. Dissed, returned to manufacturer, recalled, junked. I am fucking scrap and I never had a chance to introduce myself. I would have shared your pain. I could have done that. You must have been in pain. I could have helped. I would have wiped your face off and told you a funny story. Had I been given the chance and had I taken that chance.

I would have.

GOING OUT
•
By **Straight Up** *from*
Theoryslut

On the more serious side of the small press spectrum you'll find academic journals that offer analyses and critiques of every subject imaginable. Sure they're smart and well researched, but these journals are completely cloistered in the academic world; they rarely reach out to the wider branches of underground and mainstream culture. In short, they're boring.

Zines, on the other hand, are free to explore a wide range of theoretical discussions without the restrictions of academic thinking and turgid academic writing. Popular discussions include historical theory, situationist theory, political theory, and music theory. *Theoryslut* explores all of these, but with a strong focus on sociology. The editors of *Theoryslut* are very much sluts for theory, but they despise academia as much as they despise sexism, oppression, and fascist governments. Reading *Theoryslut* is liberating and invigorating. You'll find page after page of compelling ideas that never pretend to be anything else.

This is one of my favorite pieces: Part serious, part satire—the writers analyze the experience of "going out" with friends. People of all ages and backgrounds participate in this weekly ritual—but few understand its sociological implications.

The main way that any life at all occurs under sociocapitalism is through a process called *going out*. Other names are used to describe this structure: *finding something to do for the evening, throwing parties, dating,* etc., but it's all basically the same thing. There are so few social institutions under sociocapitalism that the System of going out is just about the only way people can get any social life at all (i.e., any intimacy or sense of community).

The basic thing about the System of going out is, unless you successfully organize or get organized into a Sociality, social life isn't going to exist. If you have no one to go out with, you *stay home alone*. This *extreme punishment* for not following the rules hangs over everyone.

There's an ideological hegemony of *object orientation*, meaning that you have to have an object goal to going out—that is, you have to be going out to do some *thing*. Close friends might be able to let each other in on the dirty little secret that they just want to see each other, but in most arrangements, even when organizers know better, an object goal like seeing a band or a movie or going to a party must be the explicit justification for going out.

Pretty much everything follows from the fact that no social life is ever guaranteed. Either you get people to go out with you, or they turn up and get you to go out with them—or you stay home alone, you're banished from the Sociality.

Among suburban family-age people, things are so far gone that there's really no going out at all. If things are not too far gone (you've got lots of people looking for mates to settle down with) or you have a lot of architecture around that allows people to talk to people (multiple roommate housing, cafes & bars, dense neighborhoods)—if you have this situation, people accumulate other people that they might reasonably expect to go out with.

We call this group of trading partners for going out *the phone list*. Common American English would use *friends* to refer to this group, but that's probably not the best word, since the word *friends* usually means something different. We'd rather save the word friend for an *intimate*, someone you'd stay close to for years, despite conflicts and long separations. The phone list is more like a group of *acquaintances*—people you're pretty familiar with and know, but aren't intimate with. (Although most people would use the word acquaintance to mean someone you've seen once or shook hands with.) But these aren't just acquaintances, because their primary importance is via the *social-business relationship,* the competitive market for trying to go out. That is, they're important because they'll reliably go out with you, not because of any desire you have to see them in particular.

You're still in competition with these trading partners. In fact, since they're the only people you interact with, you

compete with them most directly. Anytime you want to go out and have to persuade someone else to go out with you, you are in competition with your trading partners. This competition, under conditions of scarcity, creates something like a market, a *social-business relation* between people, with the usual market characteristics. But people know the rules of the market. Everybody knows the implications of concern for social value, what you have to do to fill that social calendar. For examples, see the sidebar below.

Remember, you can follow these rules to different degrees. Some of the strategies that increase social market value have an especially bad name, mainly because people hustling for career advantages use them to such excess. But, like it or not, the rules of the System apply to everyone. Those who follow the rules benefit in the heavy competition to organize socialities. And everyone follows the

KEEP THOSE INVITATIONS COMING! MAKE SURE EVERYONE KNOWS JUST EXACTLY HOW VALUABLE YOU ARE!

1. Be Cool. Hey, when you call people up to go out, don't sound needy or clingy or desperate. You wouldn't want to give the impression you ever have *any* trouble going out, 'cause then people'd think you were low value and stop calling you.

2. Always give the impression that you know millions of groovy people, even if you don't.

3. Exaggerate how well you know other people, even in your own head. If someone is an acquaintance, call them a friend. If someone you've barely met is famous, hell, call 'em a friend too.

4. Trade up. If the people on your phone list aren't valuable enough, get others if you can. And dump the old ones, so you're not judged by their lower values.

5. Keep 'em waiting! Don't call anyone too much or too regularly. Occasionally turn them down for going out, even if it means sitting home alone, cuz you want to seem kind of hard to get and valuable.

6. Always be *very very busy*, even if you aren't. You need everyone thinking you've got cool stuff going on they don't know about, so they'll call you up more thinking you're real valuable.

7. You want to be *satisfied, completely satisfied*, with the level of success you're having going out, so that any failures are attributable to a "need to be alone" rather than failure.

8. Take up useless hobbies, work real hard at groovy careers, do lots of useless errands so you can convincingly seem busy. This helps fill up free time in which you might fail to find someone to go out with, and makes you seem busy.

9. Don't try to be alone. Someone might see you not having successfully organized a going out and think you're a loser. So if you want to be alone, *hide indoors*.

10. Never ever complain about social life as a system. It would suggest *you* have trouble going out.

11. If you're alone a lot, give it up entirely. Say you're over that kid stuff (talking to people) and completely immerse yourself in work.

ONLY DO GROOVY STUFF!

Remember, in an object-oriented world your choice of object goals is being judged too, and that's really just a judgment about your market value for going out. You want to pick really high-value events to try to get people to go out to.

1. It's *where* you go out, not *who* you go out with. Remember, you can never give the impression that you would just hang out with someone for no good reason. That would make you seem *desperate*. It's much better to go see some lousy band or sit around in a place where you can't talk. And even better if you can convince yourself that's really what you wanted to do.

2. Do your research. Subscribe to magazines, fuck doormen, whatever it takes to figure out what the truly groovy and happening high-value places are.

3. If it's you who picks where to go out, maintain the illusion of it being a great thing, even if it's dull as dishwater. Say things like "Kick ass, party man," "This is so fucking cool," or "Is everyone having fun?"

4. In a town with lots to do? It doesn't matter, since to maintain a competitive edge you need to pick groovier things to do than other people. So you can only go out if the best things, the grooviest most high-valued things are happening. Even if the lower valued things seem like just as much fun, you'd better stay home instead.

rules to some extent—unless they completely withdraw from social life.

The problem is that the competition between organizers really fucks things up. It produces a constant need to demonstrate successful organizing ability—it makes social life into work, and it undermines all trust and commitment. No wonder the System produces and sustains such a high level of competition and such a low level of life.

And the funny thing is, even if you play by the rules, it's still not gonna work.

Think about parties. Think of how much effort goes into them. People who throw good parties put a lot of work into them, similar to what is needed to start a small capitalist enterprise: buying stuff, advertising, spending time on the phone. And not just anyone can throw one—you need to have enough value to throw a good one, or it'll be painfully obvious how few friends (trading partners) you have.

What do you get from a party anyway? At most it'll be drunken half conversations, focused on (mostly unsuccessful) scoring, mostly it will be people talking to who they came with, members of their phone lists. And it happens only one night and then all the people disappear until they can be gathered again months later. Totally pisspoor compared to the measliest fourteenth-century medieval village festival, the measliest eighteenth-century tavern, the measliest nineteenth-century street life.

Most of the time the System produces much worse results than a party. Usually people only get together in tiny groups: one-on-one, or maybe a few members of the phone list. You might go out every night, if you're young and groovy and good at organizing people and haven't settled down and don't live in the suburbs—but what does going out every night mean? Mostly it means spending a couple of hours getting ready, a couple of hours watching a movie or a band and then you may actually talk, what, thirty minutes the whole time. So the social life from going out is already pretty lousy, even when it's successful.

Most people don't and can't go out every night. And when organization is *unsuccessful,* the isolated organizer sits at home. So, the individual is always fighting for bare social survival. That is, the individual is always in danger of having the Social Self *murdered* as punishment for insufficient ability to organize a Sociality. This is murder in a very real sense, the murder of whole segments of your life that ought to be yours. The whole part of you that exists outside yourself keeps getting murdered. This *murder* of the Social Self is not some rare event, like, say, banishment from a village for crimes against the community.

It happens all the time. Every time you are down or depressed. Or desperate for intimacy, sex, or conversation. Or tired from work. Or fight with one or two key people on the phone list. Or there's nothing to do. Or your friends start marrying and moving off to the 'burbs. Or you just have bad luck, everyone's busy, and you didn't call early enough. No one escapes the failure to go out. For most people, failure to go out is the ordinary condition.

DON'T GIVE AWAY THE FARM—*NEVER COMMIT* TO ANYTHING OR ANYONE!

See, all commitments work against the logic of the system. Any commitment you make just lowers your value while increasing someone else's. See, if *you* commit, they can always play you against other people and try to get a better deal. So you'd rather convince *them* to commit to you, while you keep your options open.

1. Avoid anything like a regular commitment to meet at a certain time with the same person or people, or planning very far in advance. Always "keep things open." You don't want to get too "regimented" because you know you might get a better offer.

2. It's a good idea to double organize; that is, agree to do things with several people and then sift through them at the last minute for the grooviest most high-valued option.

3. Be sure to *feign bisexuality*, straight girls. A great way to get boys is to bring another girlfriend along. So talk up how valuable friendships between girls are and how maybe you ought to be a lesbian and how you two should get together. When ya get a boyfriend, clear out, don't return her calls. This trick doesn't work with straight men, because men are incapable of talking about friendships anyway.

4. Of course, you *can* commit to sexual monogamy. If you want to *settle down* you can "commit" (to not fucking anyone else, or at least to not admitting it.) But you can only do this if you're *mature* (ready to give up all social life, move to the suburbs, and start pumping out babies).

So the basic condition of the System of Competitive Organizing is a constant struggle for the survival of the

Social Self, for the survival of an actual human life, and it's a struggle that is only intermittently successful. Even when it does work, it's so competitive and undependable and pisspoor—it's almost not worth the trouble anyway.

Don't think you're gonna escape. Don't hope somehow you'll have lots of "friends" in the future or maybe have the perfect boyfriend/girlfriend or maybe you'll hit it big and have people flocking after you. That hardly ever happens. See, it won't change till this whole system changes—this whole going-out way-of-life just gets demolished and replaced with something really different.

You won't change it by just being nice to people. No, incremental changes will just get swallowed up and incorporated into the competitive logic of the System. See, if you let up, your friends will blow you off too, or you'll all go down in social status together. Naw, we'll have to bring the whole thing down at once. We'll have to make it so the Sociality is *permanently organized,* and something you count on, so you can spend your energy actually living and not just hustling up a temporary end to desperation and boredom, so you can have horrible nasty mean fighting fantastic wonderful free wheeling groovy stuff going on all the time, yeah, as a matter of course, that's what needs to happen.

Yeah, whatever. Think about it tho.

pop culture

Not all zine publishers spend their days listening to cutting-edge music and their nights running around to the trendiest clubs in town. Some zine publishers like to stay at home to watch *Nick at Nite* and obscure Hong Kong action flicks. Writing about pop culture isn't new. There have always been fan clubs and newsletters, but the new breed of pop culture fanzines is slightly different. Instead of writing about Elvis or the biggest movie stars, zines tend to focus on more obscure or cutting-edge subjects.

A bonanza of varieties of pop culture is found in zines. There's retro culture, with its emphasis on the TV shows, movies, and music of decades gone by. Hugely popular is kiddie kitsch, exploring clothing and toys that recall an earlier innocence. Recently, there's been a big resurgence in the popularity of trash culture—the kind that made a trip to the drive-in such a huge part of American leisure in the '50s. Part retro, part childhood nostalgia, trash culture embraces a part of Americana that history books would prefer to forget, but zine publishers are documenting with glee.

Critiquing movies, TV, and music can be viewed as an extension of the traditions established by science fiction fanzines. The main difference is that while science fiction fans are acutely serious, these folks take their pop culture obsession with a grain of salt and a touch of camp.

These zines explore a more personal relationship to pop culture. No gushing fannish praise, no obsessional compulsions, just simple critiques of the latest trends. Pop culture is all around us, and by exploring it in zines, publishers and readers alike are able to exercise more control over their world.

THE DAY POP CULTURE MOVED IN

●

By **Ariel Gore** *from*
Hip Mama

Parenting is, to borrow a phrase from the army, the toughest job you'll ever love. Moms have it particularly tough—damned if you stay home and take care of your kids, damned if you go back to work. You still find yourself responsible for well more than 50 percent of the work involved in raising a kid.

But there are joys too, and *Hip Mama* celebrates those joys through prose and poetry, and provides reviews and how-tos for every hip mom. Ariel Gore has been successful at getting well-known literary moms like Devorah Major and Opal Palmer Adisa to write movingly about their experiences. Not surprisingly, the publication has attracted a devoted following of readers (not all of them, I suspect, parents).

Gore is a talented writer as well as editor. This piece from her premiere issue explores how history, makeup, boy's toys, and *Beauty and the Beast* might affect her daughter's choice of boyfriend and sense of self.

HIPMAMA
Issue #1 Winter/ Spring 1994 $3.50

The Parenting Zine

what's the deal with this new generation?

Hip with four kids
See you in family court
She is going to have sex someday
Plus... Fiction, Poetry, Whirled peas... and way more

My three-year-old sits talking with an older friend. The topic of their conversation is one of their favorites: *Beauty and the Beast.*

I hear Maia tell the five-year-old that the Beast is scary and suddenly the girl announces, "I would stay with a man like that."

As my daughter nods, I cringe. It's all over. I can see the future before us—the endless stream of boyfriends from hell (none of whom turn into princes), eating disorders, maybe even cosmetic surgery as my daughter strives to emulate the plastic figurines of her childhood.

I take a deep breath and butt into the girls' conversation. "I think that story might be make-believe," I say in my calmest motherly voice. "I think beasts will be beasts no matter how long you stay with them."

I pause. *Who am I kidding?* This is my attempt at damage control, but I know it's futile. I have completely sold out. My daughter already knows these characters. The mermaid, Snow White, and *Beauty and the Beast* memorabilia (not to mention the Barbie, and pink dresses) I swore I'd never buy are everywhere in the house—books, tapes, lunch boxes, even linens are covered with images of women who have the equivalent of 18-inch waists and 36-inch busts, women who give up their voices for men, women who cook and clean in exchange for protection.

My plan to raise a pure, third-generation feminist who would wear overalls, play with trucks and Raggedy Ann, has failed horribly, and I am beside myself.

Do I burn the offending items and start over, carefully screening toys and books for appropriate messages, or do I throw in the (Little Mermaid) towel, give up, and hope for the best?

It's somewhat comforting to know I'm not alone in my exasperation. Friends who had similarly idealistic parenting plans nod in recognition when I mention my dilemma.

One mother recalls the day she realized what she was contending with—she stood with her daughter, then three, in the aisle at Target begging the child to choose a "happy-to-be-me" self-esteem doll, but the girl just clenched her jaw and crossed her arms, whispering, "It's not Barbie."

(I was prepared for rebellion when my daughter hit 16, even 13, but not 3.)

Gender roles and generation gaps have been around for thousands of years, but in the good old days cultural ideals were filtered to children through their parents and grandparents.

"At least when the moms and grandmas were making the toys—even if they were making dolls and baking sets—the characters looked like people in the family," one friend says. "We'll never look like these plastic things."

The problem got serious at the turn of the century when the profusion of mass-produced printed words and images took the place of parents in bombarding children with popular values. Mass advertising began, the plastic doll was born, and then, in the 1970s, the toy industry met feminism.

It was 1975, I was five and my mother warned me, "Commercialism is like a vacuum; if you don't be careful, it will suck you up."

She had a long list of these warnings: "Don't be the kind of girl who screams in biology class"; "Don't lose track of what's beautiful and what's plastic."

It was the great experiment in nonsexist child-rearing and hundreds of thousands of parents tried it. The plan was to combine good examples, feminist teaching, and toy censorship. I made it through most of my early years as a good tomboy, but when my daughter was born I must have let my guard down.

I think back, trying to remember owning even a single plastic doll, but I can't. (What I do remember is all the neat stuff my friends had.)

I search my mind for some rationalization that will excuse my selling out. "They have to have some cultural literacy," a friend tells me. And maybe she's right.

"Censoring can create something forbidden and they begin to think it must be really exciting," said Holly Gordon, a psychotherapist and professor of feminist psychology at New College of California. "What you can do is promote critical thinking in terms of gender, commercialization, and marketing." (Yes, damage control.)

When Maia stands before me in a pink dress and, pushing her bangs out of her face, says, "I wish I could be the real Snow White," Gordon suggests I ask, "Do you think it would be fun staying home and cooking for all those dwarfs?"

"It doesn't mean you can't have an opinion about [the toys] once you've elicited theirs," Gordon said. "Sometimes it's more important for children to feel that you respect their choices and how they want to present themselves."

But what about the beastly boyfriends? The eating disorders? Inevitable?

Probably not, according to Sara Bonnet Stein, author of *Boys and Girls: The Limits of Nonsexist Childrearing.* "How children express their gender at three is quite different from how they express it at eight or eighteen," she writes. And, "Adoring Barbie is . . . a passing event rather than a permanent condition."

I stand in Maia's bedroom and scan her collection of stuff. In the toy corner a mermaid figure, my old Curious George, a boxed wooden train set, and Barbie lie side by side. The sheets on her bed are *Beauty and the Beast* but the cover quilt is old-fashioned and handmade. The room is a decorator's nightmare and a feminist's compromise.

Maia walks in behind me. She stands confidently in her pink dress. "Mom," she begins, "I really want to go to Walgreen's."

But it is late; I am off the hook. I won't have to talk about buying purple eye makeup or dolls that turn into cupcakes tonight. "Walgreen's is closed," I tell her.

I watch as she walks toward the toy corner and carefully takes the train set out of the box, puts the track together, sets up the cars, and balances the Little Mermaid on the caboose.

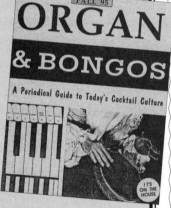

MR. BOOZE
•
By **Russell Scheidelman**
from
Organ & Bongos

Cocktail culture has hit it big in the mid-1990s. It seems like nearly everyone is enjoying exotica records and sharkskin suits or little black cocktail dresses. Hipsters are obsessed with cigars, Vegas, and drinks bartenders haven't made for decades.

Russell Scheidelman has put together a great zine to chronicle this swanky trend. *Organ & Bongos*, with its classy design and retro attitude sends dispatches from the front lines of cocktail nation. It features reviews of notable lounges around the world, recipes for swingin' cocktails, interviews with icons of the era, mouthwatering photos of neon lounge signs, and more. The premiere issue came out a few months before Dean Martin's death, and featured, presciently, this loving tribute to "Mr. Booze."

A local boy gone wayward and caught in the snares of Demon Rum, a "holy fool" in perpetual party mode, viewed with contempt, pity, and a twinge of secret envy. The advent of "mass culture," unleashed by film and radio during the early part of this century, raised the role of town drunk to a trans-local, national level. W. C. Fields, with his swollen nose and self-indulgent manner, developed the archetype for this new American folk hero/anti-hero, the National Drunk.

Fields' untimely evaporation in 1946 left a wide-open niche in the nation's cultural pantheon.

Not until ten years later, when a restless Dean Martin abandoned the comedy team of Martin and Lewis—did a serious candidate step forward to assume the Great Imbiber's soggy mantle. The Bottle was being passed to a new generation.

The National Drunk, once Dino took over the job, turned into the unabashed, urbanized Swinger. No longer did he guzzle beer or swig bootleg whiskey on the back porch of a rambling farmhouse, as a Fields character might do.

Nahh, sir. The Dino version lived in a world of fast cars, penthouse suites, and swimming pools—all bar-equipped, naturally. He was surrounded by beautiful bombshells decked out in skimpy—or elaborately revealing—attire, all longing for the chance to share a cocktail with the tanned and laid-back crooner in leisure wear. And when they did, he didn't bother their pretty heads with profound philosophical effusions. *You kidding?* Dino spoke in one-liners; between sips and oggling double takes, he drawled or sputtered quips.

Painting the Global Village Red

All of this sloppy, slaphappy indulgence in wine, women, and wine and song must have hit a nerve (and some pocketbooks) out there in the heartland, because Martin's career, instead of going dinner circuit in the wake of his split with Jerry Lewis, zoomed ever upward. He lushed his way across stage, screen, and records and into the hearts and minds of millions.

As the acknowledged vice chairman of Sinatra's Rat Pack (and I emphasize the word *vice*), Dino swung with the best and the brightest-lit carousers of the Kennedy years—Old Blue Eyes, Sammy Davis, Jr., Joey Bishop, and Peter Lawford (brother-in-law of JFK, who sometimes had occasion to join in their antics, both before and during his presidency). "The Clan" (as they were otherwise called) liked to gate-crash the nightclub acts of friends and favored performers, getting up on stage and goofing around. They would suddenly show up at favorite restaurants or watering holes (like Dino's Lodge in Hollywood) to the great astonishment and delight of the sitting customers. Frank would sometimes convene a "summit meeting" of Pack members at the Sands Casino/Hotel in Vegas (where both he and Dino held ownership interest) to hoke around and get plastered as an excuse for a (profit-making) nightclub show. And to share their rowdiness with an even wider audience (and rake in more drink money), they made a string of bad movies—*Ocean's Eleven* (1960), *Sergeant's Three* (1962), *Four for Texas* (1963), and *Robin and the Seven Hoods* (1964). Not all Clan members got to appear in these films, but Frank and Dino, who subscribed to the same philosophy of acting ("Avoid rehearsal"), romped through all of them.

Dino enjoyed the success of excess while on his own as well. By 1962 he had parlayed his drunk-onstage routine into one of the hottest club acts in Vegas. Introduced with the line, *"And now, direct from the bar,"* he'd stumble out on stage while carefully cradling his trademark and constant stage companion—a drink. Behind him, a line of plumed and scantily sequined chorus girls strutted their stuff. He'd sing a few lines, then joke about his drinking, sing a bit more, toss out more jokes (sometimes using chorus girls as props). The audiences loved it. The last act of one of these shows—filmed on location in the Copa Room at the Sands—can be seen in an otherwise pathetic 1964 movie entitled *Kiss Me, Stupid.* This nightclub scene, which opens the film, shows the National Drunk in top form.

Perhaps the outstanding cinematic treatment of Dino the high-flying lush can be seen in the four Matt Helm films he made in the mid- to late-sixties—*The Silencers* (1966), *Murderers' Row* (1966), *The Ambushers* (1967), and *The Wrecking Crew* (1969). Jumping on the spy genre bandwagon of that period, he plays an international super-sleuth/superspy/superplayboy à la James Bond, but in this

case with the Martin touch. Helm's assignments tended to take him into breweries and distilleries covering for missile sites and spy nests. He passes on the secret information by means of the drinks he orders. Although a sexual predator in the Bond mold, his priorities seem skewed in a slightly different direction. For example, when a beautiful dish-in-distress pours out her tale of woe in the privacy of his apartment or hotel suite, he is likely to offer these words of comfort while making a beeline for the liquor cabinet: "Boy, you could sure use ahh drink."

In 1965 Dino brought his campaign of conspicuous consumption to the airwaves with the NBC-TV series, *The Dean Martin Show.* Prudently assigned to an "adult" time slot (10–11 P.M.), it was probably the booziest television show in network history. The show would start with Dino sliding down a fireman's pole to a stage set that prominently featured a piano—and a bar. Once armed with a drink and a cigarette, he would joke around with the pianist and sing fragments of songs, make cracks to the viewers about drinking and sex, bring guests on (often drinking buddies or Rat Pack cronies like Sinatra), do routines with The Golddiggers (his shimmying set of big-breasted chorus girls), sing more song snippets—all the while squinting at the cue cards, fumbling words and names, looking at the wrong camera, and, on the whole, handling the TV format so clumsily that it prompted several media critics (both then and now) to analyze *The Dean Martin Show* as some sort of medium-exposing-the-medium postmodern exercise. The series was a big success, capturing a hefty 38 percent Nielsen rating at the end of its first season, and went on to televise the National Drunk's decadence for nine inglorious seasons.

Old Moderately

Was Dino's drunk schtick for real? Or was it just part of his showbiz image (as with Jack Benny's celebrated cheapness)? Several mainstream publications *(Life, Look, Time)* ran articles in the '60s portraying him as a family man (seven kids, no less; still on his second marriage) who maintained a fairly quiet, sober lifestyle. His wife and various friends and associates were quoted to the effect that his alcoholic intake was really quite modest. (Quipped Dino: "I keep a case of Moderately back in my dressing room.") Even recently, some Rat Pack veterans like *(No!)* Shirley MacLaine have asserted that all the hype about Dean's heavy drinking was just that—hype. But I look upon such timely "revelations" in the same way as I view recent disclaimers of former substance abuse by rock stars and politicians that are coming out in this newly puritan-

RS

ical, Prohibition-bent age of ours—*as just hype.* No one disputes that Dino liked to drink. While Shirley MacLaine said that the drinks he carried around on movie sets were filled with apple juice, others—like Ray *(My Favorite Martian)* Walston, who worked with him on *Kiss Me, Stupid*—swore it was really hooch. And it's hard to believe that he was anything less than crocked during his televised "reconciliation" with Jerry Lewis on the 1976 Muscular Dystrophy telethon—because he kept messing up the telephone number. (*I* saw it.) But whatever may be the truth in this matter, Dino has come to epitomize the American drinker with all of his charms and flaws. Like Salvador Dali, who claimed he didn't need drugs because "Dali *is* the drug," I think Dino has an inebriating, alcoholic quality all his own. And it has intoxicated the rest of us.

Dino is the drink. Drink up, Mr. Booze.

Even the French, we've recently heard, aren't as enamored of Jerry Lewis as they once were. We all know he's the scourge of American entertainment—but why? How did he get from the brilliance of the original *Nutty Professor* to the flop sweat that pours from him every Labor Day? *Hermenaut,* "The Digest of Heady Philosophy for Teens," may have found the reason in Lewis's unreleasable Holocaust film *The Day the Clown Cried.* A. S. Hamrah's "Thus Spake Cinderfella," from the seventh issue of *Hermenaut,* explores Jerry's long strange trip from actor to auteur.

If any zine is going to be bold enough to take on the funny half of Martin and Lewis, it has to be *Hermenaut,* one of the brainiest publications in zineland. Each issue profiles such smarties as Martin Buber, Nietzsche, and Guy Debord. But *Hermenaut* doesn't ignore TV, movies, and music, either—it applies theoretical and philosophical concepts to pop culture with highly amusing results.

THUS SPAKE CINDERFELLA
•
By **A. S. Hamrah** *from*
Hermenaut

> Who among you can laugh and be elevated at the same time?
>
> Friedrich Nietzsche

The '70s were not a good time for Jerry Lewis. After the upheaval of the late '60s, falling off roofs and yelling in a confused, strained voice seemed idiotic. Idiotic, that is, in a way Jerry didn't intend. This period saw the emergence of Woody Allen as America's cinematic king of comedy. Fake highbrow was in; fake teeth were out.

Lewis virtually went underground during the '70s—or, maybe he went someplace far weirder than underground. The things he managed to do there loom prominently, for me at least, as defining instances of the unfortunate zeitgeist of those days.

The most startling of Jerry's accomplishments in that decade has got to be his lost 1972 movie masterpiece, *The Day the Clown Cried,* a film that is by all accounts so strange and dangerous it still can't be released. Lewis, of course, starred in, wrote, and directed the film himself. Jerry went to the cinema's very heart of angst-ridden, ultra-dour filmmaking for his first foray into "serious" art. The film was shot in Sweden, and also featured Bergman-land doyenne Harriet Andersson, used here long before Woody Allen ever injected Max von Sydow into one of his tired chamber pieces. But this picture could not possibly be an Allenish Bergman knockoff, for it tells the WWII story of Helmut Doork, an aging, alcoholic circus clown who is imprisoned in a Nazi concentration camp where he is forced to entertain Jewish children on their way to the gas chamber. Jerry, you'll remember, entertained an entire generation of kids who later either marched off to Vietnam themselves or watched their peers do so.

The production of *The Day the Clown Cried* was plagued with problems. Lewis was addicted to prescription drugs, severely overworked, and had promised production money that wasn't coming in. Finally, Lewis's producer fled the movie, evidently taking with him some of the budget, and Jerry couldn't raise the needed capital for post-production. Then the lawsuits started. The writers of the source material, it seems, were unhappy with the Lewis treatment given their Holocaust story. One wonders what they expected.

A comedy about the Holocaust, conceived by the slapstick auteur of Las Vegas, was not something anyone wanted in 1972. And no one wants it now. The very idea of such an appalling, oddball, downright *creepy* thing made people wince then, just as it makes them wince today. Likely the polar opposite to 1978's watered-down TV-movie version of the Holocaust, Lewis's film is sure to throb with pain in a way that is both utterly unique and utterly unacceptable. In fact, everything ever written about the film vilifies it in no uncertain terms, even though most of those who write about it have not seen it. Unfortunately, it seems the world still isn't ready for this movie, although everyone I know is desperate to see it, something that can't be conceived of by the boomer mentality (see Bruce Handy's article in the May 1992 *Spy*, excellent illustrations by Drew Friedman). Jerry keeps the one complete copy of the film locked away, showing it only to a select few, trying to ignore the scorn, hoping someday it will be released.

Indeed, those of the hipper-than-thou generation can only express shock and anger at Lewis for even trying to make such a movie. But is *The Day the Clown Cried* really the most egregious breach of taste ever committed to celluloid? Certainly it can't be more unctuous or as numbingly mediocre as movies like *Carnal Knowledge* or *The Way We Were*, two highly regarded movies from roughly the same period. I'm sure it isn't boring, but we'll probably never know. Remember also, 1972 was the year *Pink Flamingos* was unleashed to a world that wasn't exactly waiting for it. And today we don't need John Waters to remind us that taste is the enemy of art. Indeed, *The Day the Clown Cried* takes what is one of the all-time classic images of kitsch—the sad clown so often seen painted on black velvet and hanging in your cousin's depressing rec room—and forces it to *mean something*. Jerry makes the audience grapple with the Holocaust in a way so far beyond any of the usual expectations it's clear normal considerations are out-of-frame.

The garishly original combination of a Nazi death camp for children and their sad clown was a bust. Lewis was reviled. Perhaps the Lewisian sentimentality run wild, minus the usual slapstick, plus a certain hostility and sadness kept slightly more in the background of Jerry's other films was too reflective of the '70s themselves. This kind of affirmation of life, one that cried as it laughed in the face of not only meaninglessness but the worst kind of horror, held up a mirror into which no one wanted to look. *The Day the Clown Cried* became just another reason to hate Jerry Lewis.

He still, however, had the Telethon, a prime reason he had become a culturally disreputable figure in this country in the first place, and he wasn't about to let it go. Having returned to America—perhaps he was somewhere outside Las Vegas—maybe the Valley of Fire, Jerry regrouped and was back at Caesars Palace on Labor Day 1976 to raise millions for his Kids. This was to be the famous Telethon during which Frank Sinatra himself briefly reunited Jerry and his old partner and longtime nemesis Dean Martin. The strained happiness of that moment was to give way to the grueling concentration of Lewis's yearly guilt orgy, for later that night Jerry Lewis looked America right in the eye and announced, "God goofed!" And he did this in front of eighty million people, while trying to get every single one of them to give to his special charity.

"Do you think it's normal for God to put children in steel cages?" asked Jerry, "If it is, then I say God goofed!" Told that he would lose viewers and station affiliates all over the country, Lewis then responded, "I've been told that I have offended a lot of people . . . but I still say God goofed!"

In the '70s, Woody Allen always seemed to be whining about God as if God wouldn't return his phone calls: does He like me? Why the silence? I never hear from Him! But here was the out-of-favor, supposedly-no-longer-funny, cultural dinosaur Jerry Lewis, the man David Thomson (a great writer on '70s film culture) called "the Pied Piper of the Las Vegas Sahara," announcing the death of God before the whole continent, refusing to apologize for it, and still asking for his viewers' hard-earned dollars. At that moment, the Telethon host became the anti-televangelist. And therein lies the difference between Jerry Lewis and Woody Allen, a difference that can certainly be seen in their films. Allen complains; he whines and tries to seem brainy, but can only shrug his shoulders in the face of an uncaring universe. Lewis is actively mad at God; he attempts to mold the world into a form more to his liking and completely falls apart in the face of the world's intransigence.

Anyway, he definitely holds the record for criticizing the Almighty in front of the largest number of people at once. I don't understand why this glorious moment of fantastic outlandishness isn't remembered as a high watermark of '70s strangeness. I recall it as if in a dream.

Two years after his stupendous announcement, Jerry was nominated for the Nobel Peace Prize for his work with the Muscular Dystrophy Association. The nomination was accepted by the Prize Committee of the Norwegian Parliament. It cited Lewis's sensitivity and his commitment, "which has enabled millions to express their innate desire to help their fellow man." Pretty funny, you're probably thinking, until you realize that in 1973 Henry Kissinger actually won and accepted this same Peace Prize. Maybe there isn't so great a distance separating Helmut Doork, that despised-but-fictional Nazi death camp clown who Jerry tried to bring to life, and Henry Kissinger, Nixon's all-too-nonfictional German-born secretary of state, the sad clown of Vietnam and Cambodia.

THE SKINNY ON HELLO KITTY

•

By Phoebe Harding, AKA **"Coochie Galore"** *from* ***You Sank My Battleship!***

Sometimes a zine publisher is so hooked into the zine zeitgeist that she produces something that's as close to a template for the state of zines as you're going to find. Such is the case with *You Sank My Battleship!* It's all here—an obsession with '70s culture, Generation X manifestos, and articles celebrating Taco Bell—it's almost scary. On the other hand, the articles are also stellar examples of their genres.

"The Skinny on Hello Kitty," from the first issue, finally injects some critical thinking into the cult of collecting items from a line of Japanese toys designed for six-year-olds. Writer Coochie Galore explains how she became addicted and why those pink plastic playthings just drive her wild.

Hi, my name's Coochie (Chorus: Hi, Coochie!) and I'm a Hello Kittyaholic. The first Hello Kitty thing I ever bought was a plastic backpack in Manhattan's Chinatown for $4.95, and the latest thing, a flip-top watch for $49.95. I first realized my attraction for Hello Kitty was beyond my control when, in times of greatest financial depravity, I'd start jonesin' and spend money I didn't have on Kitty action. I'd have nothing in the fridge, but lots of yummy-smelling stuff on my desk and I was strangely happy.

I have been a Hello Kitty user for almost two years now, and I'll tell you what the underlying attraction is based on: the little girl in me loves to feel spoiled. I know of no other character in cartoon history so cool, calm, and self-assured as this stocky, bikini-wearing, teddy-wielding cat.

Whereas normally I'm a pretty together individual, I lose all composure at the gates of F.A.O. Schwarz. I'm guilty of hip-checking small children who clog the Kitty aisles. I even open the off-limits employee backstock bins underneath displays to make sure everything is out, nothing is missed. I ask at the counter to see catalogs of what's available for ordering, and what's upcoming next season. And you ask, *Why?* Well, I've never been forced to detail my addiction, but now, asked to create a defense, my defense would go something like this:

1. *Olfactory Orgasm:* All the products smell of plastic and bubble gum! It's an intoxicating blend that I find irresistible, and if bottled I would be Jell-O in the hands of the wearer.

2. *Simplicity:* This sensation is not a high that comes and goes. There is nothing not to like about bright colors, bad syntax (authentic sweatshirt quote: "positively, definitely, absolutely charming she"), and the primary materials used—plastic, cardboard, and nylon.

Still with me?

3. *Fully Functional:* Hello Kitty makes stuff I need! Band-Aids, gum, coin banks, Kleenex, purses, suitcases, roll pillows, stick-on jewelry . . . all with her paw print of approval.

4. *Silly as Shit:* Even the most fully functional things are strangely stupid. For example, I have clog-shaped erasers with rubber stamps on the bottoms. There also exists clear plastic note paper with only the center primed for a small note; if you can imagine this, you'll know it's totally whack. How 'bout Kitty's latest cruise with booze? Lately, all her stuff has her holding little flowery drinks garnished with umbrellas. (Is this suitable for children?) And who hasn't noticed the rip-stop nylon Hello Kitty beeper cases, 35mm cameras, and the lip gloss that tinkles with little rock candy crystals in the base?

5. *Cheap Thrills:* Since kissing booths are history, where else can you spend $1.95 and walk away with such a big smile? Usually when something's inexpensive, you expect it to fall apart quickly, or just feel cheap. Not so with Hello Kitty! With the prices of all kitty merchandise non-negotiable (cost is stamped on at the factory), you can bet F.A.O. isn't making that much off you, right?

6. *Painstakingly Detailed and Delightful:* I know, you wince when you hear that grandmother word, but frankly these creators have gone all out to make you feel like you're a guest in Wonderland. Hello Kitty is always surrounded by presents and really weird friends. Little tiny letters and envelopes, doodads with snaps and zippers, pencil cases with thermostats (huh?), watches that flip open and spin, purses with compartment after secret compartment. You see, finally, it comes down to the . . .

7. *Small Package Theory:* As I get older, I'm increasingly coming to realize that (with the exception of Hello Kitty's head) the best things really do come in itty, bitty packages. Diamonds, checks, birth control, and Hello Kitty.

Of course, there are still many questions I have about my obsession—as any good fan will have—and I fantasize about someday running into Kitty in a crowded Manhattan sushi bar. In the event this should happen, I want to have my questions ready, like . . .

What is that fragrance you're wearing?

Are you a tiger in bed?

Hey, Puss, what's your sign?

Are you in touch with your inner kitty?

Were those real drinks, or just props for the shoot?

How did you beef up for those bathing suit layouts?

What really happened between you and Marmaduke?

And the most burning question:

When did you first learn you were a big pussy?

Unfortunately, folks, the chances of me running into her are slim, and the chances of her having an interview with little ol' me, even slimmer, 'cause you see, *HELLO KITTY HAS NO MOUTH.* Now, I've done my part, so you try to figure that one out.

There are plenty of fine publications that celebrate the 1970s—the decade of polyester, punk, and puka shells. While most '70s-obsessed zinesters were in grade school at the time, Candi

AT HOME IN THE SEVENTIES

•

By **Candi Strecker** *from*
It's a Wonderful Lifestyle

Strecker, a veteran zine maker, was in her early twenties. So instead of peeking at the '70s through the screen of childhood or TV, she chronicles it from the perspective of a young adult, just starting out and aware of all the politics and trends the time had to offer.

Candi's other zine, *Sidney Suppey's Quarterly and Confused Pet Monthly* (which, incidentally was started at the tail end of the '70s) was apparently not large enough to handle her wealth of knowledge on the subject, so she created *It's a Wonderful Lifestyle*. Subtitled "A Seventies Flashback," this thick compendium of all that's great (and terrible) about the '70s is so detailed and lovingly compiled that it's become the bible of 1970s nostalgia seekers.

In "At Home in the Seventies," from the second issue, Candi takes a look back at the sometimes-outrageous decorating decisions folks made for their living spaces. From chrome-and-glass coffee tables to the mushroom motif to waterbeds to wooden toilet seats, no room in the house escapes her eye for '70s design.

P eriod rooms" are a favorite feature at history museums these days. Visitors marvel over a series of re-created rooms: a one-room settler's cabin, a Victorian parlor, a Depression-era kitchen, and maybe a 1950s rec room. Soon these museums will realize it's time to add a Typical Room of the 1970s to the sequence, and when they do, I hope one of them gives me a call. I know exactly how a Seventies Room should be furnished right down to the last avocado-green owl-motif mug, and it goes something like this:

For maximum Seventies-ness, the room must be set up as a young single adult's *apartment.* Apartments met the lifestyle needs of the decade's new household forms: the deliberately single; the divorced; living-together couples; and young adults escaping their parents to pursue the good life of sex&drugs&rock'n'roll. *Apartment complexes* popped up all over the nation, blocky two- or three-story buildings arranged in sprawling semisuburban clusters, with ragged token landscaping and plenty of parking places.

The ideals of the Seventies took concrete form in the era's most popular household objects and furnishings. *Cheapness* decreed that a cleverly improvised object was better than one bought ready-made and mass-produced. *Casualness* demanded an informality that bordered on sloppiness. A dinner party no longer required place cards, matching fine china, or even a dinner table. Now one served spaghetti and jug wine to a gang of friends as they sprawled on cushions and pillows piled around the living room floor. And since the paramount virtue in the Seventies mind was *naturalness,* the ideal home would be one in which everything was made of non-plastic, non-synthetic, minimally processed materials. That doesn't mean that people didn't make compromises here and there. A polyester-filled pillow covered in homespun fabric was *natural enough.*

One of the most delightful things about the Seventies is that it had its own signature colors, popularly known as *Earth Tones.* These browny-greeny, muddy tints were preferred over clear primary colors. People even mocked pure, bright shades as "colors not found in nature," as if they'd never seen flamingos or parrots or poppies. The Seventies were dominated by the Earth Tones trio of *avocado, harvest gold,* and *rust* (orange-red), in order of popularity. Mixing with these were two neutrals, *white* (especially for walls) and *brown,* either a solid chocolate-bar tone or the patterned brown of grained wood.

Just as there were '70s colors, there were '70s textures. Natural materials like *wood, wicker, bamboo, rope, cork, muslin, burlap, leather, earthenware, living plants,* and *dried*

gold, rust and/or brown. Its "dirty" colors and shaggy pile forgivingly hid sloppy young tenants' crumbs and stains. Much hipper was a *bare wooden floor.* At the windows, natural choices like *split–bamboo rolled blinds* or *matchstick blinds* replaced heavy fabric curtains. In the kitchen, curtains were often made of country *gingham,* or *muslin* printed with old-timey logos to look like feed sacks.

It was possible to buy matching sets of Seventies-style *furniture*—upholstered in a plaid or tweedy blend of Earth Tones or textured off-white cotton, with lots of good wood showing in the frames—but there was something kind of square and materialistic about the whole idea. Young people usually started out with an eclectic mixture of pieces scrounged from thrift stores and Mom & Dad's attic, topped off with odds and ends left by the previous tenant. They improvised end tables and coffee tables from discarded *wooden crates, barrels,* or *round wooden telephone-cable spools.* Classic *board and brick bookshelves* suited their footloose lifestyle and expressed the virtues of the Seventies: cheap, natural, "handmade."

Ornate *Victorian furniture* switched from being the least desirable junk to the hottest antique style during the Seventies, with prices to match. *Furniture refinishing* became a trendy hobby; Victorian pieces from thrift shops, previously painted white to camouflage their curlicues, were now stripped and covered with clear varnish to reveal both wood grain and decorative lines. When all the cheap originals had been snapped up, reproductions filled the demand. Whole stores were devoted to repro round

flowers all had mildly irregular surfaces, falling somewhere between the rough and jagged and the hard and smooth. Even visually, these materials were textured, most often mottled or stippled or sprinkled with random-but-evenly-distributed flecks.

Decorating the Seventies Room begins with the background—walls and floors. Plain *white walls* were the norm, especially in boxy, generic apartments. (Flat white also provided a visual respite from the relentless texture found everywhere else in a '70s room.) As a colorful alternative, one could paint large-scale hard-edged graphic designs across a wall or two. When these stripey *supergraphics* began to appear on school and hospital corridors everywhere, they immediately fell out of fashion for home use.

Posters began the decade as cheap decor held up with thumbtacks, but ended it hung in frames and given the more dignified names of *prints* or *graphics.* Colorful flowered wallpaper was definitely out, but textured, neutral-natural *burlap* or *grasscloth* on the walls was acceptable. In rehabbed nineteenth-century buildings, an *exposed brick* wall was highly desirable. Brick was earth-toned and rich in texture, and since it was made from plain old dirt, was as natural as a thing could be. Another popular wall material was *barn siding:* raw, silver-gray wood, weathered by years of sun, rain, and wind, recycled from a real rural barn. After installing it, people learned why farmers were glad to give the stuff away: it was as rich in splinters as it was rich in texture.

Down on the floor, apartment-dwellers were usually stuck with some kind of wall-to-wall *carpet*—probably multicolor *shag carpeting* in mixed tones of avocado, harvest

pedestal tables and *golden-oak toilet seats* (with *brass hinges*). *Wicker furniture,* old or new, was prized for its natural textures; the grandiose hippie flamboyance of the giant wicker *peacock chair* was especially irresistible.

The ideal centerpiece for the "natural" living room was a *cast-iron wood-burning stove.* Popular brands included *Vermont Castings, Earth Stove,* and the colorfully enameled Swedish *Jøtul.* The wood stove embodied many '70s virtues: the nostalgia for things from Grandma's day, the cheapness and self-sufficiency of foraging for or cutting your own wood, and the ecological consciousness of using a renewable energy source. (Ironically, wood stoves are now recognized as a major source of air pollution in hippie-gentrified parts of Oregon and Colorado.)

The "natural" look called for "natural" accessories. Best of all were items reflecting any of the crafts fads of the Seventies. People scattered *baskets* here, there, and everywhere. Ceramic items with a certain crude, casual, handmade look were very big, especially speckly-brown earthenware pieces trimmed with just a bit of cobalt-blue glaze. One item swiftly became a cliché: the narrow-necked *little pottery vase* that held exactly two dried flowers. Both *living and dead plants* fit in with the '70s natural impulse. Like baskets, dried plant materials could supply visual texture and earthy tan-to-brown color. A vase filled with an armful of tall *dried weeds* you'd gathered yourself was considered creative, natural, and cheap. *Quilts* combined Granny connotations with graphic punch. If one wasn't lucky enough to inherit a whole quilt, one might patch together a calico pillow or wall hanging. And of course, the Seventies was the golden age of *macramé,* especially the rope *plant hanger* that hung from the ceiling and trailed its fringes on the floor.

If we can say that a decade has such a thing, the "metal of the Seventies" was *pewter.* Compared to hard, shiny, machine-age metals like stainless steel, pewter seemed friendly, soft, malleable, and craftable. And pewter was a natural for *Bicentennial* tie-ins. Somewhere along the line, almost every '70s household acquired at least one Spirit of '76 pewter serving platter or trivet or beer mug.

Candles conjured a nostalgic image of pre-electrical Granny dipping beeswax from a big old iron kettle. But the typical '70s candle was only remotely related to the useful, natural objects Granny used to make: mass-produced from petroleum-derived wax, artificially scented with some overpowering fruit smell, and molded to look like a hot-fudge sundae or an enormous green apple. Burning these fancy accessory candles would ruin their clever shapes, so most were never lit. Mall craftspeople entertained shoppers while making *carved candles,* using warm knives to peel down curls of wax and expose layers of color within. The *Uncandle™* consisted of a Pyrex glass cylinder and a floating wick, and burned ordinary salad oil instead of wax. These must have been popular '70s gift items, judging from the hundreds I've seen (still in their original boxes) in thrift stores down the years.

Most '70s kitchens contained at least one *Earth Tone major appliance*—avocado, harvest gold, or the popular medium brown. (Rust-red was restricted to countertop appliances.) Patterned vinyl flooring and dinette sets came in colors to match. The gourmet cooking fad in the late Seventies created a mystique around anything made of *butcher block:* cutting boards, cheese boards, dining tables. The most serious cooks diced their onions on actual butcher's blocks, huge heavy cubes of wood that stood on their own four legs in the middle of the kitchen floor.

The decade's ultimate dinnerware was genuine *hand-thrown pottery dishes,* thick-walled, speckly-brown, earthy-looking. Only rich hippies (and potters' households) could afford a full set, but everybody had at least one *clunky-crude brown mug* in the cupboard that would hold a veritable bathtub's worth of *Red Zinger™ herbal tea.* Don't think of grabbing this mug for a cup of java on the run; it was reserved for special, groovy, reflective moments.

The natural foods fad and the tough economy of the early Seventies prompted many to preserve their home-grown produce the way Grandma did, in glass *canning jars.* These jars also came in handy as casual flower vases, country-style storage canisters, or beer glasses. (Manufacturers soon offered a version with a mug handle attached, which kind of ruined the redneck-for-a-night charm of the whole idea.) Since the canning boom coincided with the Bicentennial, there was an inevitable line of jars emblazoned with the Liberty Bell. Fast-food chains and gas stations gave away millions of *promotional glasses* bearing the names of restaurants, sports teams, cartoon characters, or current movies. Coca-Cola started a fad by reproducing their old-timey *soda fountain glasses,* belled wide at the top, narrower at the bottom. 7-Up, the contrarian "UnCola," copied the shape but turned it upside down. (Clever, but harder to wash.) Glasses for TAB diet soda were belled at top and bottom, with a narrow "waist" in the middle.

Certain motifs recurred on '70s household items, especially on everyday kitchenwares. Cute 'n' cuddly *mushrooms* sprouted on plaques and kitchen towels and place mats. This unlikely icon had first been popularized as a '60s psychedelic symbol, but by the time the mushroom reached the Kmarts of the world, its threatening drug symbolism had faded away. Huggableness was a selling point for other images, like fat, puffy *strawberries* and plump, big-eyed *owls* and *frogs*. Higher-end consumers chose *herb* designs on ceramic objects like mugs, canisters, and flowerpots. Many '70s themes could be symbolically expressed by herbs: nostalgia (Grandma's lost country lore), hedonism (daring to cook with herbs your parents were too timid to try), counterculture values (alternative medicine), naturalness (green growing things, especially herbs as house plants), and recreational drugs (wasn't marijuana almost an herb?).

Hand in hand with all this herbal imagery came one of the Seventies' most characteristic scents. *Herbal* shampoos and hand lotions didn't really smell like any known plant, but consumers accepted the sharp, chemical scent that went by this name as pleasant and "natural." Intense *single-fruit fragrances* eclipsed the usual floral blends during this decade. *Strawberry, lemon,* and *"green apple"* were popular aromas for candles, colognes, shampoos, incense, and cleaning products.

In the '70s bedroom, *brass beds* had a nostalgic connotation, and their swirly Victorian lines had a satisfying psychedelic extremeness. *Old iron bed frames* were dirt cheap, needing only a do-it-yourself coat of colorful enamel. Or one could just sleep on a *mattress on the floor*—demonstrating down-to-earth antimaterialistic simplicity. The cutting edge of bed technology in the Seventies was the *waterbed*, redolent of sex and drugs. No fancy spread for any of these beds; maybe a cheap, thin *Indian cotton throw* printed in hippie-natural curry-dye colors, or a quilt.

Many pieces of '70s furniture lacked internal "spine" or structure, such as the *waterbed*, the *beanbag chair*, the *giant floor pillow*, *inflatable chairs*, and *foam-rubber cube furniture* that could be stacked and rearranged into all sorts of configurations. *Modular conversation pit sofas* let one sit at any angle, curl across a corner, laugh at the notion of posture. Unstructured furniture was especially handy when one was, shall we say, rendered temporarily boneless by recreational drug use. Stiff, stuffy, formal furniture was for uptight Mom and Dad; besides, only the young were flexible enough to slouch and sprawl in a beanbag.

It's A Wonderful Lifestyle
A Seventies Flashback ☺ Part Two

$4.00

The *hot tub* sums up the feel of the Seventies in a single object—hedonism, sexual liberation, California-ness, communal activity, do-it-yourselfitude, wood splinters in your butt. Hippies first took big old oaken California wine barrels, cut them in half, and put them in the backyard to be filled with hot water for a nice pore-opening Japanese-style soak. Shrewd manufacturers stripped away the hot tub's funky elements, reinvented it as a ready-made indoor fiberglass tub with built-in Jacuzzi bubblers, and mass-marketed it to wild-and-crazy suburbanites.

Although the natural look predominated in the Seventies, the opposite style came on strong late in the decade— a visually and texturally *"hard" look*. It was machined and mass-manufactured instead of natural and craftsy, looked to the urban instead of the rural, and took its nostalgia cue from the Art Deco 1930s instead of the agrarian-Granny 1800s. It was cool, not warm; night, not day; bachelor pad, not earth mother. One might think that the Natural and the Hard styles were hostile or mutually exclusive, but thousands of decor-magazine photos prove that elements from both these trends frequently mingled in the same room.

Some characteristic elements of the smooth and shiny hard style were *mirrors, glass, chrome, anything silvery, white and frosted pastel colors, regular geometric shapes, glitter*. A room's decor might start with a wall of *stick-on mirror tiles* or a *metallic wallpaper*. The punch of *supergraphics* also suited this bold look. Windows were covered up and played down for a feel of perpetual night. *Plastic furniture*

or a *modular sofa grouping* sat on the *white shag carpet*. The *smoke-gray acrylic plastic* used to make dust covers for stereo turntables was adapted for accessories like magazine racks, ice buckets, and cylindrical planter pots. *Chrome-and-glass* coffee tables and wall-storage units were also popular. A trendy *chrome gooseneck floor lamp* rose in one giant curve from its base on the floor to peep its bobbing head over your shoulder. Instead of earthy mushrooms and strawberries, the hard-edge style used *images from nostalgic cinema:* the faces of Mae West, W. C. Fields, Charlie Chaplin, and Humphrey Bogart became black-and-white patterns on posters, wallpaper, and gift wrap.

A *"good stereo"* was mandatory in every '70s household, no matter what its style. A minimal Good Stereo setup consisted of a separate turntable, amplifier, and speakers. This *component* arrangement let one upgrade the system piece-by-piece, the way audiophiles did. Chains of new stores sprang up in the Seventies to supply millions of baby boomers with mid-price stereo gear by *Marantz, TEAC, Superscope, Bose, Harman-Kardon, Technics, Sansui, Onkyo,* and *Sanyo.* Certain gimmicks appealed to buyers, like multiple knobs, dials, and readouts, or *speakers with foam front panels* instead of grille cloth. The "best" stereo equipment was encased in wood, as if this material somehow imparted positive natural vibrations to sounds. Few people knew what *Dolby™* actually was, but this buzzword was the mark of quality on tape decks.

Blood-pressure cuffs always remind me of the look, feel, and smell of those big, fat *Koss stereo headphones* everybody had during the Seventies. Two big ear-cups, of thin vinyl over foam padding, were joined by a head band that kept them firmly in place, enclosing the listener in a soothing acoustical space. They let young people hear rock the way they wanted, loud and visceral, without parents or neighbors yelling, "Turn that goddamn stereo down!" When the *Sony Walkman* was introduced in 1979, the thing that impressed people most wasn't the breakthrough tiny size of the tape-player, but the fact that those little

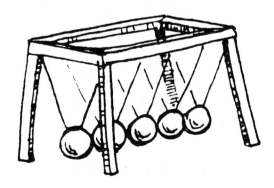

open headphones worked as well as the giant Koss ear-muffs. It was like switching from a corset to a bikini. Other audiophile necessities were an array of record cleaners, wipers, brushes, and *anti-static guns*, with weird names like *D-Stat, Parastat, Zerostat, Discwasher, Vac-O-Rec,* and *The Preener.* Record storage units in the form of repro *fruit crates*, complete with colorful end-labels, nicely combined the appeals of natural wood and graphic nostalgia.

The great audio boondoggle of the Seventies was *quadraphonic sound.* Four-speaker quad was supposed to supersede stereo the way stereo had replaced monaural hi-fi in the Fifties. FM rock stations quickly made the switch, boasting, "We're broadcasting in quad," but consumers hesitated when they found they had to buy more than just an extra pair of speakers. One also needed a *quadraphonic decoder receiver* and all new quad records. (Funny how the first record to appear in any new format is always Pink Floyd's *Dark Side of the Moon.*) To make matters worse, there were three incompatible systems of quad sound: *SQ, QS,* and *CD-4* (backed by Columbia, Sansui, and RCA, respectively). The *vinyl shortage* of 1974 may have dealt the final blow to quadraphonic sound; record companies barely had enough vinyl to meet the demand for regular stereo records, and they weren't about to divert scarce materials to riskier formats.

The audiophile reel-to-reel tape decks of the Sixties gradually gave way to two friendlier formats in the Seventies: the *8-track cartridge* and the *audio cassette* still in use today. Invented by the same Bill Lear who gave his name to the Lear Jet, 8-tracks were the first recorded-music option for automobiles. People were delighted to have an alternative to the car radio, and added 8-track players to their home stereos as well, but soon discovered this format's drawbacks. The sound quality of 8-track tapes was mediocre, and most decks were play-only units that didn't record. Worst of all, the long "symphonic suites" rock musicians were recording in the Seventies just didn't fit onto 8-track tapes. When an album had a single continuous piece of music on one side (like Mike Oldfield's *Tubular Bells* or Yes's live album *Yessongs*), the 8-track player paused inelegantly in the middle of a song to switch tracks: sudden fade-out, silence, *chhKUNK*, silence, fade in . . . Meanwhile, audio cassettes leapt ahead of 8-tracks in sound quality, and manufacturers wisely included recording capability with most cassette decks. Even before the Seventies ended, record companies were cutting back production of 8-tracks. The introduction of the cassette-only Walkman finally sent the 8-track to the trash heap of history.

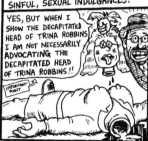

In the late '80s and early '90s you couldn't open up a zine without finding at least one comic strip from Ace Backwords. Fewer zines were being published back then and it seemed like Ace Backwords supplied every one of them with his hilarious, politically oriented Twisted Image cartoons. But things have changed for Ace. The zine explosion brought him, instead of increased popularity, an increased measure of obscurity. After suffering through some roller-coaster love affairs, emotional stress, and tight finances, he put *Twisted Image* on hold. Last I heard, he sublet his apartment, grabbed a tent, packed up a backpack, and headed off to the woods for a while. He's still checking in and offering back issue sets of *Twisted Image* for $20. This is one of my favorite Ace pages, a brutal (but loving) tribute to fellow cartoonist Robert Crumb, created several years before the surprise hit film *Crumb*.

PICKING UP (JACK) CHICKS

•

By **Dan Kelly** *from*

Schlock: The Journal of Low-Brow Cinema and Culture

Trash culture gets little respect in this world. Look what's happening to the home of trash culture, Times Square in New York City. It's being completely scrubbed clean and sanitized so tourists from Kansas can go there without fear. Well there *are* some folks who care about trashy movies, pulpy novels, and forgotten records—and these people write about their obsession in zines like *Schlock*. Each issue recalls an earlier era when triple bills at the downtown theater attracted a large enough audience to keep it going. Although it primarily focuses on B-movies, *Schlock* explores the full spectrum of trash culture. In this piece, contributor Dan Kelly writes about the strange miniature comic books produced by Jack Chick.

There's a strong affinity between zines and these tiny comics that present Jack Chick's unique vision of Christianity. While Mr. Chick probably prints hundreds of thousands of his booklets, they still fall between the cracks of mainstream literature. You can't buy them at your local newsstands; instead, you'll find them serendipitously in bus stations and phone booths. Zine publishers must also find alternate methods of distribution, employing as much ingenuity as Jack Chick's followers.

Another surprise is how Chick Publications often provides a gallery of ready-made clip art for the anxious zine maker. Many a zine publisher has "borrowed" a panel or two from one of Jack Chick's proselytizing stories and adapted it by replacing the comic's words with their own. You might even find a Jack Chick book stuffed into the envelope along with a zine that you ordered.

THE SISSY?

KEEP ON TRUCKIN'

J.T.C.

Dan Kelly is one of the most committed zine publishers. He has at least five titles to his credit, including *Chum, Evil ®, Vox Canis, Ugly Illinoisian,* and *Danger.* He somehow found time to compose this comprehensive overview of Chick Publications for *Schlock* wherein he lists some of his favorite Chick comics. Look for them around town, or you can even try ordering them from the address Dan provides.

"When he had finished saying this, the thief
Shaped his fists into figs and raised them high
And cried: "Here, God, I've shaped them just
for you!

Dante, The Divine Comedy, Vol. I: Inferno

I t's happened to you at least once in your lifetime. Whether you were walking down the street, visiting the state fair, or waiting for the next bus to arrive, you've been subjected to . . . The Approach. The Approach involves one of your fellow human beings walking up to you with an inane grin on his face, shoving a wad of pamphlets into your hand and attempting to strike up a conversation about the big guy, Jesus Christ. Unfortunately, one teeny little obstacle lies in the brambly path to your redemption. Namely, you're not listening to a damned word they're saying. Yep, despite their practiced spiels, freshly scrubbed fingernails, and regular baths in Lysol and Mr. Clean, you've already placed these people in the same league as lepers and insurance salesmen. The only thing you want to get from them is away.

That's too bad, because in terms of pure rhetorical fun, you can't beat the testimonies of the born-again set.

Regrettably, in a few such cases, the Son o' God's basic message of peace, love, and understanding occasionally becomes lost in transit. Nowhere is this more apparent than in the hollow-pointed biblical bullets of Christian propaganda produced by one Mr. Jack T. Chick. Chick, a former designer, has been producing his 2³/₄″ x 5″ comic tracts since 1972, when he produced on his kitchen table the first of many tracts. Since then, Chick has managed to parlay his comics for Christ into a million-dollar-a-year industry, the tracts have been translated into at least 30 languages, from Russian to Tagalog, and there doesn't seem to be an end in sight. Chick continues to grind out new tracts every few months, each one addressing some concern, be it homosexuality, drugs, the occult, or whatever, with the same tender refrain: "Turn to the Lord and his infinite love . . . or burn in Hell forever."

Chick's show-no-mercy interpretation of the scriptures and refusal to accept any other system or lifestyle but his own haven't won him many friends over the years (particularly among the Catholics; Chick ranks with Tony Almo in vitriolic attacks on the Vatican). Nevertheless, his bite-sized chunks of Christian zealotry, combined with his erratic, scratchy cartoonic style, make for an attractive witnessing package for most would-be evangelists out there. Unlike the narcotizing, crammed-to-the-gills pamphlets of the Free Tract Society and other Christian propagandists, the average sinner will actually take time to read a Chick tract—long enough either to become enraged over the spiritual venom lying within or (shudder) long enough to convert.

Chick has confessed that he got the original idea for the tracts from the Communist Chinese, who propagated the words of Mao in similar illustrated books, apparently to great effect. It's easy to see why. The tracts are an irresistible read, and whether they turn you Christian or not, their psychological impact is undeniable. To this day, my blood still curdles and my mouth hangs agape after reading a Chick classic like *Bewitched?* (Young Debbie Wilson is targeted by Satan and his minions, given LSD flash-

backs of her face melting and dies horribly . . . but not before her grandma turns her on to Jesus, Praise be God!) or the incredibly saccharine, love-it-or-hate-it *Somebody Loves Me* (wherein a little kid with Walter Keane eyes as big as hubcaps is forced to beg in the freezing rain, has the shit kicked out of him by his drunken father, and shortly thereafter dies of exposure . . . but not before he turns to Jesus, Praise be God!).

What follows is a selection of some of Chick's better tracts. By "better" I mean those that are the most amusing and/or horrifying and therefore the most eminently collectible. Look for them on your next encounter with "The Approach," but also remember that Chick has charged his lackeys with full-time revival duty, selecting for them a plethora of cunning drop sites. Whether they're in a library book, a public restroom, or a phone booth, the tracts usually find you before you find them.

THIS WAS YOUR LIFE! One of Chick's classics, this particular tract has been translated into umpty-ump languages, annoying and disturbing people the world over. *TWYL!* shows your basic Rapture premise. Essentially, when you die, an angel comes and takes you to God's throne (made all the more embarrassing by the fact that you have no clothes on) where a film of your life is played for all to see. Not only is every dirty little deed you've ever performed viewed by everyone who's ever lived, but your mind is read too. Uh-oh. If this is true, I suspect that a lot of people will be jockeying to stand behind guys like Hitler and Stalin, if only to make their own sins look slightly more lackluster.

THE HUNTER A particularly wrenching tract that seems to attempt an anti-drug message but is too steeped in bizarre imagery to be taken seriously. The premise: Cool guy Curt, the captain of the high school football team and the local drug pusher, suckers "straight" kids Bob and Jim into using every drug under the sun. Why? Because the

rich folks that back him have received direct orders from Satan himself to increase soul quotas from Curt's high school. Particularly memorable images include Bob freaking out on angel dust and Jim's greeting in Hell by Satan (who is apparently having a bad hair day).

THE TRICK Ever wonder why, when you went trick-or-treating as a kid, some houses had all the lights turned out at 6 P.M. and nobody came to the door no matter how hard you knocked? *The Trick* might explain why. In this tract, the local Satanists, people who look just like you and me (gasp!), prepare Halloween treats with incantations, drugs, crushed glass and razor blades. After eating treated Snickers bars and Bit-O-Honeys, one kid dies (the one dressed as the Devil—subtle, huh?) and the others suffer from internal bleeding and an uncontrollable desire to disobey their parents. Fortunately, Becky, another former witch for Jesus, converts the neighborhood in time.

BAD BOB Every Chick tract has the basic message of "Love Jesus or burn in Hell," but a few are tailored to specific types of people. For example, there are tracts for Mormons, Jehovah's Witnesses, Truck Drivers, and so on. "Bad Bob" is evidently geared toward Hell's Angels and other people likely to kick your ass if you witness to them. Bob is a no-good, mean sumbitch who sells drugs and pours drinks on waitresses' heads. Luckily for him, he almost burns to death in a jailhouse fire, putting the Lake of Fire into perspective and striking him Christian.

THE BULL Another specialized tract, this one is geared toward prisoners. The Bull, who looks like a cross between The Thing and The Pillsbury Dough Boy, is the shot-caller of the prison. He gets thrown into solitary where he finds a conveniently placed copy of "Somebody Loves Me." (The only instance where I've found Chick to be self-referential. Interesting . . .) Anyway, when The Bull

leaves the hole (do I detect a "coming out of the darkness" metaphor here?), he's mad as Hell and orders everyone to repent, delivering such bon mots as, "I hate sin and I won't put up with it anymore," and "There will be no more raping, because I just found out that God hates sodomy."

THE BEAST Ka-Booooooom!!! One thing you have to give Christianity . . . for all its tepidity and dreariness right now, they sure do have a helluva party lined up for the end of the world! The Beast! The Antichrist! The eventual laser-imprinting of 666 on everybody's foreheads! Public guillotining! Vampirism! Tribulation! Locusts! The Four Horsemen! Seas of blood! Armageddon! The Millennium! Parousia coming out of our goddamned ears! Call Ticketmaster right now for the ultimate Battle of Monster Trucks! Roarrrrrr!

HOLOCAUST Not funny in the least little bit, but especially worth checking out because Chick throws a little conspiratorial thinking in with his usual line. This one was done in conjunction with Dr. Alberto Rivera, a supposed former Jesuit who learned of the true inner workings of the Vatican. Rivera and Chick were in trouble a few years back for their nasty-nasty "Alberto" comics, which depicted Catholics as a bunch of Mary-worshipping bastards intent on dragging the good Protestants of the world to Hell with them. Chick is convinced that the Vatican is the true Whore of Babylon and the pope is the tremendously charismatic Antichrist destined to lead the world to flames and Perdition. In light of the troubles the Catholic Church has been experiencing lately, you do have to admit that they're doing a pretty piss-poor job of conversion.

Holocaust states that the gassing of the Jews was little more than another Inquisition, and Hitler was acting on the orders of the Vatican. There's more, including claims that the Department of Immigration is intentionally letting more Catholics in than any other religious group, plans are already under way to make Catholicism the "official" religion of the U.S., etc., but it really has to be seen to be believed.

Of course, I was raised Roman Catholic, so I would say all this, wouldn't I? Hmmmm . . .

In conclusion: For those who like to do things in one whack, write to Chick Publications, PO Box 662, Chino, CA 91708-0662 to receive their free catalog. If you have no compunctions about giving them money, a fine selection of mind-bending books and tracts are readily available to you.

Now get thee hence, in Jesus' name! (Matt. 4:10)

sex

People write about what interests them, and what subject could be more universally appealing than sex? Practically every adult on earth has done it (some more than others).

Always popular in *Factsheet Five* are the descriptions of zines devoted to sexuality and erotica. We don't print any dirty pictures, but over the years we've been rejected by several printers purely because of the zines that we write about. What might you find in these controversial sex zines? Lots of erotic images, of course, but you'll also find a surprising array of personal, political, and theoretical discussions about sexuality.

Why are sex zines so popular and ubiquitous? It's not that there's any shortage of sexually oriented magazines on the market, it's just that the mainstream magazines don't offer all that much variety. Sure you can find magazines devoted to big butts or breasts, but the sexual landscape is much more vast and complex than that. If a person has a sexual fetish that isn't satisfied by what he (or she) finds at the local porn shop, he or she might be inclined to start an erotic publication of their own. "I've seen it all" just doesn't work with sex zines, as there's always something new that will surprise even the most jaded or open-minded individual.

Some of the more interesting sexually oriented writing isn't erotic at all. The most engaging stuff is usually the true-life stories about what sex is really like. Included here are some of the more compelling pieces I've come across. It's a unique selection of writing that you're unlikely to find anywhere else.

FORESKINS FOREVER!

CIRCUMCISION

IS MUTILATION

●

By **J. P. Slee(z)e** *from*

Batteries Not Included

Walk into almost any convenience store and you're bound to find a bonanza of slick sex mags. They range from the relatively tame girl-next-door *Playboy* to the more graphically explicit *Hustler.* The zine underground also offers plenty of sex-oriented publications, but, like *Batteries Not Included,* they tend to be more personal, more from the heart, more about real experiences with real people.

Batteries Not Included is primarily devoted to reviewing erotic videotapes. Editor Richard Freeman is a long-time zine publisher and a long-time fan of erotica. The result is a simple fanzine that celebrates sex. Richard really opens things up, inviting all his friends and fellow writers to talk about their favorite videotapes. Like many of the folks who contributed to *Batteries Not Included,* J. P. Slee(z)e is a prolific zine publisher who has produced a wide variety of pamplets and zines. The one thing she hasn't published is a zine about her sexual experiences. Richard gave her the opportunity to write a more personal sexual essay, and she turned in this piece, which reveals her appreciation of the uncircumcised penis.

My boyfriend is uncircumcised and I love it. I have been against circumcision since I attended a two-hour lecture at the 1991 Annual Men's Conference at the C.U. campus in Boulder. I was taking a course called "Sex and Gender." We were assigned to go to the lecture of our choice, so I looked for the weirdest, wildest one in the schedule. I picked "Circumcision: Cleanliness or Child Abuse?" I went to the lecture chuckling at the idea that they would even consider circumcision as child abuse. I assumed the argument would be flimsy at best. Two hours later, I left the room wide-eyed and slack-jawed; enlightened. I had no idea genital mutilation was so widespread around the world, especially in a first-world country like the U.S. I learned that circumcision is sadistic, completely unnecessary, and severely traumatic to the baby. They also talked about female genital mutilation in Africa. I respect the culture, but I will never condone *that*.

I fully support the banishment of circumcision. It's an outdated custom still performed in hospitals across America for the financial gain of doctors. Many parents don't even realize they have a choice. And an uncircumcised penis is just as clean as a standard circumcised one, believe me. After two years of going out with my boyfriend, I should know.

Now for the *fun* part in my anti-circumcision rant: *sex!* Once you've had foreskin, you'll never go back. It's a hundred times more fun to play with: pulling the skin forward and back, back and forth, is the fastest way to turn *him* on (built-in friction!). Sucking it really works. I've nicknamed it my Chinese Water Snake (remember those toys?). I can even blow it up like a balloon. I have to do it quickly because as soon as my lips wrap around his dick

cumcision rate. I think the rate is around 75 percent here in the U.S. Happily, it's decreasing. But how many foreskins do you remember seeing in the shower in gym class, guys? My guess, after talking to male friends, is not many. Recently, I'm happy to say I have prevented the circumcision of one baby boy by advising a pregnant friend against it.

About a year ago, I saw a TV talk show featuring circumcised men who were traumatized by botched surgery and who went to doctors to regain their lost foreskin. Only a tiny handful of doctors would even perform the surgery. These liberal doctors claim men with foreskin have up to ten times more sensitivity in the tip of their penis, and as a result have more intense orgasms. Whether this is true or not, we'll probably never know, the question is too sub-

and blow into the foreskin, it's on its way to hard-dom, and the balloon trick only works on a soft snake. It's a very fun trick, especially in the shower. You can't do that with a "regular" cock!

When flaccid, it looks like an elephant trunk, and when fully erect, it's a dead ringer for a standard circumcised willy. To make that anteater into a fireman at full attention, I like to suck up all the skin as far as it will go, then slowly push it down all the way with my lips until the hidden jewel pokes its pink self out.

I imagine there are a lot of people who have never seen a real live uncircumcised cock. European porn is a good place to scout for it, as they have a meager 6 percent cir-

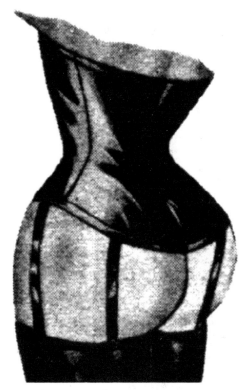

jective. But I can't help feeling a shade sorry for all the boys and men walking around with exposed heads! Baby boys are born with protective skin just for that purpose— to protect their pecker. Why on earth cut it off?

My boyfriend is grateful his father saved him from the knife and coincidentally is now in a band named Foreskin 500. Check your favorite record store, and oh yeah, if you have to know, he is the only one in the band with skin. He's DJ Fogboy, and maybe he'll let you see his snake next time they stop in your town.

PUSSY GALORE

•

By **Sarah-Katherine Lewis** *from*

Pasty

Newspapers and TV would have you think that a person's sexual orientation is set in stone. It's much easier to deal with controversial subjects like gay rights when you can box everyone into categories of "heterosexual" and "homosexual." The reality is that sexual identity is much more fluid than that. Reading zines you get a feel for how sexuality functions in the real world. Sex with men, sex with women, sex with a group of people, and sex by yourself—when it comes to sexual expression, labels just get in the way.

While Sarah-Katherine is interested in many different forms of sexual expression, she never gets up on a pedestal and declares her sexual identity. In her zine she writes about penis size, attracting boys, riot grrrl politics, and working at a condom store, all without the grandstanding that you might expect from such an outspoken individual.

It's every man's fantasy to explore the secrets of an all-girl sex club, but it's through Sarah-Katherine's cynical eyes that we find out what really goes on behind closed doors. What happens there is not quite as exciting as one would have thought, but it's still very intriguing. No glitz, no fantasy, just real-life sex (or lack thereof).

New! Improved! 100% more expensive!

PASTY

No. 6

A few more pages at TWICE the price!

poetry-free since 1994

I went to this grrrls-only sex party called Pussy Galore that was organized by some friends of my (now ex-) girlfriend. It was happening at the South End Steam Baths, which are located about three blocks from where I'm staying—nice and convenient, huh?

I wasn't sure what to expect, but what was even more stressful was that I wasn't sure what to WEAR. Don't laugh—I'm not just being vain—but really, what DO you wear to a sex party? A robe? Shorts and a T-shirt? Sexy undies? I considered all these options (and more) all day Saturday, boring and exasperating my coworkers to death by asking for suggestions and then rejecting them. The WORST suggestion was to go buck naked—I mean, I'm sorry, but this isn't a *National Geographic* pictorial. I wanted to look seductive, not educational.

I finally settled on a black underwire lacy bra and a pair of pants made of flowy rayon (black, too). I figured I had kind of an Arabian Nights look going, and also the pants hid my cellulite. Excellent! I tried on jewelry, but nothing really looked right, so I wrapped my hair back in a scarf and called it done. I ended up with kind of a dirty Princess Jasmine look.

Since it was raining HARD, I added a few sensible layers of sweaters before I set out on the walk to the Baths. This was not a very sexy addition to my outfit, and if I were doing it all over again, I'd've taken a cab. By the time I got to the Baths I was wet and cold and NOT sexy-feeling at all. As a matter of fact, I was regretting the whole thing and seriously considering calling it off.

Instead, I mustered up my flagging libido and went in. It was HOT and STEAMY and DARK, and not to be rude, it smelled like the owners of the Baths hadn't had them cleaned since they'd opened. The floor was sticky, and I tried not to think of the millions of sperm cells that had met their deaths on the floor and were now adhering to my shoes.

Girls were packed in the narrow hallways, some naked, some in various stages of undress. Everyone smelled like bodies and chlorine from the hot tubs. Music pounded. I tried to be cool, casually removing my layers of wet wool to reveal my foundation garments. SHIT! No one else was wearing pants—it was too HOT! But I'd be damned if MY pants were coming off!

I wandered. There was a tiny pool, with naked girls floating in it. There were a few "performance" rooms, with various sex acts occurring for my viewing pleasure. Lots of

S/M, a few lone masturbators. I watched one girl with a vibrator for a while, but lost interest before she came.

I became fascinated by the wide variety of breasts on display. Not one girl had the kind of breasts you see in pornography—huge but pointing at the ceiling. Most girls' breasts pointed down, like little deflating balloons. I met one girl who had had silicone implants, and her tits were, in a word, awesome. They did not move or jiggle at all like normal breasts, instead, they stayed rock hard and still. When she squeezed them, they briefly indented like rubber balls, and quickly returned to shape. I am so glad my breasts are un-siliconed—hers looked like they weren't even part of her body. Also, she said she lost most of the sensation in her nipples after the operation. FORGET it!

About an hour after arriving, I starting to think about getting laid. There were many attractive women there (DUH, that was the point)—but I wasn't really sure how to get anything started. Actually, I wasn't really sure if, in my heart of hearts, I even wanted to get laid. It was more like I felt I should.

At this point, Laura (one of the women who organized the party) handed me a little green slip of paper, which I have graciously copied for you:

10 Tips for Cruising a Girl

1. Make eye contact. You know, if she looks at you, don't look away.
2. Ask before you touch. If she grabs you and starts working it, go directly to #5.
3. If you are too scared to talk to her, write her a message.
4. Be serious. Want it. Cum in your pants.
5. Be safe. Go for it. Get the Big O! This is not a potluck.
6. Know what you want.
7. Be open to suggestions.
8. Tell her how pretty she is.
9. Show her how pretty your ass is.
10. Don't be afraid of rejection. Try again.
Get It Girl! You've Got 12 Hours!

Oh my god! It was so intense! "Get the Big O!" All of a sudden I was feeling as sheepish as a premature ejaculator. How could I get the Big O in front of all these people? I'd have to take off my PANTS!

I decided that getting laid was NOT my mission for the evening. Instead, I walked around for another hour watching OTHER people get laid.

At midnight, a professional performer from New York (hired by the Pussy Galore organizers to keep things interesting) took the floor in the pool room. She did various tricks with her body that were pretty impressive displays of muscular control, like bending over and making her asshole move in and out like an automatic-focus camera lens. After this, she fisted herself, which brought down the house. I couldn't figure out how she pulled that off—she must've had really long arms, and double-jointed wrists. To me, her act was more weird than sexy, but a lot of other women seemed to really get off on her whole show.

Around two o'clock in the morning, I had had enough of unbridled sensuality. I wanted a hot shower, flannel pajamas, and bed. Also, I was very hungry. Hey, it's hard work watching other people get it on! So that was my big Sex Party experience.

The work of gay and lesbian cartoonists has undergone a real renaissance the past few years. Thanks to alternative papers around the country and small publishing companies like Giant Ass Publishing, gay and lesbian cartoonists are finally getting their work out.

PRIVATE CLUB
●
By **Robert Kirby**; *Story by* **Orland Outland** *from*
Strange-Looking Exile

This wonderful comic, from the final issue of *Strange-Looking Exile*, explores the bathhouse sex scene from the point of view of an original queer punk. Robert Kirby has done some wonderful work over the years, editing and illustrating his comix *Strange-Looking Exile* and *Boy Trouble*. Orland Outland has been similarly busy—publishing his zine *Adversary*, writing columns for the *San Francisco Bay Area Reporter*, and running for a seat on the San Francisco Board of Supervisors.

Queer punk culture has finally come out of the closet, and Orland Outland explains how it started for him, more than sixteen years ago.

Private Club

© 1993 by Robert Kirby
story by Orland Outland

WE NEVER WENT TO THE BATHS FOR SEX. WE WOULD ALL GATHER IN THE EVENING AT STEVE'S, ALL OF US 18 YEARS OLD IN 1981, AND GET READY TO GO OUT. IF YOU REMEMBER THAT BACK THEN, WEARING A LONG TATTY BLACK COAT, A RIPPED T-SHIRT AND A PAIR OF OLD-MAN/THRIFT STORE PANTS, YOUR HAIR DYED BLACK WITH ONE BLOND "**MAD MAX**" STREAK, WAS KIND OF SHOCKING. STILL SHOCKING, THEN, IN SAN FRANCISCO, AND WE WERE DOING IT IN RENO, NEVADA.

WE'D LISTEN TO **NunSexMonkRock** AND KRAFTWERK IN SOME ROACH-INFESTED LOW-BUDGET APARTMENT, EAT SOME MACARONI AND CHEESE (UNLESS SOMEONE WAS WORKING AS A CASINO RESTAURANT WAITER, IN WHICH CASE WE'D GO EAT FOR FREE). THEN, TOO YOUNG TO GO ANYWHERE ELSE, WE'D GO TO THE BATHS.

WE HATED RENO WITH THE RIGHTEOUS PASSION OF THE YOUNG, BRILLIANT AND TRAPPED. NO ONE AT THE BATHS WOULD SLEEP WITH US—THEY WERE CLONES, THEY WERE MEN. WE WERE FAGGOTS, AND PROUD OF IT, LONG BEFORE ANYBODY EVER INVENTED QUEERS. NO, WE WENT TO THE BATHS FOR THE MUSIC.

AT THE SAN FRANCISCO BATHS LOTS OF HOT MEN WERE FUCKING THEIR BRAINS OUT, BUT MORE IMPORTANTLY, THERE WAS A D.J. THERE MAKING TAPES OF THE BEST MUSIC IN THE WORLD, WHICH HE SENT TO THE CLUB BATHS IN RENO. WHERE ELSE COULD WE HEAR THE MUSIC WE NEEDED? A.M. RADIO RULED THE WORLD, WITH POCKETS OF HEAVY METAL ON F.M. AS THE ONLY ALTERNATIVE. SO WE'D GO TO THE BATHS AND DANCE THROUGH THE HALLS, RUNNING INTO EACH OTHER'S ROOMS TO ASK, "WHO DOES THAT SONG?" AND SMOKE CIGARETTES AND SHRIEK LIKE THE 18-YEAR-OLD MISSIES WE WERE.

IT'S WHERE I FIRST HEARD JOY DIVISION AND THE FIRST NEW ORDER SONGS, LIKE "CEREMONY" AND "EVERYTHING'S GONE GREEN." KLAUS NOMI AND GARY NUMAN AND OMD, SO LONG BEFORE ALL OF THEM WERE ANYBODY ANYONE HAD HEARD OF BUT US.

SOME SONGS, WE NEVER FOUND THE ARTIST. I WOULD PAY A FORTUNE FOR THE ONE THAT GOES "CAN I HAVE A TASTE OF YOUR ICE CREAM / CAN I LICK THE CRUMBS FROM YOUR TABLE / CAN I INTERFERE IN YOUR CRISIS?" THAT SONG WAS OUR MANTRA; OUR RELIGIOUS DUTY WAS TO SING IT ON BUSY DOWN-TOWN STREETS, TERRIFYING TOURISTS WHO EXPECTED NONE OF THIS IN THE BIGGEST LITTLE CITY.

SMALL WONDER I DIDN'T GET INFECTED UNTIL 1989 — I WAS TOO BUSY DANCING AND SCREAMING TO HAVE TIME FOR SEX. WHEN THEY CLOSED THE BATHS IN S.F. THERE WERE NO MORE TAPES. FOR A WHILE THEY PLAYED THE OLD ONES, BUT ONE DAY I WENT IN AND THEY WERE PLAYING THE A.M. STATION - EVER TRY TO WANDER A DARK HALLWAY IN YOUR TOWEL, TRY-ING TO LOOK EXOTIC AND FORBIDDING, TO THE STRAINS OF "MY BABY TAKES THE MORNING TRAIN"?

BESIDES, WE WEREN'T 18 ANYMORE, ABLE TO GET IN-TO BARS, AND NO LONGER QUITE SO SCARED OF MEN. WORST OF ALL, IT WASN'T SCARY TO BE PUNK ANYMORE- EVERY SUBURBAN MALL RAT WHOSE LIFE CHANGED WITH HIS FIRST DEPECHE MODE RECORD THOUGHT HE INVEN-TED **THE PUNK LIFE**. I GUESS WE WERE LUCKY TO HAVE HAD OUR SECRET WORLD, PUNK FAGS IN THE MIDDLE OF NOWHERE; AT LEAST WE LOST OUR WORLD TO TIME AND OTHER FACTORS AND NOT TO THE MACHINERY THAT EATS ALL TRENDS AND MAKES THEM SOFT ENOUGH FOR MASS CONSUMPTION.

I SHOULD HAVE LOVED CLUB URANUS WHEN IT OPENED, DISCOVERED THE WORLD OF PUNK FAG-GOTRY REBORN THERE, BUT IT WAS TOO LATE. I'D DONE IT, IT WAS OVER, AND BESIDES, IT WAS AN S.F. THING, WHICH MEANT IT WAS ABOUT BEING PRETTY MORE THAN ABOUT BEING PUNK. THEY COULD HAVE PLAYED THOSE OLD TAPES AT URANUS ONE NIGHT AND THEY'D'VE SOUNDED JUST AS FABULOUS, BUT IT COULD NEVER BE THE SAME.

TRUE CONFESSIONS

•

By **Bill Brent** *from*
Black Sheets

Bill Brent is one busy dude. In 1992 he published the first edition of *The Black Book,* an annual resource guide to the many sexual-oriented products and services available in the United States. In April '93 he published the first issue of his quarterly sex zine, *Black Sheets.* And just last year he started up a new publication, *Porno Pen,* a resource guide for writers of erotica.

**   *Black Sheets* is one of my favorite sex zines. Bill combines true sex stories with fantasy-driven erotic fiction and anything else he feels like putting in each issue. While it primarily explores bisexual experiences, *Black Sheets* captures the attitude that sex is simply sex, without assigning arbitrary gay/straight labels to it. This piece, borrowed from the "Sex and Productivity" issue, reveals a couple of affairs that may not necessarily be on the list of Bill's top sexual experiences.**

Twice in my life I've been paid for sex. One time was in 1984, when I was living in a room in back of a garage in San Francisco's Glen Park. My curiosity took me to Esta Noche, a gay Latino bar in the Mission. All night long I cruised hunky Latino boys, but they all seemed to be uninterested or taken. After last call, a bloated, fortyish black guy came on to me, and I let him drive me home, more because I wanted the ride and also because I took pity on him. He was a wine salesman, I believe. On the way, he told me stories about how a boyfriend of his had known Prince in the Midwest and had pictures of him playing with another guy. Big deal. Is this supposed to impress me, I wondered. The longer he talked, the more desperate he seemed. We got to my room, and the sex was so uneventful, I can't even remember whether we came, or what we even did. Probably blow jobs. This was definitely a mercy fuck. I thought that was the end of it, but then he began stalking me. I would come home from work and find him parked outside my building. I gave him the brush-off twice, but he was really persistent. The third time, out of sheer exasperation, I told him I'd have sex with him, just to get rid of him (big mistake!), but it was going to cost him. He said he'd give me $20. I took him inside and perched him atop my bed. I stood in the doorway, about 10 feet away, and I jacked off. I was so turned off that it was one of the few times in my life I couldn't even pop a boner, much less cum. After five or ten minutes of jerking my limp dick, I got sore and tired, and I told him that was it. Well, then he started bitching at me and wanted $10 back because I was so lame. He felt that, for $20, I should at least cum. In theory, I agreed with him, but the guy had been such a pest, I refused on principle to give him a refund. Then he began to get really ugly, and I told him that if he didn't leave immediately, I'd start shouting and alert my landlady upstairs. He finally relented and left, and fortunately, he never came back. I guess I finally pissed him off.

The second time was in 1987, when I was living in the Mission and went prowling in Mission News' video arcade, before the management turned into the Sex Gestapo and made it impossible to get laid there. It was a typically slow weeknight. This older white guy (late 50s) came on to me. His breath smelled of alcohol. I was about to tell him to fuck off when he offered me cash if he could play with my dick. Well, I was pretty broke that week (a typical situation), so I told him he could do it if he gave me $20. We went into a booth and locked the door. He fished out $20 from an envelope and I pocketed it. I had a hunch that he wasn't working and had just gotten his allotment from some government program.

Even though I wasn't attracted to the guy, I can get hard in almost any situation, so he jerked on my stiff meat for a bit and then decided he wanted to blow me. I told him that would cost him an extra $10. He didn't seem too thrilled about it, but I held my ground and he gave me another $10. I was grossed out by his drunkenness, but he was actually giving me pretty good head—so good, in fact, that I eventually came in his mouth. I got his consent to do that, but I guess the taste shocked him, because up came his lunch. Fortunately, I anticipated his gag reflex and pulled out of his mouth just in time to avoid coating my crotch with his puke.

I watched him heave his guts out and then handed him some tissues I had in my pocket. I know it sounds weird, but I got a perverse thrill out of having such an impact on him, albeit a negative one. I tried to clean him up a bit, but it was useless. After I determined that he wasn't going to choke to death, I zipped myself up, managing to avoid the puddle of spreading vomit, and left the booth, which had begun to smell really fetid. I breezed out the front door and left him there. I couldn't really help him any further in his condition, and telling the management would have just added to his problems. I figured maybe he'd pull himself together if I left him alone. The manager would find out about the puke soon enough, anyway, and I didn't see the point in getting tangled up in some sorry drunk's drama.

On my way home, I went to the supermarket and spent about half the money on groceries. It felt deliciously wicked to walk into an innocent setting and spend my ill-gotten gain on the things I needed. I felt great, no longer broke, and very powerful, in a way that is hard to explain. I didn't feel angry at the guy for puking, just sorry for him, and happy for me.

Sex work is rarely discussed objectively or without hysteria in the mainstream media. Prostitution, lap dancing, stripping, phone sex—we know it's all out there, but most people would rather not talk about it. For many years, the publication *Whorezine* acted as the de facto industry trade journal. Created by and for sex workers, this lively zine explored practical topics (like legal issues, AIDS, and other hazards), but also included more humorous writing.

This piece from *Snevil* would have been right at home in *Whorezine*. It paints a true portrait of what's really happening at the other end of the phone sex line when you call for some hot chat. Popular culture would have us believe that phone sex operators are either lingerie-clad models lounging on penthouse-apartment waterbeds or fifty-year-old trailer-trash divorcées. In actuality they're just hardworking women, trying to pay for school, raise their kids, or simply earn a living.

I WAS A PHONE SEX GIRL

•

By **Connie L.** *from Snevil*

"Hello, you have reached 970-????. The charge for this call is $30 unless you hang up now. Would you like to speak with a girl?"

That's how we were instructed to answer the phone. No screening operator, no computer setup, just some girls in a hot dark room with a couple of ratty phones and old chairs.

The first phone sex place I worked, let's call it Company X, was a dumpy little place run by a tyrannical woman who listened in on the calls from her home. The girls lived in fear of her. No one was allowed to work part-time, everyone worked 8-hour shifts with no breaks, 5 days a week. Many of the girls worked 7 days, some double shifts. They must have had expensive drug habits, because nothing in the world could make me work these phones every day. Unless you've actually done it, you cannot imagine how stressful being a "fantasy phone girl" (as we were known) can be, especially with some crazy broad critiquing you after some of your calls.

When I was hired, a few things were explained to me: you had to work a minimum of five days a week. If you were sick, you had to get a replacement. There were no personal calls. You could not leave to get coffee or food. You had to stay on your line until the next shift came to replace you. You had to spend $2\frac{1}{2}$ hours on each of the three lines run by this firm—the local $30 line, the 900 national line, and the local party line. You could not leave the party line unattended, so you could not run to the bathroom. You could read a book, but you could not nap in the office. Pay was $6 an hour, and you got paid once a month, at the end of the month. You set up your schedule at the beginning of the month, and you could not deviate from that. If you needed a week off, you were responsible for getting replacements. Got all that?

Naturally, there was very little mention of what I should actually do when I got on the phone. There were a few rules. If you get someone who sounds young, ask them when they graduated high school. If they can actually answer that question satisfactorily, ask them if their parents know they're calling a $30 phone line. They would usually hang up then. The other rule was that on the national line we were not to actually bring up the topic of sex. If the guy mentioned it first, we could go along with it. The crazy broad who owned the company thought that MCI was trying to shut down her national lines and so would sometimes call. Apparently, the MCI stooges would not say anything sexually explicit over the phones, so we couldn't, either. Unless the guy started. Oh. And the other rule. Your name had to have an "s" or "sh" sound. All the girls were named Cheryl, Cindy, Sandy, Shala. And you had to say you were tall and blond. No black girls, no Spanish girls.

The trainer forgot to mention one important fact to me, which I found out later. All the girls live in a townhouse on the Upper East Side of Manhattan. We live there for free in exchange for answering the phone. We don't get paid. We like doing this work. And by the way, I have a piece of property in Baja that I'm sure you'd be interested in buying.

My first call was pretty standard. I was reading Tom Robbin's *Skinny Legs and All*, so I was pretty annoyed to hear my phone ringing. I picked it up and went into my spiel. When I got to "Would you like to talk to a girl?" the guy had the nerve to say "Is Sheila there?" Sheila? Sheila! Don't I sound good enough? I asked him to hold on and asked the trainer if there was a Sheila here. No, of course there isn't. "Well, " I drawled, "Sheila isn't here. Would you like to talk to me?" "Sure, why not." Gawd, what a way to start off.

When I got my first call, I hadn't been told all the rules yet, so I told "Mark" (as he identified himself) that my name was Yvette and I had long dark hair, dark eyes, and was 5'5", 38-24-36. He thought I sounded cute ("You sound just like an ex of mine," he said, "only cuter."), so we continued.

Mark asked me if I had ever been with two guys at once. Oh, sure I had, only once though, but it was really hot. And had I ever been with a black guy? Well, Mark, it's funny that you mention that, because one of the two guys was a big dark stud with a rock hard bod and a big black prick to match. I then proceeded to describe how I orally excited my Nubian prince and our third party blond boy did the PeeWee while watching us. And just as Mr. African American shot his hot steamy Clorox-and-buttermilk cocktail past my soft moist lips, Mark muttered "Thank you" and hung up. Only five minutes and he paid for thirty. Put your feet on the desk, doll, and smoke a butt.

The evening progressed in that manner until I got on the party line. The party line is $15 for ten minutes, it gets disconnected automatically, and sometimes there's more than one guy on the line. It can get very confusing. There are a lot of regulars on the party line. The one that stands out is this guy that the other girls call "The Director." He liked it best when there were other guys on the line, and he would tell everyone where to put what and the call would proceed from there. Like, "Jose, stick it in her ass, and you, Mike, you get her mouth." I never spoke to the Director, but I did get a lot of guys who just wanted to listen to me talk to someone else or to myself. People on the party line were into behaviors I know nothing about, so I began to feel a little lost. One guy wanted to be fisted, and at this point I started to wish that there was a manual around to tell me what to say. Ten long minutes of fisting, and in that time I got my whole hand up his ass without the use of Crisco or surgical gloves.

One thing I learned from the party line is that guys like to hear stories. You with other guys, you with other girls, you alone, you in cars, in the park, on the bus, almost getting caught. They don't want to hear about what you'd be doing if you were together, though. It's all about voyeurism. They want to pretend to be looking in your bedroom window while you go down on your Spanish girlfriend, or walking by your car while you fuck some stranger. There is never any mention of condoms, of course.

Not all phone sex companies are like this. One place I called advertised for astrology line operators. It turned out to be a very well-known adult publishing company that runs a lot of phone sex lines. Yes, they were starting a new astrology line, but would I be interested in doing phone sex? The woman I spoke to there was so stupid that when I mentioned I had worked sexually explicit phone lines before, she said, "Well, how do you feel about doing phone sex?" That's what I said I did, bitch. This particular place did have nicer offices, however, with air conditioning and everything. But the pay was lower and the hours just as bad—no part-time, full-time only.

And what about the girls who do phone sex? They all said they do it for the money. But c'mon, $6 an hour? And under those conditions? You'd get as much working at Macy's and an employee discount, too. Most of the girls were young and reasonably attractive. So much for the myth of the grandma who does phone sex. The girls were actresses, students, writers. One claimed to be a psych major who was doing this for research. Only a few had been there for more than six months, and these were the "old-timers"—they were already considered managers, which means that they did very few phone calls. Is this demeaning work? I guess it can be. It's boring as hell. One thing I did find out, though. The line that advertises beautiful women with big cocks? It's not even gay men you're talking to. It's the same girls you get on the other lines.

LAPPSAPOPPIN':
SELWYN HARRIS LAP
DANCES AROUND NYC

•

By **Selwyn Harris** *from*
Happyland

In the early days of this century, New York's Broadway and 42nd Street symbolized the pinnacle of the entertainment industry. Vaudeville stages, legitimate theaters, and movie houses all lined these famed roads. It was in the '60s and '70s that B-grade movies and the sex industry took over Times Square.

In recent years, big corporations, in conjunction with the city government, have waged a war for the soul of 42nd Street, forcing out the strip clubs and making the area safe for high-priced hotels. While some might celebrate the shiny facelift given to this vibrant neighborhood, many are saddened by its sterile Disney-esque future, a future sure to be devoid of any gritty human character.

Many zine publishers have romanticized the heyday of 42nd Street movie houses, with their bargain-priced triple features of bizarre low-budget B-movies. None are more devoted than Selwyn Harris, whose nom de plume was borrowed from a couple of his favorite theaters along 42nd Street. In his zine, *Happyland*, Selwyn looks fondly back on the early days of "The Deuce," before the Walt Disney Company took all the fun out of it. In this piece, Selwyn visits some of the "adult entertainment" clubs that line the strip, taking in a lap dance or two (purely for journalistic research, of course). Unbeknownst to him, just a few months later, the Time Square Redevelopment Program would change all this, turning this consumer guide into a swan song to a lost era.

Lap dancing, Mardi Gras, Tease-n-Squeeze, Greasing Prettied-Up Palms for the Pleasure of Having a Cottage-Cheese Caboose Booming Up & Down on Your Bone-On: call it what you will, it seems to be some sort of rage in the Big Apple these days, a rage of which the borough of *Happyland* wholeheartedly approves. Our support is so enthusiastic (and costly), that we recently received yet another letter from The New York Savings Bank inquiring as to why we haven't added so much as a measly cent in more than six months to the $8.72 that keeps our account open. Ha!—they'd be better off asking one (or a dozen) of the delightfully colorful seat-level entertainers who labor in these new lascivitoriums about the whereabouts of my finances: the *ladies* don't seem to have any difficulty whatsoever in extracting cash from yours truly; in fact, the friggin' bank should be more concerned with keeping their mitts on the measly eight-bucks-and-change in the first place: Certainly my newly beloved couch-cuties need it more than they do, and woe unto he who would ask me which of those parties (the bank or the bone-boomers) I need more. How about you?

Compadres, a cancer has spread in our city this past Winter. Ugly cancer, misogynist cancer: the kind of cancer that forces women to starve themselves, to put plastic in their tits, to waste their money on pore-clogging warpaint. Among the tumors that cropped up in light of this infection were Goldfingers, Scores, Stringfellows, Pure Plat-inum, and a whole bunch of others that advertise in the *Newsday* sports pages. These loathsome pits are high-tech, sanitized versions of what pencil-dicks in $1,200 suits think a tit bar should be, complete with "carving board" buffet tables, walls of TV monitors beaming out every sports event going on the planet at any given time (just to let the girls know that, sure, their tits are okay, but they ain't worth shit compared to Bobby Bonilla), and, of course, scads of bim-bolines who brought their Barbie dolls to some quack plastic surgeon so that he could use them as a model as he chipped away any part of their bodies that didn't look like it was manufactured by Mattel.

But what I have come to report to you on this day concerns a benevolent, countercancer that grew alongside the one described above. For a few weeks there, it seemed that for every "Trump's Tush Mahal" that was opening up, some dank, sleazy spot sprang to life for a brief, but infinitely fruitful life span. These foreboding-to-all-but-the-truest-of-believers holes allowed women to really be women—in all their pudged-up, unshaven glory—and allowed men to be the powerless, worshipful slaves-to-punani cretins that we are (and that shit-pits like Scores go all out to make it seem like we aren't). A little honesty, particularly on that level, goes a long way in my book, so believe me when I tell you that my intrepid travails in these establishments were purely for both anthropological and supportive purposes, as well as to inform you, my reading audience, about new and intriguing trends in the field of female-male relations; in short, prurience was never a part of the equation. A lesser fanzine, now, would follow that preceding sentence above with the colloquialism "Not." But we're better than that. And so are you.

Not.

Fantasy in Motion

Label me as you will, but I prefer my lady friends, both professional and otherwise, on the heavy side (not that, in a pinch, I don't ravenously devour whatever's set out in front of me, but . . .). Imagine my delight, then, when after paying Fantasy in Motion's weighty ten dollar entrance fee, I locked eyes with an even weightier blond bouillabaisse spilling over the sides of a folding chair with my name practically written all over her cellulite. Excited, I shot her my finest little-boy-lost-in-the-big-city-with-only-his-fat-wallet-to-protect-him-and-his-hard-on. Unimpressed, she shot back, "I'm on break," which shot me right the hell down.

But then my dark angel swooped down upon me as in salvation. She was bone-thin, black, and pretty. She seemed happy to see me; I figured it was because since she probably dealt with so many obese, ugly fifty-year-olds all day, she was grateful to have a strapping young buck like myself. But then she turned to the girthy glamourpuss still on break and said, "This is cool. Now I can give you back that ten dollars I owe you as soon as he's finished." Oh.

The lingerie-clad skeleton led me not to one of the many rows of folding, auditorium-style chairs that were lined up in front as if they would soon be filled by proud and annoyed parents forced into sitting through the Christmas pageant, but to a locker-type cubicle, inside of which was a pane of Plexiglas that separated me from the booth she went into. All I'd be groping was my own stinking self! FUCK!

She told me that a "naked show" would only cost me the ten-spot that she owed to the chubby lovely outside. Hell, why didn't she just cut out the middleman, I wondered, but I only sought to ask her where the fucking Lap Dance was—or actually, "LAPP DANCE," as it was spelled—that the sign in the front window had lured me in with.

She explained that they had been having "license troubles," so the lap dancing was put temporarily on hold. *License trouble?!?* What, did some underage broad with only a temporary permit get caught operating a crotch while not in the presence of a Licensed Lapper? Did they fail the written test? What the fuck? I was too disgusted to even think about it. All I could do was shoot a load. Which I did. Thinking about my Heavy Honey on the stool out there, waiting for *my* ten dollars as she dreamt about the entire pizza she was gonna buy with it. I exited dripping and pissed off. And thinking about her thinking about the pizza made me hungry.

Laps

To enter Laps you must pay a steep $8 admission fee, after which you ascend an even steeper, long, and not overly well-lit staircase (decorated with "Sweetheart Cinema" wallpaper that porn-goers of a bygone era have etched in their wet dreams and/or anguished consciences and for which you would pay any price to own a yard of. Fuck that, an inch), of which that takes you up to a theater lobby where a couple of girls sit around talking. Naked. Well, almost.

A hulking presence perched by an open doorway (who by its scent alone you can tell is male, and from its presentation—and, face it, location—you decide is a felon) points you toward a half-open Dutch door behind which sits a kid at a desk who's maybe all of fifteen (maybe) and he's ham-ham-ham-hammerin' away on his GameBoy

with a vengeance to be envied by the power-palmists from the theater's halcyon days of handlove. He looks up, visibly annoyed that you have plucked him out of Super Mario World and readies a hospital-style wristband for you (which you're used to wearing from the Coney Island Sideshows and detox). "You give me ten dollars now," he commands. "The girl gets ten dollars. And you give the wristband back after!!!" He affixes the plastic tag to you and the realization strikes that what he was saying was that you are now twenty-eight dollars into a hole that could only get deeper *(too* deep, you hope) and you brave on. In the name of science.

The mountainous chap grunts out something instructional-sounding in tone, so you saunter past him and into the auditorium. You see a bikini. That's all you need to see.

You are seated in a cocktail party chair, there is a significant weight straining your midsection. Then your hostess joins you on your lap. She's biggish, though still not *BUF* magazine big (like you like 'em), because most of her seems to be dense, black curly hair that was apparently styled with grease and which clogs your every breathing portal.

About five minutes into the procedures, you begin to rethink your Chubby-Chasing ways. You are in pain. The problem may not actually lie, however, in your enchantress's heft, but her technique, which consists of pneumatic bouncing that grinds her G-string-covered mystery spot into your lap with such force it nearly crushes your thighbones. She obviously thinks this is somehow "erotique." It's not. It hurts.

This is agony, misery. Pain. As the song reaches its peak, her depth charges, to your incredulity, actually increase in both their power and urgency. Your legbones are being pummeled with wrecking-ball force; you fear they will snap.

When you sense the song petering out, you heave a sigh of gratitude. You are both exhausted. To your colossal relief, she slithers off you. You have been assaulted, devastated. A few minutes later, as you are still recovering, the first image that greets your tearstained eyes is yet another bikini, on yet another crotch attendant. She speaks: "You want to try a lap dance with meee, bay-bee?"

You run for your fucking life.

Capri Theatre

It has been said that the candle that burns brightest also burns shortest. How true, how true. Allow me, now, to add a corollary: that the scum-pit that festers filthiest also festers most quickly out of commission. 'Tis true, too. And a pity.

The Capri Theatre, one of those seemingly indestructible little porn toilets that have littered Eighth Avenue for decades, was just such a scum-pit.

The Capri is actually less of an out-and-out pit than its neighbor, the Venus, but then, the Venus is the type of place where the germs have actually sprouted wings and have to be swatted off when you enter like swarming insects, so your average homeless shelter urinal is less of a pit than the Venus. In addition, the Capri's setup is strangely similar to a theater in a suburban multiplex, with its narrow rows of plastic seats facing a small, bright screen and its decently kept lavatory and its squads of blow job junkies wandering around inquiring if you need any "help" (which, in light of the "No Ladies Admitted" sign hanging in the box office, I can state forthrightly that I've never partaken of). But it is a nice service for those who are interested. Kinda like stewardesses. Well, okay, maybe it's not *that* much like a mall theater, but it still seemed a damned odd choice for the installation of lap lovelies. A choice that, for the ultra-reasonable five-clam admission fee, I'd be investigating. And did. Very much the manchild in what would turn out to be very, very, *very* much the promised land.

Remember the fire-and-brimstone, Cecil B. DeMille–scale dens of debauchery that you envisioned Adult Entertainment Centers to be when you were first old enough to realize what they were? Ladies and gentlemen, I tell you this was it: a funhouse of filth, a two-tiered (the balcony was open, though, as a sign stated, "For Movie Viewing Only"—ha!) panorama of perversions. Dante's Duplex. Nothing less. I was in heaven.

Saint Peter, the gatekeeper, turned out to be a fat old guy rotating on a barstool, picking his exposed ass-crack, and biting his nails. Yum. He was perched at the top of the auditorium's downhill slope, accosting what at first I thought was a chubby black kid (He later appeared to be in his forties. Then he looked thirteen again. Maybe he was some kind of magical shape-shifter . . . or an angel!) for being a pain in the ass to the lap lassies who were lined up along the interior wall. My eyes hadn't yet adjusted to the dark (though the porn images projected on the screen up front did cast a luster of daylight onto objects—and objectifiers—below), but I could smell the ladies, even through the jizz fumes. That alone got me hard.

Then I felt one. By mistake. As I was fumbling in the theater's pitch blackness down the center aisle I clasped the wall next to me for support. Only it wasn't the wall. It was Clara. It was her tit. It was her beautiful, bulging, *naked* tit. It was love at first fondle.

I learned her name as she escorted me to a seat and one of her fellows cheered her on. She went. I came. Here's how:

She led me into one of the rows of seats, whereupon I gained my night vision at last. It was then that I learned, in fact, that the theater's seemingly excellent sound system had not been cranked up, but that the ear-splitting wails of passion and moans were rising up from the *audience itself*.

Thirty people were situated in the theater that night—half of them pathetic, desperate, forlorn fools (the men), the other half savvy, surreptitious seat-Shivas (the women). And among them, fifteen unholy, unashamed, unhampered, unsullied, *unbelievable* unsafe sex acts were taking place all around me.

Get the picture.

There were writhing bodies, *nude* bodies, intertwined everywhere. Nude. Stroking. Nude. Blowing. Nude. Fucking. Nude. Coming. Nude. Really. Nude. In movie theater seats. Nude. Really Really Really. Nude Nude Nude. Clara sat me down and invited us to join them.

For ten bucks.

She had a taker.

We didn't get nude right away (though Clara was halfway there from the giddyap, she took some time to get to know my Levi's first, butt first, of course).

Her melons swung in front of my face like a hypnotist's you-are-getting-*verrrrry*-sleeeepy-watch. A string of drool escaping from my mouth gave me away.

"What?" she asked. "Your mama didn't breast-feed you when you was baby?"

"Nyaaah-ah-ah-ah-ahhh," was the best response I could muster.

She wrapped her arms around me, cradling my head with one hand and cradling her hoot with the other.

"I give you what your mommy didn't, then, bay-bee." There was a sudden nipple in my mouth. "Eat . . . eeeat."

Gluttonous does not begin to describe the "eat, eeeeating" I did.

We sat in a squirming, stripped-to-the-waist ball of quiver-bliss for the next few minutes. I had a hard-on you could drive railroad spikes with. And she had these . . . hands. Her bazooms and belly and backside were devastating enough, but her hands! They were like warm, wet tarantulas and they were everywhere. And, oh, their sting!

"You know I love to play with your beautiful cock bay-bee," Miss Touchy Feely told me, "but if you want me to kees it, you got to pay extra."

And then, I swear to BabyJesusGodMotherMary-AllTheAngelsAndSaintsAndAllThem, John Holmes stopped fucking onscreen, looked right at me, and stated, flat out, "NO!"

I shook my head spasmodically in the fashion of a bewildered Elmer Fudd. When I reopened my eyes, the colossal Mr. Holmes was back to bone-ness as usual. I decided the hallucination was some kind of omen, anyway, so to Clara's invitation I offered my now standard reply of "Nyaah-ah-ah-ahahahah." She understood. But that didn't stop her from finally de-pantsing me altogether. Nor should it have.

There were now *sixteen* stark nude, unholiest of matrimonies going down (in some cases, all too literally) in the Capri's majestic aisles. Ooops—the fat eighty-year-old guy in front of me with a little blonde sucking his considerable tits just blasted such a geyser of goop that it hit an exit sign and broke the lightbulb! Back to fifteen. And among them, of course, was the refined Madame Clara and your intrepid working boy. Who now believed he was falling in love.

I felt the curves and planes of Clara's magnificent face and I slipped my hands down and felt my betrothed's back. I felt her sumptuous love handles and I felt the folds of her belly with my frantic fingers and I felt those afore-celebrated mitts of hers caressing my whole being and I felt like I was in the clutches of no one less than the Alpha-and-Omega of Goddess-Bitch-Mommy-Angel-Whore-Teacher-Amazon-Baby-Slut-Girl-Lady-Woman-Womynhood and I felt like I said like I was in love and I felt in a way like I don't think I've ever felt it before. And certainly not since.

My cock—engorged like it hadn't been since the episode of *Blossom* wherein the title character takes a hot tub with her buddy "Six"—was jammed into Clara's navel, seemingly trying to open a new orifice. I moved it out . . .

"Bay-bee, to fuck I only charge you twenty dollars. You got?"

. . . and up . . .

"Y-y-y-esss. Here."

. . . and in.

I felt a clamp like a hunter's steel leg trap slam down violently onto my sack. I looked in terror and saw, to my utter fright and repulsion, a hand. A male hand. Squeezing. Hard. Hard enough to make me think something would pop. My eyes DID pop, and I used them to follow the trail up the arm and saw who it was attached to:

Mike Brady. Robert Reed. His ghost. No shit.

"Asshole," the apparition said. What? Did he want me to give Clara sodomy? Okay, I was game. I parted her holiest-of-holys . . .

Someone slapped me across the face. I turned and saw Rock Hudson. "Dickboy," he said. I buried my shvantz as deep as possible into Clara (who was doing such a bang-up job in the fake orgasm department that she hadn't even noticed our guests), in hope that the scent of over-worked vadge would repel my attackers. Then the seat in front of me popped straight into the air like something out of James Bond's car.

Valentino Wladziu Liberace emerged from the hole where the chair had been. The string of obscenities he shrieked at me were unprintable, even for *Happyland*. His brother George was with him.

Suddenly, *all* the seats in the Capri were exploding or being upended or propelled rocket-like toward the ceiling. The dead rose from the ground beneath them in George Romero–scale hordes: Roy Cohn, Keith Haring, Malcolm Forbes, Chad Lowe as his *Life Goes On* character, the big black dude from *Predator* and *Harry and the Hendersons*, and lots more. They hovered around me in a terrifying circle chanting, "One of us . . . one of us . . . one of us . . . " until the ritual had conjured the ultimate HIV hobgoblin. From beneath my seat emerged Gaetan Dugas, the notorious "Patient Zero" credited with bringing a wacky new virus to North America.

The former airline steward leaned into my face and bellowed, "What's your fucking problem, shit-for-brains? Where's your condom? *Didn't ya ever hear of AIDS!?!*"

He added, "Nice legs, though." An instant later, the gaggle of ghosts swooped down upon me and rushed me out the door. I dressed myself as I ran, like a kid caught at a Norman Rockwell swimming hole. I was a-scared. But, as I sat a few minutes later in an Eighth Avenue peep-booth *safely* finishing what the clandestine Miss Clara had started, I was grateful. You should be, too. A world with AIDS is bad enough, but, I don't care what they say, I won't live in a world without *Happyland*.

PUZZLING THROUGH THE PEEP SHOW

•

By **Sasha Cagen** *from*

Cupsize

While the heyday of the 42nd Street strip clubs is long since gone, a few peep shows can still be found scattered around the Deuce. Because nude women are the main attraction at these shows, the audience is almost exclusively male.

Sasha and her friend Becca, two bisexual women, ruffled a few feathers when they tried to invade this bastion of the male experience. Searching out a lesbian sex show, what they found instead were a handful of bored, low-wage sex workers just trying to earn a meager living. This piece from *Cupsize* raises a lot of questions about how the peep show experience affects the women who work there and the men who experience this form of alienating sexual experience.

Forty-second Street, the Deuce, the association is immediate and I think you know what I mean. Flashing lights, the neon outline of a curvaceous female figure, girls, X, girls, X, girls and X and X. For a good, long while, I've wanted to step inside these red smoky dens that live only in my grrrl mind's eye. Smoky and dim by default, because I couldn't clearly envision what was inside. These imagined parlors have been the subject of pages of analysis and countless debates, and I'd never even been inside even one peep show, bordello, strip joint, you fill in the blank. When I was in my late teens, I would walk by at a quickened pace, with my head turned, eyes averted. But as I age, I've become more curious and head-strong. I now pause for an instant on the sidewalk, crane my neck and peer beyond the doorman to the action inside. I want to see for myself.

But you know, I never found a partner in crime—a feminist who shares an appetite for the occasional porno-

graphic adventure. Maybe I was too shy to ask, to inquire about likely candidates, or maybe it's just rare that I meet that special person.

I got to go quite accidentally . . . which pleased me very much. I would have been depressed if I had painstakingly mapped out the excursion, if I had to work at going to the peep show. One June afternoon, my friend Becca and I were making a pilgrimage to the biggest Salvation Army in Manhattan, a few avenues west of the sex hub. Whenever you go to the midtown "Sally's," you wind up traveling through the epicenter of the adult entertainment fray. On the way back, Becca mentioned that she wanted to see the "lesbian" sex show advertised at the "Playpen." Needless to say, I wanted to see it, too.

After some hemming and hawing, some giggling on the sweaty, grimy New York street, and a couple of Snapples inside Port Authority, we psyched ourselves up and committed to the "project." We walked back to Eighth Avenue and wandered haltingly into the lobby of the Playpen, a house of love, a mirrored, bejeweled carniva-lesque hallway. From behind a yellow booth, a woman was selling gold tokens, as if she was selling tickets to see the bearded lady. As we approached the counter, she told us that we weren't allowed inside without a male escort. Orders from the male boss, legislated for our protection. Becca told her, reflexively, "That's discrimination." Becca almost tried to duke it out with her, but I piped up with a surly good-bye and steered us out to the street. I had made the correct assumption that there were plenty of other lesbian sex shows within a stone's throw away.

When we entered the other peep shows, the doormen didn't feel the need to protect us. Pausing at the white frame door of the peep show half a block away, I asked a loitering-looking guy if we could go in. "Yeah, sure."

I was wearing the wrong clothes for the occasion. I looked like a country bumpkin, completely innocent and naive, in the dowdy floral skirt I had ripped to the knees and the Birkenstocks I was wearing because I had furious blisters on my heels. I was already paranoid about body fluids dripping on me: in these stupid sandals, I also had to worry about my unprotected feet. I imagined that we would watch a sex show in the kind of place where fluids would pool unnoticed, seated on the frayed upholstery of a sagging row of seats, ogling two people performing sexual acts on a dusty black stage. I couldn't have been more off. The insides of these places were gleaming, plastic, and pristine. No body fluids, instead the tiles were shiny and practically antiseptic.

As far as I could tell, this is how the work was organized. The setting: a wide, open space of warehouse proportions. Circular clusters of bright red booths dotted the floor like the mushroom cottages of a Smurf village: half-dressed women were casually traveling between them. The booths looked modern, like huge red kitchen cabinets or Formica coffins soldered together and propped erect with blue handles attached to open them. Though the management advertised a stage show, I saw no evidence of a stage or a show. I think they counted the interior of the circle of booths as a stage and the women inside as a show. Becca and I tried to assume the appropriate mien and demeanor (whatever that would be) as we bought two tokens and entered our separate plastic booths. We dropped our tokens into video game–type slots; a small sheet of plastic opened to reveal a paneless window.

Inside the circle were four women. Three of them were sitting, just languishing on chairs, while the other was peeling off her teddy. But this was hardly a sexy or sexual act: disrobing was just preparation for nudity, an element of her job description. Two women were smoking, looking pretty bored. One woman, the most attractive one, looked at me and asked if I was tipping. If I had been, she would have walked to my window and I could have touched her. I was so unprepared for the question that it would have taken me the full minute to fumble for a bill in my wallet. It was all I could to form the word "No." The next fifty seconds in time slowed down to a near standstill: fifty awkward and unpleasant seconds.

The woman studied me with challenging eyes. I had to fight the urge to look through my wallet or bite my nails, anything to find an alternate focus for *my* eyes. Assembled in this naked, plastic ennui, more at ease in the flesh than I was in my clothes, not doing anything particularly erotic, the women inside were much more comfortable than I was on the other side of the window. I could have been passing time on the benches of a locker room with them. But I couldn't kid myself into that false camaraderie, because in the booth to my right, another customer had come to tip. One of the women went to his window and he reached in and fingered her inner thigh and her cunt.

A disembodied limb, a hairy arm reaching into the crotch of a woman whose eyes were fixed to the ceiling, staring to pass the time. I'm hesitant to describe the pathos I saw in this scene, because I don't want to rob this woman of her subjectivity; I don't know her, and I don't know best for all women. Perhaps she prefers sex work to less lucrative positions and otherwise demeaning jobs. I'll simply say that a lump swelled in my throat when I watched her look away as he reached between her legs. *Could* she have

chosen other work or other forms of sex work?

Perhaps if the interaction seemed a little more human and less fractured, I wouldn't have been as unsettled. Even for the paying customer, what was the appeal? I could be equally sad for *him*: alienation in the late twentieth century and all that. But how can I waste my tears on the owner of that hairy arm? Even if the women seemed more comfortable and "in control" in the middle of the space, male money opens and shuts the window on the peep show. And male managers define the terms of the industry.

I have described a very particular context, a 42nd Street peep show. I need to say very plainly that I believe that sex work is a perfectly valid occupation, sometimes far more profitable than other "pink-collar" professions. But working conditions and power relations make the biggest of differences, and this street and this place did disturb me, I won't lie.

I shouldn't have been surprised that many of the customers were well-dressed, professional-looking men. Even though I expected this demographic, I was struck by the affluence all the same. The excursion seemed so completely habitual and routine. These men bought their tokens unabashedly, a ten-minute bite of sex, then lunch, and back for conference calls in the corner office. When I mentioned the preponderance of well-dressed men to my roommate Jill, who works at MTV, she said that she suspected that at least half of the men in the building where she works patronize the Playpens of 42nd street on their lunch hours. That number may be inflated and rhetorical, but until the Disney takeover of Times Square, there were probably enough stalls in the Playpens to accommodate them.

Can you imagine the same availability of lunch-hour sexcursions for the female employees at MTV? The female executives, secretaries, publicity managers, or Tabitha Soren? Imagine if I, a twenty-two-year-old woman, could pay seventy-five cents to stroke a warm body before I bought a slice of quiche, a bottle of lemonade; before I dashed back to work. I can't imagine it. At all.

MY SO-CALLED SEX LIFE

•

By **Sky Ryan** *from*

How Perfectly Goddamn Delightful It All Is, to Be Sure

Self-publishing allows people to do just about anything they want with their publications. So, while *Time* magazine has been published continuously since 1898, reporting the news in the same old style the whole time, some folks, like Sky Ryan, prefer instead to change the character and title of their zine with every issue.

So far we've seen *Fuck Off and Die, Schmooze, 1985, Cryptic Crap,* and this one, *How Perfectly Goddamn Delightful It All Is, to Be Sure.* If the title of this zine sounds familiar to you, it should. It was borrowed from a favorite phrase of the late Charles Crumb, as highlighted in the documentary film *Crumb.*

While in earlier publications Sky explored her appreciation for "Weird" Al Yankovic, recently she's been writing about her experiences as a homeless vagabond, traveling up and down the West Coast. This piece is one of the most disturbing confessionals I've ever read in a zine. Sexual experimentation seems to be a major component of a lot of people's life progressions, but Sky seems to have gone a bit overboard the past few years. She documented it all here—as a diary, as a confessional, or maybe as a warning.

I lost my virginity in january 1994 when i was eighteen. here it is, not even two years later, and I've slept with twenty-two guys and a couple of girls since then! even scarier, not one has been a boyfriend/girlfriend. most have been one-night stands and I don't even know the last names of over half the people I've had sex with! so here it is the low low low way lowdown on just how special my relationship with each and every one of my partners was!

1. MICKEY KIRBY—the first guy i ever fukked. he was my boss at wendy's in new york and i pursued him. we made it one night in his single bed at his parents' house and he told me to give him a blow job or get outta his bed. i obliged, but the next day he dumped me anyway.

2. JOE WOLF—my best friend's brother-in-law!!!! we fucked at Bagby Hotsprings when we were both falling-down drunk. during sex, i looked over my shoulder and noticed there was this old hippie dude sitting on a bench behind us watching. after joe got off he sat down next to the old fart and got smoked out. i puked.

3. ROD MILLER—one of my few sex partners who wasn't a one-nighter. i was 18 and he was 32 and married when we started seeing each other. he could only spend time with me on tuesday (the one day a week his wife worked) and we'd run around and do his errands that day, then at the end of it he'd fuck me in the back seat of his car, drop me off, and i wouldn't see or hear from him again 'til the following week.

4. JOHN—met him the same night I fucked him for hours on end in his car. when he'd had enough, we went our separate ways.

5. CURT PERRY—he came up to me at a show and screamed in my ear or maybe i screamed in his first, i can't remember which. but we screamed and screamed at each other and then he took me home to his mommy and daddy's house and we talked for five hours and found out we had a lot in common and so, then, well, uh you know how it goes—we wound up having five-minute high school sex on the couch. the next morning he bought me taco bell and gave me bus fare.

6. SKADEE—stupid little 15-year-old I fucked off and on for a couple of months. it was one of those relationships where you just call each other only when you're really horny and desperate, and then you arrange to get together for the night and that's that until next time.

7 & 8. JAKE HAYERS & NICK—my first 3some was with curt's homey jake and this chick nick. oh, it was so erotic. nick and i were both on the rag and jake kept losing it.

9 & 10.—another threesome. i had this one with IAN and RED. we all fucked in red's boyfriend's bed. he walked in on us. the three of us got kicked out in the middle of the night.

11.—fucked DAVID in red's backyard the first night i met him. red's mom came out while we was doin' the nasty, kicked us out, and then we decided to get married! davey boy and i lived together for a week then split.

12. SOL—gutter punk. what a fuck. jesus christ hard fast huge and he could keep going and going and he was so aggressive. he'd slam me down and throw me around and pull my hair and put me in all kinds of crazy positions. drove me wild! he looked good to me and tasted good too. i still sometimes get hungry for him but then i remember his body, and what he does with it is the only, ONLY thing that's appetizing about him.

13. JESSE LAME—was sol's best friend and i fucked him as a favor to sol. one night in portland they took turns fucking me and that was pretty fun. another time in san francisco i fucked jesse in golden gate park and then stole a twelve-pack of beer from cala foods for us to drink. when i came outta the store after successfully swiping the booze, jesse grabbed it away from me and took off in his punk fuck friend's car with it!

14. MURRY—thanks for the herpes, pal! and for taking off to san francisco without telling me.

15. DITTO—a dumb little lovable punk who never leaves golden gate. he was sweet to me and we were gonna hitch to new hampshire and fuck and shit on gg allin's grave but then i left him and he left me with bugs.

16. ISAAC—met him at manache's in berkeley. i was super high and had a lot of cash. we did it on the roof of the chateau and i gave him this speed and smoked him out and gave him $ for pool games but he was too demanding so i left.

17 and 18. I met PIERRE and this chick whose name i forgot outside epicenter in san francisco. i gave them a copy of my zine and a few days later saw him again outside the bart station in berkeley and pierre ran up and hugged me and said he loved my zine so much he wanted to fuck me. so me and pierre and this chick friend of his fucked in an alley. he wanted to urinate in my mouth but i wouldn't let him.

19. SARAH—ok, sarah and her boyfriend were these crackheads who were cashing all these stolen checks for me. one night we three got a motel room, smoked a bunch of crack, and when we were high her boyfriend said he wanted to watch us (sarah and i) fuck so we did and he was ordering us around and at one point calling us trash and sluts and then started babbling this religious "we're all going to hell for this" shit but i did what he said went along with it for 3 or 4 hours and then i wanted to stop i was sore inside and had enough but they wouldn't let me.

20. JUSTIN—met this horny little homeboy on broadway in seattle, went back to the motel room he shared with his buddy, fucked him, then got kicked out in the middle of the night cuz i wouldn't put out for his homey too.

21. ROBERT—was this little nug dealer i met on upper haight. we had fun fucking even though we were surrounded by like 20 people (the love pile!) in buena vista park.

22. BOBBY—my fucking hillbilly wingnut sex slave from arkansas. this boy told me i treated him like a whore and i did. i despise the stupid fuck and the only thing he was good for was going down on me. only fuck who ever came close to making me come.

23. JOSH—this guy's such an ass. he works at this tat shop in venice on the boardwalk. everybody who works there is a junkie. this guy gave me a place to crash and i gave him my body.

24. IAN—this stupid head i hitched a ride with to santa cruz. his come-on lines were "do you believe in free love?" and "i want to experience you."

25. JEFF—another dumb horny hippie I went on phish tour with for a while. we hated each other and i guess that's why we fucked.

music

By far the most prevalent type of zine is the music zine. Music fanzines evolved back in the '60s and '70s because music fans craved thoughtful critiques of the exciting new trends in rock and roll.

Back then, music journalism was almost unheard of, except for the trade press like *Billboard.* Since the mainstream press was virtually ignoring the new artists like Dylan and Hendrix, folks started up their own fanzines to document and explore this musical revolution. Now, in the '90s, the popularity of music fanzines continues to grow, primarily because fans feel that the mainstream press isn't adequately covering the underground music scene.

There are two main types of music fanzines. Those that are modeled after the fan club newsletter—created by fans for other fans to report on concerts and new releases from a favorite performer. Then there are the general interest music zines, which feature interviews and record reviews from enthusiastic and personal viewpoints. General interest music zines are currently the most popular type of zine. Filling in the gaps left by *Rolling Stone* and *Spin,* they cover the music that diehard fans are excited about—without the influence of the powerful record conglomerates and their large advertising budgets.

Of course, no one can dispute the power of free stuff. Many a zinester has started a music fanzine partially (if not predominantly) to scam free CDs from the record companies. When you think about it, it's a match made in heaven. The record companies are starved for any mention of their latest pop sensation. Empty-pocketed teens crave new disks to add to their collections. With CDs costing about 50 cents to manufacture but going for close to 20 bucks at the local mall, who can argue with this strategy?

Most music zines devote the bulk of their space to record reviews and band interviews. No wonder—this is precisely the kind of writing that keeps the free CDs flowing. But more important, it allows the fan to chat with their favorite musicians and to present opinions about their favorite (or least favorite) new album.

While record reviews and interviews seem to be everywhere, I tried to avoid choosing that type of writing for this section. Whatever is popular today will most likely be forgotten by tomorrow, making music writing the most ephemeral of all zine topics.

THRIFT STORE RECORD SHOPPING
•
By **Kim Cooper and Richard Hutt** *from*

Scram

While the typical music zine primarily features interviews with bands no one ever heard of and reviews of records few people will ever buy, the editors of *Scram* seem to have little regard for this sort of music culture. They are more interested in compiling the finest writing about music, while ignoring the current crop of hopefuls.

In the past few years, zine publishers (and everybody else) have discovered the treasure trove of vinyl records hidden in thrift stores. We are all well aware of the financial situation of the typical zine publisher—broke. That predicament has led many a zinester to the local Salvation Army to procure household goods, clothing, reading material, home appliances, and especially bizarre outdated music, forgotten pop albums, and archaic instructional volumes. It's hard work digging through dusty bins of scratchy vinyl, but sometimes you hit paydirt. Kim Cooper and Richard Hutt assembled this informative guide to get you started. Take their advice and head off to those cluttered stores on the other side of town. You might come away with some treasures of your own.

scram No. 4 $4.00

Tiny Tim
Lisa Carver
Mary Lou Lord
Dame Darcy and
Dennis Eichhorn
The Go-nuts
Junk Food
Vinyl

Townes Van Zandt
Wacky Cannibals
Boyce & Hart
ZOG
Pin-ups
...and more
Helpful Hints
from Chas

Have you ever noticed peculiar record jackets in coffee table books, then seen some of the same discs on a wall in a record store sporting hefty double-digit price tags? Or perhaps you paid a visit to a pal's bachelor pad and were startled to see a row of records longer than your arm, or your car, for that matter. A whisker of jealousy curled about your nose, and you wondered, "Do I have what it takes to be a disgusting old record raccoon (so-called due to the curled-hand clawing motion required to flip through a stack of records)—overweight, unloved, slave to a vast collection that gradually takes over my entire life?" Or you might just think it would be neat to hear something that can't in any way be described as "cuddle core" or "new wave of new wave." Either way, you've developed an interest in that fine, obsolete format, the vinyl disc. But not just any old garage sale record like Foghat, ABBA, or Loverboy will do.

Nope, you're keen on the weird 'uns.

And so you should be. Because, honestly, chances are you'll continue getting your rock'n'roll the same way you always have: from "alternative" radio and the new CDs that Columbia House sends to "Mr. Abdul P. Housefly" at

your address. Which is fine. It's never been easy to build a decent rock collection without frequenting specialty shops and spending real money, but there's plenty of other stuff out there, in grubby little thrift shops in your very town. Soon you will learn to love them like we do, to swerve across three lanes of traffic when you spy the magic T-H-R-I-F-T letters on an unfamiliar storefront (and to swerve right back should it prove to be a bank or bakery outlet).

But first, you must eliminate any of the following notions from your mental repertoire:

- ❧ Only other people's relatives shop in thrift stores.
- ❧ It's all been picked over already by people cooler than me.
- ❧ If there was anything good in there, it wouldn't *be* in there.
- ❧ It smells.

While there is a certain amount of truth to every one of these assertions, being fatalistic is not going to make you happy. You might as well just skip on down to your nearest junk emporium—remembering to breathe through your mouth and try not to touch anything velour.

Forget that guy with the sprawling collection of great, obscure records that sound like wild picnics on Mars and feature kinky cover art you'd have to hide from your mom. Chances are it wasn't so very long ago that he had just a short stack of vinyl to call his own, and half of it was probably by Queen! Okay, repeat after us: "*My* thrift store record library will put them all to shame!" Better still, it needn't cost more than a dinner for two at your favorite coat-and-tie prime ribbery. But to do it up right, you'll need to need my advice. These rules are designed to save you many shekels and spare you the trauma of bringing home bad records that you can't sell or even give away.

The main thing to remember is the three reasons rule, or 3RR. Quite sim-

ply, you should have at least three good reasons for purchasing any unknown record. (The only exceptions are in the case of mystic genre classics; records that feature the words beatnik, rat-fink, bubblegum, gremmie, teenage, exotica, LSD-25, rumble, bongo, hot-rod, jungle, or Banana Splits anywhere on their jackets must be purchased immediately.) But when a record is a complete mystery to you, the 3RR is your special friend, the one you can (figuratively speaking) turn to in a crowded Goodwill and ask, "What do you think the odds are of this being a total piece of shit?" (Actually, come to think of it, that statement doesn't *have* to be figurative—another great thing about thrift stores is their high level of tolerance for insane babbling and untoward behavior. This even includes a reluctance to impose the death penalty for such classic thrift exchanges as—First student: "Hey look at me, I'm from the Seventies!" Second student: "Huh huh. You should like totally buy it.") If you can't come up with three good reasons for taking a

chance, you're likely to be disappointed with your purchase. But if you find those reasons, you're gonna have some fun tonight.

Okay, great, but what exactly constitutes a "good" reason? Any number of things, actually, and your reasons won't be the same as ours. Say the songwriting credits someone you already dig, that's one. A cover photo of a gorgeous dame with a mermaid's tail would be an-

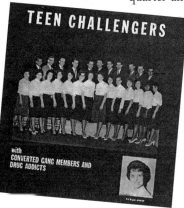

other. Unusual song titles or lyrics. Also be on the lookout for blatant exploitation of trashy popular culture, like the hippie movement or CB craze; a guaranteed hoot, the more clueless the better. A reason can be as vague as liking the particular shade of green of the lettering, or as specific as "background vocals by Casey Kasem." The important thing is that they're your reasons, which is why the records you bring home belong in your unique collection. If you feel compelled to buy every mock-psychedelic astrological record of the years 1968–1973, that's a drive no psychiatrist would ask you to squelch. Gotta have all three Mrs. Miller albums? Terrific, only don't ask us 'round for a listening party. Let your collection reflect your inner self, with all the messed-up glory that it entails.

The other important thing is to *remember where you are.* You are in a thrift store, where there is no such thing as a "collectible," "collectable," or even a "colectubul." Somebody threw all this stuff away! Records in thrift stores should not cost more than 99¢. Singles should cost a quarter and 78s should be *really* fucking cheap, because the odds are about 50/50 that the "helpful" counter staffperson will break them while forcing them into an old plastic bread bag. Stores that put $3.95 stickers on Pablo Cruise albums or

RICHARD'S GUIDE TO OMNIPRESENT THRIFT STORE RECORDS

FOGHAT—Rock and Roll Outlaws

THE J.F.K. MEMORIAL RECORD—(often under the counter as a "collectible"—presumably for collectors of *stuff that's as rare and valuable as empty beef jerky wrappers*)

AMERICA—The one with the retarded hand drawn cover

E.L.O.—Out of the Blue

ANDRE KOSTELNATZ and his BAND OF TRAVELING APES—Music To Drink Martinis with Strange Looking Ladies by Candlelight To

ISAAC HAYES—Live at the Sahara Club in quadraphonic (not that this is a bad thing)

A BAND YOU HAVE VAGUE MEMORIES OF SEEING ONE DRUNKEN NIGHT IN 1988, THAT MAY HAVE INCLUDED SOMEONE YOU KIND OF KNOW—Some Foolish Looking Record

SEALS AND CROFTS—Kill Me

BARBRA STREISAND—Color Me Dead

NAT FINKLESTEIN AND THE BANANA SPLITS—Teenage Beatnik L.S.D. Riot

And there you have it, a few guidelines with which you can set about building a collection so dementedly cool that your pal with the wall of records will come sniffing around asking if he can make some tapes. The only other things you need to know is that, unfortunately, nearly every thrift store has a dirty old piss-smelling guy who was already looking through the records when you got there and won't be finished when you leave, and that you must always, always, take a record out of its sleeve to be sure it's what it says it is and that no one's gouged "Ricky + Emily 4-EVR" into the grooves. We'll leave you with two snappy lists of some disks you're likely to encounter frequently as you commence your new hobby, and the admonition that, henceforth, you ever strive to advance the cause of thrifting in word and in deed. Happy hunting!

RICHARD'S GUIDE TO RECORDS YOU ALWAYS SEE IN THRIFT STORES THAT ARE ACTUALLY GOOD

BEE GEES—Any and every pre-SNF LP

ARTHUR LYMAN—Yellow Bird, et al.

PAUL REVERE & THE RAIDERS—Midnight Ride

ISAAC HAYES—*Shaft* soundtrack

EARTHA KITT—Live, somewhere or other

RICHARD HARRIS—A Tramp Shining

THE AMERICAN BREED—Pumpkin Powder Scarlet & Green

THE BEACH BOYS—All Summer Long

NEIL DIAMOND—His early stuff on Bang Records

EMITT RHODES—Same

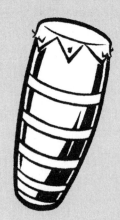

price trashed and crappy doo-wop records based on the "near mint" price in the Goldmine book do not deserve your business. However, these same shops will often price truly cool stuff at the bottom of their inflated price range, and only a fool would pass up a $3 copy of *My Son the Surf Nut* on general principles.

DIARY OF A MAD TRACKER

•

By **Malcolm Riviera** *from*
8-Track Mind

Some people have become so obsessed with how CDs have destroyed the market for vinyl albums that they have completely forgotten about another music format that has been cast aside. The humble 8-track, once the king of the car stereo, has fallen into such a state of neglect that most thrift stores won't even place them out on the sales floor and instead keep them hidden in the back.

Since 1990, Russ Forster has been fighting to keep the 8-track format alive with his surprisingly engaging zine *8-Track Mind*. He isn't going at it alone—each 40-page issue is filled with memories of 8-tracks past and recent reports from avid collectors. It's a surprisingly varied publication, with articles ranging from tips on repairing broken cartridges to reports on the world's most sought-after 8-track (the first Sex Pistols album). Be sure to catch Russ's documentary film, *So Right They're Wrong,* about 8-track tape collectors.

The rock band Gumball is famous in 8-track circles for acquiring a mountain of 25,000 8-track tapes off a former wholesaler in Lancaster, Pennsylvania. In this piece, Gumball member Malcolm Riviera describes some of his major scores over the years. Alice Cooper, Partridge Family, Cheap Trick, and Foreigner—not quite like finding original Elvis 78s, but fun nevertheless.

7/12/92, FORESTVILLE, MD. Went to Memory Lane, a tape and record collector's shop. In front of and surrounding the cashier was an incredible sight: probably over 1,000 8-tracks, over half of them still sealed. Unfortunately, the guy that runs the shop is a total miser and has them priced at $3.99 EACH and up! Some of them were over ten dollars! The guy is totally out of touch with reality. I bought a sealed copy of Slade *Slayed* but refused to part with any more cash. $4 for a tape that I could probably get for a quarter at a flea market!

10/12/92, TAYLORSVILLE, NC, MY HOME-TOWN. Went to the old FCX feed store that used to sell 8-tracks when I was a kid. Hadn't been there in 8–9 years probably. An amazing sight greeted my eyes when I entered the place: over in the far corner, covered in dust and cobwebs (with spiders) were 2 of the old 8-track display cases, the kind with hand holes for browsing cut out of the clear lucite front. Both cases were crammed full of brand-new 8-track tapes! They were mostly early '80s titles, the last years that 8-track tapes were made. These tapes had been in those cases for years and still had the original prices on

them, although the owner had marked them down to 4 for $12 several years ago (WAY too expensive). I can't imagine the last time anyone actually bought a tape, from the way the place looked. I don't think the cashier even knew what they were, or that they no longer made 8-track tapes or players. The lady at the cash register wouldn't bargain with me, so I left empty-handed, but I'll be back. They also had several new-in-the-box car players!

11/3/92, FLEA MARKET IN LAUREL, MD. A crusty old guy had a table with mostly country & western 8-tracks, but I got a few good rock ones (Grand Funk, Alice Cooper). I bought an 8-track carousel from him, too, for 5 bucks (he was reluctant to sell it to start with because they are basically his display case). He spontaneously started talking about 8-tracks after I bought the tapes, said he thought that "8-tracks are better than cassettes any day —just put 'em side by side, you can tell the difference," he said. Then the guy at the next table said, "But you can't get any new music on 8-tracks!" The old guy said, "I don't want any new music. I got thousands of tapes at home and that's all I need!"

1/12/93. My housemate came home today with a veritable treasure trove of 8-track goodies that she'd salvaged from her parents' basement: a carousel and two tape boxes with handles, both crammed full of tapes! A lot of homemade tapes, which I know some people are into (but not me); also some good rock stuff including Elvis, Foghat, Foreigner, and Ted Nugent. This is a good way to build your collection. Just let people know you'll take their 8-track tapes off their hands and they seem to get into it and actually give you quite a few tapes over the years!

1/18/93, LANCASTER, PA. Major score today at Stan's Records and Tapes, my first visit to the store. New, in-the-cellophane 8-tracks—4 for a dollar! What a score! Really unusual stuff, like Spanish and German language instructional tapes, soundtracks, weird '60s bands I've never heard of, etc. These tapes were covered in so much dust it must be original dirt from the '70s!

1/19/93. Another still-in-the-wrapper score today in Lancaster! Porter's, this old antiques/junk store, had hundreds of new 8-tracks, 2 for a dollar. Mostly bogus titles of has-beens or never-weres, but I did pick up some choice Slade tapes and three different Zager & Evans. One of the guys that works there claims that the owner has a whole garage full but just puts new ones out when the supply dips. A garage full—yikes!

2/20/93, ANNANDALE, VA. Good score today: found what must have been a recent delivery of 8-tracks to the Salvation Army. Snagged 36 tapes, including several Chicago, Sonny & Cher, and Glen Campbell. Got a nice holder, which they agreed to throw in. I've noticed that frequently if you take your tapes to the cash register in a box, they'll throw the box in for free. Anyway, notable finds included *A Partridge Family Christmas* and *The Magic Organ* (I'm a sucker for sleazy instrumental organ tapes). This one sounded like those organs at '70s shopping malls with the cheesy built-in drum machine.

3/1/93, GOODWILL IN HARRISBURG, PA. Good score! Picked up 18 tapes, 4 for a dollar, several still sealed. Found a "Fonzie" tape and quite a few good rock tapes (ELP and Stones bootlegs, KISS, and Frank Sinatra). Also, my friend Jay picked up a Beach Boys bootleg tape that was actually just a studio band playing Beach Boys songs! I have noticed this phenomenon and value these tapes above all others. It's such a surreal concept to record another band's album and then release it as if no one will notice the difference! This never happened with cassettes, LPs, or CDs to my knowledge. Later, in Lancaster, I spotted a nice GE Portable with AM/FM, which I talked the guy down to $12 dollars for. Should have been $5 at the most, but it did work and looks nice in my bedroom. I now have an 8-track player in every room of my apartment. Just need one for the car (I'm working on that!).

3/7/93, LAUREL, MD. Went to the Value Thrift, a pretty huge store that usually has a small 8-track selection. Found 8 tapes today, including 2 more for my Chicago collection (I am working on getting the complete set, although I don't know which of the 21 Chicago albums was the last to be released on 8-track tape). The posted price was 3 for $2, but they lowered the price to 35 cents each at the register. Picked up *Chipmunks Christmas*, Vol. 1 & 2. Bonus!

3/13/93. Bought a nice Elkin portable player for $5, but needed a new belt. I robbed the belt off another player I had lying around. This is a good reason to never throw away portables that don't work: you can always rob them for parts (speakers, belts, etc.).

3/24/93, Laurel, MD., again. Amvets Thrift Store: scored an addition to my Chicago Collection, *Chicago VIII!* I now need only the fourth album to complete the first 10 albums (and Vol. 1 of *Live at Carnegie.*) Also picked up Cheap Trick *Live at Buddachan,* an *Elvis Live* tape, and a nifty Radio Shack plastic storage box. Ah, Radio Shack, the last bastion of Trackdom! I think they were the last company to carry any type of 8-track players, accessories, and blank tapes. A moment of silence, please, in honor of those lost years.

6/25/93, Silver Spring, MD. Went to a great new store today, Big Al's Trading Post. Not only did he have very nice condition 8-tracks for sale, he had 3–4 killer players, one of which I snapped up. The deck I bought was a portable Ross stereo AM/FM, the type that had two pieces hinged together. Sounds great! He also had a great little Sears portable, but at $20 I decided to wait. Big Al turned out to be quite the dude, totally into tracks and was floored to find out about *8-Track Mind* magazine.

6/27/93. Saw an ad today for "250 8-track tapes in a box, $350." Way too expensive, but maybe I'll call her in a week and offer her $100 for the lot.

6/28/93. Slim pickings today: Bowie *Heroes* at a small "antique" store in Brunswick, MD. The lady had a bunch of home-recorded tapes, but I wasn't in the mood.

7/1/93, Silver Spring, MD. Back to Big Al's today: took him a copy of *8-Track Mind* and he totally dug it, along with the other two dudes that work there. Picked up Beatles *Second Album* and *Something New* in really great shape, Pretenders 1 & 2, and Stones *Exile on Main Street.* All the tapes were $1 apiece, but in really good shape and good titles. He says he has 800 tapes he wants to sell, but at $1 that would be kind of pricey. Great shop, though!

7/18/93, Dundalk, MD. Went to a great indoor flea market, found a number of good tapes and also a lady selling carousels 4 for $5! I only bought one, though. Probably should have bought them all. Bought 7 tapes for $1.25 at one stand, then somehow lost them before returning home. Damn! Must have set them down somewhere. Also found a guy selling still-sealed bootlegs for $3 each—way too much, especially since the titles sucked.

7/21/93, Goodwill in Harrisburg, PA. Two good boots: Cars *Candy-O* with Day-Glo orange label and a Dolly Parton Mexican bootleg (Cool!). Also Supertramp *Breakfast in America* (I used to like them). Slim pickings overall.

7/23/93, Lancaster, MD. Today will go down as probably a world record for 8-track tape purchases for this humble writer. Let me start at the beginning: Don Fleming and I went back to Porter's to scope for tapes, and I noticed that they had fewer tapes than usual (they typically have several hundred still-sealed tapes, but usually pretty bad titles). I asked the owner what happened to the tapes, and he said, "Want some tapes? We've got 20 or 30 THOUSAND in a garage around the corner!" This boggled our minds, of course, and we realized this number of 8-tracks was completely insane. Don and I talked a bit, and finally asked him if he would sell just 1,000 tapes; he said, "Make me an offer." So we said how about 10 cents each? He laughed and said, "No way," especially since we wanted to dig through them all and just get the ones we want. Then the other guy that works there said, "Tell you what—I'll sell you the whole lot for $450!" We started thinking, and realized that was something like 2 cents a tape. First, we needed to see them, so the guy took us to the garage. What a sight awaited us! Three walls were filled with tapes, 2 and 3 deep; there were boxes, bags, and crates of tapes; tapes lying around spilled everywhere—we estimated that there were 25,000 tapes there, about what he said. So we called Rummy, told him about the deal, and asked if he was in. He said, "Yes!" with little argument, so Don put up $200 and Rummy and I put up $125 each and we bought the suckers! I think the guy was amazed that we did it, since those tapes had been sitting there for years with no prospects for sale. So we started hauling them out of there by the carload, bought about 60 trash bags and started bagging the rest, got a guy in a pickup truck to haul some, and still haven't got them all yet. I guess there are 7 or 8 thousand still down there, which we'll go back and get on Monday. We're putting them up in our rehearsal space (thank God for the freight elevator!) and even began an attempt at alphabetizing them (no way will we finish it—why did we start?). The number of duplicates is overwhelming, of course: over 100 copies of some (Andrea True Connection, Richard Betts, Zager & Evans, Ace, etc.) but some real gems including Sun Ra, Mahavishnu Orchestra, Ravi Shankar, Jo Jo Gunne, Elvis, Silver Apples, Can, etc. Also tons of great bootlegs, including the highly sought after *Excerpts from Tommy by the Who: Played by the Decibels, Vol. 2* (3 copies so far). I think it's going to be some time before we will be able to assess the full impact of our purchase. What a day! We've decided that all future purchases must be in bulk, 5,000 minimum!

HEY SONY— WHAT MAKES THOSE CDs SO DARN POPULAR?

•

By **Negativland** *from*

Sony Free

Walk into any music store these days and you'll be greeted with rack upon rack of freshly wrapped CDs. What happened to all those lovely 12" vinyl albums that they used to sell? Thinking back, the change seemed to happen overnight. One day the stores were filled with records, the next day they had transformed the entire store so that it only stocked CDs. Everyone seemed to follow suit and get brand-new CD players so that they could listen to all their new purchases. Now the only place you seem to be able to find vinyl records is at a thrift store or a tiny music specialty shop.

A few years ago, in the North Carolina Triangle area, the Sony corporation sponsored a local "independent" music festival. Lots of local bands were scheduled to play, giving the whole thing a down-home community feel. It turns out that Sony got involved primarily to promote their *new* music format—the Mini-Disc. The editors of the zine *Stay Free* got together and published a single issue of *Sony Free* to report on all the controversy that surrounded the music festival and to critique Sony's plan to introduce yet *another* recorded music format to the public.

The experimental music group Negativland contributed this great exposé on how CDs became so popular so quickly. They describe how, in the spring of 1989, the record distributors changed their return policy on vinyl LPs. This virtually forced record stores to stop carrying vinyl because they couldn't afford the financial risk. This piece was originally intended for *CMJ: the College Music Journal,* which refused to print it. It's been selected for this book because it perfectly illustrates how the music industry tightly controls the way people listen to music.

aybe you already know this story, but the answer certainly surprised us.

In the early eighties, sales of vinyl, cassettes, turntables, and cassette players were "flat." This means that sales were stable, not rising or falling. For the makers of all this hardware and software, that wasn't quite good enough. They needed a new angle. A new way to sell music and the stuff to play it on. Luckily, someone at the Phillips Corporation (owner of PolyGram Music and Island Records and one of the world's top defense contractors) had the bright idea that it would be good for their stockholders and investors if they could get the music-consuming public excited about buying music again by introducing a new format and a new machine to play it on (i.e., how can you convince that aging baby-boomer to buy yet another copy of *Deja Vu* by Crosby, Stills, Nash and Young when *they already have one?*)

Thus was born THE COMPACT DISC in all its shiny, aluminum, plastic, digital glory. Its maximum playing time, about 75 minutes, was chosen because the president of the company wanted something that could play his favorite piece of music, Beethoven's 9th Symphony, all the way through without stopping.

Well, compact discs weren't as successful as they had hoped. For one thing, their price was too high. The higher price was blamed both on the fact that they were mostly being made in Japan and that they had a high defect rate, with approximately one out of every three discs being tossed out before even leaving the CD factory. Early on, the economics of this led to an industry-wide decision to continue paying recording artists a royalty rate based on the sale price of vinyl instead of the higher sale price of compact discs. And nobody was buying those new CD players, either, because they were just too darned expensive.

But then, in the spring of 1989, something wonderful happened for the music industry. Everything changed! Almost overnight, CDs were everywhere! Suddenly they were a huge success and suddenly it became almost impossible to get anything on vinyl *at all.*

This change must have occurred because it was what the consumer wanted . . . right? We live in a market-driven economy and the market was demanding more compact discs . . . right?

Wrong. What actually happened was this—a flexible return policy had always existed between record stores and the seven major distributors, i.e., stores could "buy" something from a distributor, and if it didn't sell, they could return it. This allowed stores to take more chances on new releases or on things they were not so familiar with, because if it didn't sell, they could always send it back. Well, in the spring of 1989 all seven major label distributors announced that they would *no longer* accept "returns" on vinyl, and they also began *deleting* much of the vinyl versions of their back catalog. These actions literally *forced* record stores to stop carrying vinyl. They could not afford the financial risk of carrying those releases that were on vinyl, because if they didn't sell they would be stuck with them. Very quickly, almost all record stores *had* to convert to CDs. The net effect of this was that we consumers no longer had a choice, because the choice had been made for us. High-priced compact discs were being shoved down our throats, whether we knew it or liked it or not.

As we mentioned earlier, record labels were paying artists a royalty rate on sales of CDs based upon the $8.98 or $9.98 list price of vinyl (or achieved the same end result by using contractual tricks like "packaging deductions"). As CDs took over and the majors all acquired their own domestic CD pressing plants and the defect rate dropped to almost zero, the cost of manufacturing compact discs dropped dramatically as well. One would have expected the price of CDs also to drop and for the profits now to be split evenly and fairly with the musicians who were making all the music.

This, of course, never happened. CD prices have continued to rise to a now unbelievable $16.98 list price (soon to be $17.98!), while manufacturing costs have dropped to *less* than what it costs to manufacture a $9.98 vinyl release. A CD, with its plastic jewel box, printed booklet, and tray card now costs a major label about 80 cents each to make (or less) and a small independent label between $1.50 and $2.00. Meaning that a CD should now cost the consumer *less* than their original price *over* a decade ago, not more. But the music business got consumers used to the idea of paying the higher price and the labels got used to the idea of their higher profit margin, *and* record labels continue *to this day* to pay almost all artists a royalty rate as if they're selling CDs for the list price of vinyl. That extra 4 or 5 or 6 bucks goes right into the pockets of the record labels. It is not shared with musicians. And of course, we all had to go out and buy a CD player (which had mysteriously dropped to a more reasonable price) if we wanted to hear any of the music on this "popular" new format. So, all in all, it's no wonder that the record industry and stereo manufacturers *loved* the compact disc. In fact, the following year (when our economy was supposedly in a recession) the music industry had its biggest profits ever!

If any of this bothers you as much as it does us, then you might be wondering why you've never heard about any of this or why no antitrust action was ever taken against major label distributors. The answer to this is quite simple. Most of the reporting on the inner workings of the record business comes from the music press, and the music press is almost totally reliant on the advertising dollars and goodwill of the business they're writing about. So, in the interest of not wanting to "rock the boat" or anger the folks who essentially bankroll their publishing ventures, this story would, and will continue to remain, unreported.

Which brings us to . . . THE MINI-DISC. The music

industry is essentially trying to replay their grand economic success with compact discs *all over again.* So far, they haven't had much success with Mini-Discs, but that doesn't mean that they've given up trying . . . which is what brings THE SONY CORPORATION to Chapel Hill. They're hoping to get you kids excited about Mini-Discs (i.e., how can we get those Genslackeration X kids to buy another copy of their favorite Pearl Jam release when they already have it on CD?).

So good luck, have fun at the Triangle Music Fest and don't forget—BUY THOSE MINI-DISCS!!

Note from Negativland: A slightly different version of this was originally written for CMJ: the College Music Journal, *which asked us to write a guest article for their weekly "TECH" column. Their legal advisor took one look at this and proclaimed it to be a dangerous and libelous piece of writing. We pointed out that no names were named and that everything in it was quite factually based upon the knowledge we had gained from our many years of being in a band, running our own record label, being on someone else's record label, and dealing with hundreds of different people involved in all aspects of the independent and corporate music industry. They refused to print it.*

MY LITTLE PIECE OF KURT

By **Megan Kelso** *from*

Girlfrenzy

Nothing shocked and galvanized the zine community more than the death of Kurt Cobain. For *months* following his death, every zine publisher on earth wrote about what that talented musician had meant to them. While on the surface, this might seem like simple fan commentary, the connection between Cobain and zine culture goes much deeper.

Nirvana's first record label, Sub Pop, started out as a music fanzine, *Subterranean Pop,* which branched out first into 7-inch singles and then full-length albums. Nirvana's huge success, and the resurgence of interest in underground music, helped propel zines into greater prominence. In turn, zine publishers embraced Nirvana as an underground band that finally got the recognition it deserved.

In this piece from the British riot grrrl–oriented comic zine *Girlfrenzy*, Megan Kelso illustrates the hold that Cobain and Nirvana held over so many people. She was "crazy in love with that band," as were many people. They were fun, friendly, and really rocked out. The music scene hasn't been the same since.

My Little Piece of Kurt

Megan Kelso 1994

wanna hear MY Kurt Cobain Story?

Spring 1988 Olympia, WA

Psst! party at the Glass House, Lush and Nirvana

Psst. Party at the Glass House Nirvana's Playing

There was a buzz about Nirvana from the beginning

who could resist punk rock boys playing heavy metal pop songs about recess and swap meets?

is this Lush or Nirvana?

it seemed like everyone in Oly was a fan.

Nirvana single is out!

Nirvana single's out

Would you believe me when I tell you... you are the Queen of my heart?

Summer 1989, NYC

ooh, white vinyl!

BLEACH

visiting my sis

now while I'm out of town, don't go out at night alone or anything, ok?

yeah, no problem.

Wow! Nirvana's playin' at some club in Hoboken!

Village Voice

a couple nights later...

LOSER

is this the train to Hoboken?

Yup.

they opened for Tad to a crowd of about 100 or so.

No Recess

they smashed their stuff

kurt said hello

aren't you from Olympia?

I made it back to NYC unscathed...

crazy in love with that band.

zzz

THE INVISIBLE LINK
•
By **Al Aronowitz** *from*
Long Shot

Back in 1982, before I even knew what a zine was, I picked up the first issue of *Long Shot* in a small literary bookstore in New York City. I had been in college for a few years and was familiar with literary journals, but I'd never before found one that spoke to me, that printed poems and stories that *I* found compelling. Editor Danny Shot assembles this vibrant literary publication with recent and classic pieces of literature, many of which were inspired by the original Beats. Allen Ginsberg, Amiri Baraka, Charles Bukowski, Eileen Myles, Cookie Mueller, Anne Waldman, and Richard Hell have all appeared in the pages of *Long Shot*.

Writing about jazz and the Beats in the '50s and '60s for many publications, including the *New York Post,* Al Aronowitz eventually landed a columnist position in 1969 writing about pop music for the *Post*. This continued for three years, until 1972, when he was essentially blacklisted in the publishing industry by a vindictive editor. He's now starting to get back into things by publishing his writing in small journals like *Long Shot* and on the World Wide Web. This piece is a treasured memory of the connection between jazz and the Beat literary scene. Al was there (and many other places) and is now finally bringing some of these moments to light.

It was while I was researching the Beat Generation series for the *Post* back in 1959 that Billie Holiday introduced me to Miles Davis on the same night I introduced Billie to the Beat Generation. Miles was playing at Birdland with his *Kind of Blue* quintet; John Coltrane on tenor, Paul Chambers on bass, Elvin Jones on drums, and Bill Evans on piano, or was it Wynton Kelly? It was at Billie's suggestion that we all piled into my station wagon and drove to the club. In the Birdland men's room, I asked Miles what he thought of the Beat Generation. Coltrane, two urinals away, snickered. With his usual sneer, Miles growled in his famous half-hiss and half-real of a voice: "The Beat Generation ain't nothin' but just more synthetic white shit!"

This was during a time when a writer named Bill Dufty worked as my colleague in the so-called Poets Corner of the *New York Post* city room. Bill, later to be the husband of aging silent screen star Gloria Swanson, was then still married to Maele Dufty, a remarkable woman to whom I will always remain deeply indebted. In 1959, husband Bill Dufty was riding high after ghostwriting Billie Holiday's autobiography, *Lady Sings the Blues,* which starts out: "Mom and Pop were just a couple of kids when they got married. He was 15, she was 16, and I was three." By the time Bill completed work on Billie's book, Billie had adopted Maele as her "white sister" and the two of them became as tight as twins. It soon was apparent to me that the Beats were so much in awe of the jazz avant-garde underground that their adoration of Billie Holiday in 1959 was at least as intense as the teenybopper screeches for the Beatles five years later. All I wanted was to ask Billie what she thought of the Beats, but Maele immediately invited my wife, Ann, and me over to one of Maele's gourmet, home-cooked dinners at the Dufty apartment so we could meet Billie.

As worn-out as Billie looked, she radiated a magical charisma, which I imagine is the kind of stuff that halos are made of. I remember especially how tall she looked, much taller than her five feet and seven inches, even with heels. Tall, slender, and majestic, she still drooped in the same way a drape sags. On the one hand, there was enough baggage under her eyes to need some help from a redcap. On the other hand, her stardom shone through her droopy, done-in disguise like the moon through tree branches on a romantic night in May. As a kid feature writer, I was really just another adoring fan, but I was also impressed with Billie's *hamishness.* She talked with a junkie's drawl, but she had an easy-to-get-to-know kind of charm.

It was after dinner that we went down to Birdland to see Miles, and it was after Birdland that I suggested we all go over to the Seven Arts Coffee Gallery, on the second floor of 596 Ninth Avenue, around the corner from 42nd Street in Hell's Kitchen. The Beat poets were giving a reading there, but when I pulled up in front of the coffee gallery, Billie suddenly decided she didn't want to get out of the station wagon to go upstairs. Instead, two of the poets, Joel Oppenheimer and LeRoi Jones, came down to meet her. LeRoi Jones is called Amiri Baraka now and Joel is deceased. The two of them both tried to stick their heads in through the partly rolled-down window of the backseat, where Billie was sitting.

"Thanks!" Joel Oppenheimer said. "Just, thanks. That's all I can say is thanks. Thanks! Thanks! Thanks! Thank you, thank you, thank you, thank you, thanks. Just thank you for being you."

He said something like that. He said it as if he were reciting a poem—a poem with a power that, to me, overshadowed what Amiri said, which, although I can't recall Amiri's exact words, expressed a similar gratitude for Billie's existence. The last time I asked Amiri, he said he didn't remember what he said to Billie, either. Or, maybe he remembers but just won't tell me. It was, after all, a momentous occasion for Joel, for Amiri, for my wife and for me, too. In the backseat of the station wagon, Billie told Maele that Amiri looked cute and then she added, "Come on, let's get the fuck out of here!"

That night is one of the most treasured in my memory. With my wife in the front seat with me, I turned and asked Billie, "How come you never recorded"—and I sang

the title—"*My Man's Gone Now?*" That's one of my all-time favorites, you know, from *Porgy and Bess*. By George Gershwin. His brother, Ira, wrote the words."

As I've already indicated, this was at a time when drugs had just about finished wringing Billie out. Because she drawled and mumbled so much, it was hard for me to follow what she was saying.

"Ah know! Ah know! They asked me to play the part of the girl who sings that song when they opened that show."

"Who asked you?"

"The Gershwins. Both of 'em."

The girl who sings *My Man's Gone Now* in *Porgy and Bess* is a character named Serena. She sings the song after learning that the villain, Crown, has murdered her husband. We were nearing Columbus Circle and Billie drawled from the backseat, "Naw, I couldn't sing that song night after night after night. It's too sad. It's the saddest song ever sung. That song breaks your heart. It woulda killed me. It killed the girl who got the part. She sang it night after night after night and she died. It broke her heart. Singing that song woulda killed me, too."

And then, Billie began to sing it, a cappella, in the backseat. She sang it as I have never heard it sung before or since. She sang it as only Billie could sing it, turning the corners with mournful bluesy catches of the throat. Out of the gravel of her voice and the slurred mush of her enunciation, the clear and beautiful sound of her singing rose up to fill me with thrills and cover me with goose pimples:

> *My man's gone now*
> *Ain't no use in listenin'*
> *For his tired footsteps*
> *Climbin' up the stairs . . .*

I had to wipe the tears from my eyes because I couldn't see to drive around Columbus Circle. Then Billie asked me to take her to her favorite Chinese restaurant so she could get some food to go. Her speech was so strung out that I could just about decipher what she was saying, but she made a big fuss about how necessary it was for her to get a takeout from this particular Chinese restaurant. I've always wondered whether the takeout included a hit of junk. Billie died only a few months later.

politics

W hile this country has a powerful Constitutional amendment protecting free and open speech, you wouldn't know it from checking out the magazines at your local newsstand. Row upon row of slick glossy magazines await you there—all selling cigarettes and booze, all toeing the same lifeless party line.

It's always been a struggle for people with nonmainstream political beliefs to find an audience for their ideas. Thankfully, the zine revolution has made things a whole lot easier for people to get their message out. Through the magic of desktop publishing and cheap Xeroxing, people can quickly write up a

screed about what's wrong with the government. Then, through the effective use of the zine network, they can spread the word to their many sympathetic (and some not-so-sympathetic) readers.

Anarchy, libertarianism, Marxism, and militia movements all find a voice in the vast landscape of zines. You do occasionally come across a zine that actively supports the dominant centrist party line, but that's a rare occasion. It's the voices that are silenced in our telegenic political age, the people with strong convictions but minority opinions who take the most active role in zine publishing.

Taking a look back, it seems like the history of zines is almost the

history of America itself. Thomas Paine, Ben Franklin, Thomas Jefferson, and many others created political pamphlets to "rally the troops." These early opinionated political pamphlets were much like our modern-day political zines.

This selection of articles is just a small smattering of the political topics discussed in zines. Similar to the group *Project Censored* (the activist collective who exposes the mass media's failures in reporting controversial news stories of vital public interest), zines often explore subjects not fully covered in newspapers and TV. Use this as a starting point to discover the broad spectrum of opinions and ideas.

THE *LIES* KEY TO U.S. POLITICS, CIRCA 1996

•

By **Jon Worley** *from*

Lies

Politicians have a way of taking seemingly simple problems and offering the most off-the-wall offbeat and convoluted solutions to them. Take the pressing issue of our growing national debt and deficit. All of a sudden, the solution to governmental bankruptcy is to cut its main source of revenue . . . taxes. Huh? Inside zines you'll often find more rational, logical solutions about our current political problems. Many of these solutions are so rational that you'll never find the mainstream media talking about them. They're just *too radical.*

Lies is a very lively zine that covers everything from pop music to poetry to politics. This piece was borrowed from their "By George, We're Gettin' Political" issue, which was published in December '95. While this chart of political situations is more than a year old, the problems listed are still current (and probably will remain current for *years* to come). I've always felt it was best to look at political crises with a humorous eye.

PRESUMED PROBLEM	PRESUMED SOLUTION	REAL PROBLEM	REAL SOLUTION
Welfare and Medicare are bank-rupting the country	Kill all the poor people	Defense spending is bankrupting the country	Kill half the generals and half the weapons programs
The nation is facing a moral crisis	Life without parole for possession of a joint	The nation is facing a hypocrisy crisis	The death penalty for censorship; life without parole for attempted censorship
Immigrants are stealing our jobs and our way of life	Kill anyone who looks like they weren't born in Simi Valley	Rich white people are taking advantage of legal and illegal immigrants	Nuke Simi Valley, Mission Hills (KS), Rio Rancho (NM), Clear-water (FL), Salt Lake City, and other centers of whitebread land
Affirmative action is taking jobs away from deserving white men	Reward rich white guys for whin-ing loudly and taking advantage of everyone else	Rich white guys whining causes cancer in lab rats	Send Rush, Gordo, and company on a special mission to the afore-mentioned centers of whitebread land
Kids can't pray in school; thus they turn to shooting each other	Mandate state-sponsored prayer and the posting of religious law	Kids think Jee-zus is the latest comic book superhero (Come down from heaven, gonna kick your ass!)	Real teaching of religion as culture and philosophy
Hollywood keeps putting out movies, records, and games full of sex and violence	"Shame" the big companies into acting "responsibly"	Most of the movies, records, and games Hollywood puts out suck	Don't pay for the shit
Too many children are being born out of wedlock	Legislate morality	Too many children are being born out of wedlock	More and better teaching of birth-control methods (including abstinence)
Environmental regulations are strangling business	Let companies pollute as much as they want	Air and water pollution may have been reduced, but there is still a problem	Keep the current laws; they seem to be doing a good job
Schools suck	Bring God back into the class-room and pay kids to attend pri-vate school	Schools suck	Encourage public school choice and pay teachers more money
The country is quickly going to hell in a handbasket	Buy Republican snake oil	The Republicans are goddamned annoying	Find a way to transmit AIDS on $100 bills and start bribing freely

MURDER BY CHARITY

●

By **Lucy Gwin** *from*

Mouth: The Voice of Disability Rights

Zines and other forms of independent publishing give voice to people who often have trouble being heard. One such group is disabled people. After years of being stuck with phony spokespeople like Jerry Lewis, disabled people now have zines like *Mouth,* which brings important issues into the open.

Mouth is a brilliant empowerment zine; it's funny, intelligent, and thought-provoking. It has the potential to change my (and possibly your) thinking. The magazine is mostly composed of short personal essays by community members that cut right to the heart of their anger (or however they feel emotionally). Rants against the system are done with a humorous and angry spirit that makes me laugh out loud. In this article, editor-publisher Lucy Gwin explores the process of plasma donation from the recipient's point of view. Back in the early days of AIDS, it was called GRID (Gay-Related Immune Deficiency) and it primarily struck the three H's— Haitians, Homosexuals, and Hemophiliacs. Lucy's article explains how money and politics allowed this tragic disease to spread so widely in the hemophiliac community.

A crowd of well-dressed, angry people surrounds the National Hemophilia Foundation's annual meeting.

Parents who just this month had to watch their child die stand vigil now beside a sleek, white, rented hearse. They lift a banner that reads CORPORATE NEGLIGENCE KILLS 10,000.

Brenda Walls, a quiet, middle-class mother, lost her hemophiliac son Jason to AIDS due to use of a blood product endorsed by the foundation. She carries a sign framed in bloody handprints. The sign says DR. LOU ALEDORT—THE BLOOD OF 10,000 IS ON YOUR HANDS.

What you see at this demonstration and in similar actions across the country is evidence of the radicalization of quiet, law-abiding citizens. They are people who, until now, kept silent about their hemophilia and trusted a charity organization to look out for their interests. These people were betrayed. These people and the people they love have been murdered by charity.

For years, the National Hemophilia Foundation has shushed its members when they spoke the A-word. Now members and their families are dying of AIDS. Although this charitable foundation knew the probable dangers of the blood product (called *clotting factor*), its bulletins, conferences, and newsletters did not even warn members against transmitting the disease to wives and sexual partners; they continued to play down the dangers and, on occasion, urged the continued use of the deadly clotting factor compound.

According to the NHF's Patient Alert #1: "It is important to note that at this time the risk of contracting this immuno-suppressive agent is minimal and CDC [Centers for Disease Control] is not recommending any change in blood product use."

Alert #1 was issued on July 14, 1982, eight days after Dr. Louis Aledort, chief scientific advisor to the foundation, had been advised of the dangers by the CDC itself.

1982 was a turning point in AIDS investigation. Until that year, AIDS had no name, no category. Its methods of transmission were not yet known. There were as yet no means to test for it, nor had its source been identified as a blood-borne virus. The Federal Centers for Disease Control had begun to investigate an alarming outbreak of often fatal opportunistic infections among homosexual men and intravenous drug users.

Suddenly, hemophiliacs joined the at-risk groups when two men with hemophilia died and another became gravely ill due to severe immune dysfunctions. These cases were a critical clue that the disease was blood-borne, infectious, and caused by a virus, according to Dr. Don Francis, a CDC researcher.

The discovery of these cases was a "real zinger," Dr. Francis has said.

Soon the CDC found that workers in the blood products industry had also been infected with the virus. A wave of death had begun to wash ashore.

Michael Rosenberg, a hemophiliac infected by the HIV virus and brother of a man who died of AIDS after exposure to blood products recommended by the National Hemophilia Foundation, says that the hemophilia/AIDS epidemic amounts to "the worst medically induced epidemic in history."

Rosenberg, who today as president of the Hemophilia/HIV Peer Association publishes *Action Now,* says that this was "the preventable plague."

"The giant pharmaceutical companies continued to market a plasma concentrate that they knew as early as 1968 to be extremely dangerous" because the concentrate contained viral agents, Rosenberg says.

"No viral inactivation methods were applied to the concentrates until it was too late. These methods were known years before HIV entered the public bloodstream, but the pharmaceutical companies would not spend the time or money to change a product that was already producing great profits. Hemophiliacs were sitting ducks for any new virus in the blood supply."

Thomas Drees, former president of the Alpha Therapeutic Corporation, a manufacturer of the concentrate used by people with hemophilia, confirmed the industry's concern over profits. He says his firm sought to restrict blood donors, but other makers of Factor VIII fought changes in the way they collected blood. "They were worried about losing donors," Drees said.

The plasma collection process relied principally on collection units sited in locations convenient to people living in poverty such as inner-city skid row districts, U.S.-Mexico border towns, and prisons. Here plasma was collected from paid donors whose poverty made them easy targets for diseases such as Hepatitis B and, subsequently, HIV.

Once collected, this questionable plasma was subjected, according to *Action Now,* to a manufacturing process geared not to safety but to the economies of scale. The result was that a hazardous product—not subject to any viral disease inactivation process—was manufactured and sold for infusion into people with hemophilia.

The activities of the multibillion-dollar American plasma industry reached around the globe. "The U.S. is the OPEC of the plasma business," said Thomas O. Hecht, chairman and CEO of Continental Pharma Cryosan, a Montreal-based distributor of plasma products.

According to Michael Rosenberg, "The U.S. plasma industry was the engine that powered the dissemination of AIDS among people with hemophilia around the world. In Japan, for example, hemophiliacs constitute the largest AIDS group."

Rosenberg says he does not wish to imply that the spread of AIDS was the intent of the clotting factor manufacturers. "But it was the predictable consequence of a pattern of choices that consistently placed commercial considerations above the safety of consumers."

At the time plasma marketing decisions were made, Drees said, "I don't think there was anybody in the blood products community who doubted that AIDS was spread by blood, that it was a virus, and that it was fatal. A lot of people being sued today won't admit it, but everybody knew it."

"Everybody" apparently included the National Hemophilia Foundation.

Rosenberg and the Hemophilia/HIV Peer Association call attention to the peculiar role of the National Hemophilia Foundation, presumably the advocate for Americans with hemophilia.

Rosenberg has obtained 1989 federal tax returns for the National Hemophilia Foundation, which show that Factor VIII makers donated $970,300 to NHF—about 20 percent of the foundation's budget that year. In 1990 the largest private grant source was Armour Pharmaceutical Company, which gave NHF $555,937 in that year.

Some families of hemophiliacs infected with HIV have brought suits against manufacturers of the clotting factor concentrate. Most such cases have been lost, due in part to the testimony of expert witnesses. Most such witnesses are physicians affiliated with the National Hemophilia Foundation.

One expert witness is Dr. Louis Aledort, the NHF medical director notified in the July 1982 letter from the Centers for Disease Control of the dangers of blood products to hemophiliacs and their families. Expert witnesses are often paid a minimum of $10,000 for testimony in such cases.

Meanwhile, other quiet Americans with hemophilia are breaking the silence. "Seven members of Loras Goedken's family have died of AIDS. In the last six years, the Houston man has lost four brothers, all hemophiliacs, to AIDS. One of the brothers gave the AIDS virus to his wife, who passed it to their baby at birth. Mother and child have died. Goedken himself unwittingly passed the virus to his wife, Jan, who died of AIDS at age 50. "It's the death after death after death that really gets you," Goedken says.

Now, Goedken and other people with hemophilia are getting angry, speaking out, filing lawsuits, and taking it to the streets.

The National Hemophilia Foundation recently released this statistic: approximately 30 hemophiliacs are dying from AIDS each month.

GET FAT, DON'T DIE

•

By **Michael C. Botkin** *from*

Diseased Pariah News

A consistent source of good writing, vital reporting, and strong politics, *Diseased Pariah News* is an uncompromisingly good zine that explores issues of interest to people with AIDS, people with HIV, and their sympathizers. Boldly angry and hilariously trenchant, *Diseased Pariah News* provides everything from cranky-but-informed rants against the bad guys (gouging drug companies, evil conservative politicians) to edgy poetry and prose. Best of all, it isn't just angry, it's horny, too, with features like Porn Potato's dirty movie reviews, centerfolds that feature hot naked guys, erotic tales, and safe-sex tips.

Diseased Pariah News is also a handbook for survival, full of information, from the first issue's "PWA Primer"—financial and medical information for people with AIDS—to the recent "Well-Fed Welfare Queen"—how to survive when you're on a limited income. In a similar vein, Biffy Mae's "Get Fat, Don't Die" column has been a mainstay for the five years *Diseased Pariah News* has been published. Avoiding weight loss is a big part of staying healthy for the person with HIV, and Biffy Mae's tempting high-fat recipes help people with sketchy appetites keep the weight on.

Michael C. Botkin, "Sleazy Editrix and Protector of the Streets" died August of 1996 from AIDS-related causes. An elegant writer and a guiding force behind the magazine (and the pseudonymous Biffy Mae), he will definitely be missed.

What you will see in this hallowed column probably flies in the face of everything that you have learned about nutrition. While we're not knocking what Mizz Johnson taught you about the four basic food groups, the truth is that classic dietary guidelines often fail to address the specific needs of people living with HIV and AIDS.

Malnutrition and weight loss can be a significant problem for us folks. There's the obvious problem of dropping weight due to some nasty infection, but being too tired to cook or changes in taste perception due to certain medications (including our favorite, AZT) can take their toll as well. Not only does being undernourished reduce your chances of getting lucky at that next orgy, it can make you much more susceptible to illness, and we'll have none of that.

GET FAT, Don't Die! presents strategies for dealing with HIV- and AIDS-related dietary problems. In addition, we'll publish our readers' own taste-tempting high-calorie recipes.

Speaking of Fat . . .

A high-fat, high-protein diet is recommended for people with AIDS. There are a couple of reasons for this. First of all, when you suddenly drop weight, you tend to lose about 10 to 15 percent of what you originally weighed, regardless of what your original weight was. If you are already underweight, this is even more dangerous, so it's best to be at or a little over what the insurance company's charts say you should weigh. Secondly, a fortified diet will help you recover from a bout of illness. This is especially true if your appetite is weak, and every bit of food you can choke down must work to its full advantage.

Here are some ways that dieticians recommend to boost calories and protein:

- Add lots of butter, margarine, cream cheese, sour cream, cheese, and mayonnaise to your vegetables and starchy foods.
- Use whole milk, cream, half-and-half, or a high-calorie non-dairy creamer in cooking and on cereal.
- Add whipped cream or frosting to desserts.
- Bread and fry fish, meat, and chicken.
- Drizzle liberal amounts of sauce or gravy over your food.
- Use honey on toast and cereal, and in coffee or tea.
- Add dry milk to foods to boost calories and protein.
- Spice up cereals and desserts with raisins, dates, dried fruit, chopped nuts, granola, or brown sugar.

Piggies beware! Although this is your carte blanche to eat heartily, don't snarf those marshmallow pies and Ho-Ho's at the expense of good nutrition. It's also a good idea to check with your physician before making any radical changes to your diet. He or she might have some suggestions for tailoring a diet to your special needs.

And now, mouthwatering recipes from Biffy Mae's Secret Archives. Let me know what you think —B.T.

Austin Mae's Vanilla Poached Pears

4 Bosc or firm Comice pears
2¹/₂ cups water
³/₄ cups sugar
¹/₂ vanilla bean, slit lengthwise
3¹/₂-in. strip lemon peel

Peel the pears and cut in half. Use a spoon to carefully remove the seeds and narrow fibrous core. Bring water to boil with sugar, vanilla bean, and lemon peel. Stir to dissolve sugar, then lower heat to a simmer. Add pears and cook them gently until they are translucent around the edges; then remove and place in a bowl. Scrape the seeds out of the cooked vanilla bean and place the pod in the bowl with the pears. Pour the poaching syrup back over the pears, discarding the lemon peel, and refrigerate until chilled. Serve with a small scoop of Häagen Dazs vanilla bean ice cream. Very elegant and sure to win that twinkie's heart.

Biffy Mae's Gingerbread Pudding

4 cups stale gingerbread (recipe follows), cut into ³/₄-in. cubes
3 eggs
¹/₂ cup sugar
1 teaspoon vanilla extract
2¹/₂ cups whole milk

Preheat oven to 350° F. Place cubed gingerbread in a deep 2-quart baking pan or soufflé dish. Mix eggs, sugar, vanilla, and milk. Pour over gingerbread in dish. Place dish in a larger baking pan filled with just enough hot water to reach halfway up the sides of the pudding dish. Bake pudding for 30–45 minutes, or until a knife inserted off-center comes out clean. Serve warm or cold.

Stale Gingerbread

¹/₃ cup shortening
¹/₂ cup sugar
1 well-beaten egg
³/₄ cup molasses
2 cups all-purpose flour, sifted
¹/₂ teaspoon salt
2 teaspoons baking powder
¹/₂ teaspoon baking soda
2 teaspoons powdered ginger
1 teaspoon cinnamon
¹/₄ teaspoon powdered cloves
1 cup regular applesauce

Preheat oven to 350° F. Grease a 9-in. square pan. Cream shortening with sugar until fluffy. Add egg and molasses and mix well. In separate bowl, sift together flour, salt, baking powder, soda, and spices. Alternately add applesauce and dry ingredients to egg mixture. Beat well. Pour into baking pan and bake for approximately 50 minutes, or until a knife inserted off-center comes out clean. Let sit around for about a week to get nice and dry.

The worst form of terrorist action that our government is currently engaged in has got to be the so-called war on drugs. What can only be described as a war against our own citizens has resulted in the shredding of the Bill of Rights, the loss of effective medical treatment, the corruption of our police forces, and the highest per capita prison population of any civilized nation. All this to fight the consumption of mild intoxicants like marijuana, which has never caused a single death.

It was President Jimmy Carter who said in 1978 in a statement to Congress: "Penalties against possession of a drug should not be more damaging to an individual than the use of the drug itself." In the '90s, at the height of drug war hysteria, former Los Angeles police chief Daryl Gates went on record saying that casual drug users should be taken out and shot, since they are traitors in the war on drugs.

The most talked about problem of the day is crime, and the most feared crime has arguably got to be homicide. A stolen TV set can be replaced, bruises from a vicious mugging can heal, but nothing can replace the murder of a child or other loved one. Kirby R. Cundiff earned his Ph.D. in theoretical physics but wrote this compelling essay, which explores the connection between intoxicant prohibition and the U.S. homicide rate.

Sure, there's a problem with crime. Sure, the murder rate is way too high. (Any murder is one too many.) In this essay, first published in the political zine *Claustrophobia,* Kirby tries to ascertain whether the murder rate is caused by the intoxicants in question or laws prohibiting them.

Crack, heroin, and other drugs are taking their toll on America's cities. But maybe it's the lust for profits and the battles with police that are leading people to arm themselves with AK-47s. Everyone is gonna have an opinion about the drug problem. The best we can hope for is for an *informed* opinion.

CRIME AND THE DRUG WAR
•
By **Kirby R. Cundiff, Ph.D.** *from*
Claustrophobia

In 1907, when Georgia and Oklahoma made the manufacture, sale, and transportation of intoxicating liquors illegal statewide, the homicide rate in the United States was one person per 100,000 per year. Before the end of the decade, 13 states plus Alaska, Puerto Rico, and the District of Columbia had gone dry. By 1919—when the Eighteenth Amendment was passed, making alcohol use illegal nationwide—the homicide rate had grown to eight per 100,000. The murder rate climbed steadily until it peaked at ten per 100,000 around 1933, when our nation admitted its mistake, and repealed the Eighteenth Amendment. By 1943 the homicide rate had drastically shrunk to five per 100,000 and stayed near that level until 1964, when the United States made the same mistake all over again.

In December of 1964, having been ratified by forty countries, the Single Convention on Narcotic Drugs went into effect restricting narcotic drug use to medical and scientific purposes. It also internationally banned narcotic drug trade outside of government monopolies. History was about to repeat itself. From 1964 to 1970 in the United States, the number of state prisoners incarcerated for drug offenses more than doubled, from 3,079 to 6,596 (it was 90,000 in 1989), with this new concentration on enforcing victimless crimes. At the same time, the homicide rate began to skyrocket. Between 1964 and 1970 the homicide rate doubled from five per 100,000 to ten per 100,000, where it has remained, with minor fluctuations, until today. Lyndon Johnson had declared War on Drugs, to be followed by Richard Nixon declaring War on Drugs in 1969, Ronald Reagan declaring War on Drugs in 1982, and George Bush declaring War on Drugs in 1989

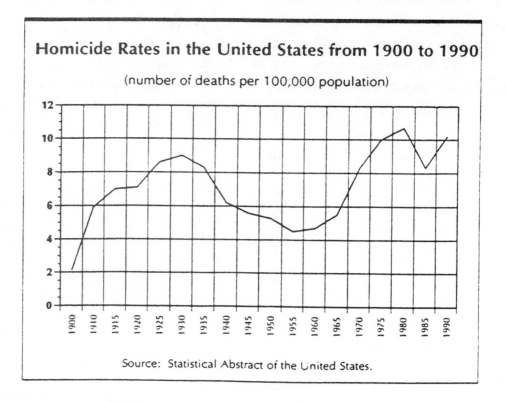

Homicide Rates in the United States from 1900 to 1990

(number of deaths per 100,000 population)

Source: Statistical Abstract of the United States.

At the turn of the century, both heroin and aspirin were legally available and sold for approximately the same amount. Today aspirin can be purchased at the corner drugstore for 10 cents per gram, while heroin costs $50 per gram. The price of heroin rose drastically after it was made illegal due to the dangers involved in its sale. Dealers are willing to kill each other for profits obtained from such a lucrative market; junkies are willing to rob and kill for money to support their habit—money, if drugs were legal and cheap, that they could easily obtain by working at McDonald's. You and I, through high crime rates caused by the War on Drugs and high tax rates used to support the War on Drugs, pay the price.

During Prohibition, "liquor store" owners murdered each other to protect their turf just as drug dealers do today. Today, liquor store owners are generally peaceful. Eliminating the enormous profits involved in black-market businesses eliminates the motive for violent crime, and therefore the violent crime.

More law enforcement is commonly touted as the answer to America's violent crime problem. Since 1970 the percentage of the American population in prison has tripled with no noticeable effect on the homicide rate. More than 1.3 million citizens are now in jail. In fact, the United States has a larger percentage of its population in prison than any other nation, and still maintains the highest homicide rate in the industrialized world.

Furthermore, we have thrown away parts of our Constitution in the name of fighting crime. Asset forfeiture laws allow law enforcement officers to seize the property of American citizens without even charging them with a crime. Over $2.4 billion in assets have been seized since 1985, $664 million in 1994 alone—and in 80 percent of the cases no charges were ever filed.

Disparities between the poor and the rich are often considered causes of our high crime rate, but the United States has not only one of the world's highest crime rates, but also one of the world's largest middle classes. The religious Right claims America's huge crime rate is caused by a breakdown of family values. This would require family values breaking down suddenly in 1907, returning in 1933, and suddenly breaking down again in 1964. Many liberals believe that America's large crime rate is due to our lack of gun-control laws, but America's gun-control policy has changed little throughout this century. The United States government's substance-control policies are the only answer. The only way to lower America's violent crime rate, short of turning the United States into a totalitarian police state, is through ending the War on Drugs.

BARTER FAIRES: WHY USE MONEY AT ALL?

●

By **Zachary D. Lyons** *from*

Boycott Quarterly

 community gathered for its semiannual Barter Faire in the Okanagon Hills in mid-October. They came from Washington and British Columbia; from Oregon, Idaho, Montana, and California— even Alberta and beyond. They came from a region—a bio-region that they call "Cascadia"—to trade the fruits of their labors of the previous six months.

The Okanagon Hills truly make one wonder why we have this silly border between the U.S. and Canada. The hills, and the people who inhabited them before the Europeans came, have no such boundary lines. The hills simply roll northward from Central Washington into British Columbia, creating an "inland empire" far from the problems and congestion of the densely populated coastal slopes of the Pacific Northwest.

In the spirit of the first people to have settled on the hills of the Okanagon countryside, this community gathers twice a year with their bounty to trade and to share—and to sustain a lifestyle the cities have long since forgotten.

My friend Steve and I arrived in the Okanagon Hills at midnight that Friday, stopped for directions to the Barter Faire at the local co-op, and headed up Washington Route 20 to locate a place to pitch a tent. The season's first snows were falling upon the higher hills, and a bone-chilling fog danced in the moonlight over the lake behind our site. We broke out our extra layers, set up our tent, and settled in for the night.

A cold morning greeted us with a frozen car-starter, but with a push from some deer hunters out for opening day, we were on our way. We arrived at the Faire and strategically parked the car with the starter in mind. Then we hiked into the circle.

What immediately struck us was that you could literally find anything there, save the few things clearly banned at the entrance: alcohol, guns, and fireworks. And though we had erroneously expected only "hippies," what we found were people of every background and persuasion you could think of.

It was, in fact, a small temporary village, and the name of the game at this village was trade. Trading what you have for what someone else has that you want or need. We used only a little cash all weekend.

The beauty of the Barter Faire is learning the courage to allow yourself to be told "no," and having it be OK. After all, just because you want what someone else has, it should not follow that they want what you have. And thus it is even more important that one learns how to say "no," lest you go home with a lot of stuff you don't want, and little of the stuff you need—in other words, poor!

I found that the Barter Faire recharged my spirit—my very soul. It was more than just being out in the country, far from the big city, surrounded by a crowd of "alternative-thinking" people. While it was good to be with a large group of people passionate about operating outside of traditional economic channels, something else—something very personal—was taking place. It was like an opportunity to develop individual strength—a real sense of self-worth—through trade. I had with me the fruits of my labor: *Boycott Quarterly*. That was my currency for the weekend. And I determined what that currency was worth to me. Was it worth a candle? Or a jar of blackberry preserves? Perhaps a few would be worth a sack of potatoes.

For once in my life my work had some truly tangible value. Steve and I bought our meals with magazines. And with them I stockpiled food for winter.

I could look at my magazines and envision not dollars but weeks of food.

And I knew that my work was worth more than just a full stomach, because the people who traded me the food had toiled in the fields all year to produce it. They were truly giving of themselves when they traded. And that is how I knew that my work meant something to them. It wasn't some dirty old bill that has seen a thousand wallets being handed to me—it was a piece of themselves.

In a shopping mall, the products are marked with monetary prices. If you want something on the shelf, you

must fork over that many dollars. There is no discussion about the price. You either pay it or you don't. The price is determined by some computer that has meticulously calculated all of the assorted factors such as rent, wholesale price, wages and benefits, depreciation and so on. The person who created the product could be half a world away. The salesperson could not care less whether I like what I am purchasing. It means little to them.

At the Barter Faire the products have been grown, prepared, processed, collected, and constructed by the very person who is offering them up for trade. And that person knows exactly what their needs and wants are and what

their work is worth to them. That is why my feelings were not hurt by those who did not want to trade for my magazine. Some people—believe it or not—are not interested in boycotts and the lot, so they understandably want to save what they have to trade for something they do want. Others use the Barter Faire as a primary means of getting the goods and services they require to sustain their lives, and magazines are simply a lower priority on that list. Still others see the Faire as a rare opportunity to generate much needed cash—yes, cash is used at the Faire—when they simply cannot afford to trade. After all, in a society built around banks and federal currency, it is almost impossible to completely avoid the use of money.

One of the more challenging activities we participated in at the Barter Faire was the "cross-trade." You see, sometimes a person has something you want, and they do not want what you have, but they do want something that someone else has. So you go trade for that item elsewhere and use it to trade for the original item of interest to you. For instance, a man had dried sea kelp—a tasty snack that makes delicious soup—but he didn't want *BQ*. He did want, however, dried fruit. As luck would have it, I have yet to develop a taste for dried fruit, but a couple who had dried fruit to trade did have a taste for *BQ*. So I traded them magazines for dried fruit, and then I traded dried fruit for dried sea kelp.

One man that I met actually was trading one item for another, over and over, just to see how many times he could make trades over the course of the weekend. He was not attempting to amass his winter stash. Instead, he was enjoying the interactions generated by the bartering, amassing countless new stories and new friends. I have to admit that I did not trade with him because the item in his possession when we met was not something I needed.

Nevertheless, by the end of the weekend I just gave him several copies because he had indeed given me something: his spirit.

Much like farmers' markets, I knew where the products I was acquiring at the Barter Faire had come from and how they had been produced. I knew that they were produced without undue hardship for Earth or the laborers. I knew it was fresh and healthy. I knew who produced them. And I knew who would benefit from the wealth I traded for the products.

Steve and I only came with magazines this past October. We thought we were poor—with little cash, little to trade. We discovered that we had plenty of wealth—things we no longer had use for that someone else could use, or things we had created that others sought out. And now we knew what to bring to the next Barter Faire.

riot grrrls

An exciting new development in the community of zines is the group of young women acquiring angry attitudes and taking arms against oppression wherever they find it—in school, in the media, or in domestic home life. These "Riot Grrrls" have created a new form of feminism that makes sense for the '90s.

The Riot Grrrl movement originally grew out of the alternative music scene. The Riot Grrrl zines were created as an extension to the female-fronted rock bands like Bikini Kill, 7-Year Bitch, Huggy Bear, and Tribe 8. Often at these concerts, the bands allowed and encouraged the showgoers to set up tables and sell/trade/give away their zines. Riot Grrrl zines now thrive on their own, covering music, sexism, politics, health, and anything else they damn well feel like.

But Riot Grrrls aren't the only women to make their own zines. There's a long tradition of informal writings on the topics of empowerment and health issues that have circulated among feminists since the beginning of the second wave.

Today's female-oriented zines cover just about anything. You can find features on lesbian issues, sexual politics, academic criticism, and contemporary culture. Modern girls aren't even afraid to look at subjects covered by the mainstream women's magazines (and thus reviled by traditional feminists), like fashion and beauty.

Like zines made by fans of punk rock, Riot Grrrl zines tend to have a brutal aesthetic and literary sense. However, the writing collected here is a bit more polished that what you'll find in the typical Riot Grrrl zine. Though true to the Riot Grrrl spirit, these essays are a bit more organized, looking at both the new and the old traditions in feminist attitudes.

THE DAY MY HAIR FELL OFF

●

By **Lisa Palac** *from*

Bust

Its audience has been described as "too old for *Sassy* and too sassy for *Cosmo.*" But *Bust* is much more than just a *Sassy* for the twentysomething generation. It's a popular zine full of entertaining writing from extra-brainy women with strong pro-grrrl attitudes. Editors Celina Hex and Betty Boob encourage their contributors to get down on paper intense, nostalgic, and very personal essays for each themed issue.

When the zine first started, most of its contributors wrote under pseudonyms, presumably because the material they were writing about was very honest, and often very sexual. But after it took off in both popularity and esteem, lots of talented and celebrity scribes wanted to write for it, including performers like Ann Magnuson and Courtney Love.

In the fashion issue—subtitled "Our Lipstick, Ourselves"—cyber-writer and former editor of *Future Sex* Lisa Palac shares a horrifying and hilarious story about just what happens when you leave bleach on your hair too long. You'll laugh, you'll cry, you'll never change your hair color again.

Whenever there's a really big change in my life, my hair changes, too. Fresh start, fresh head, you know? Unfortunately, it usually turns out to be a disaster. I end up crying, and kneeling on the floor, clutching the pre-chemically treated, snipped-off bits of my tresses. Why didn't I just leave it alone! Then I always swear that I'll never do anything to my hair again—except wash it—until time slowly scrubs away the bad memories and I start itching for a change.

My last major hair debacle took place almost six years ago, to give you a sense of how long it takes me to recover from this kind of calamity. I'd just gotten back from traveling around in Europe for almost a year. My hair was past my shoulders and curly, with shiny gold highlights fed by the Grecian sun. But it looked so normal. I wasn't reflecting that, Hey, I am part of the counterculture, the people-who-only-wear-black crowd, the edge scene. I thought dreadlocks would be more fitting.

I have fine hair, I'm not black, and I wasn't willing to go for months without a shampoo, yet I was convinced by a stylist friend that I could attain the desired hairdo with a technique she'd invented. The Spiral Dreadlock Perm. It involved taking tiny sections of hair, ratting it, twisting it, then rolling it up and perming it. It would give me that Dave Pirner/Soul Asylum look. But when the rollers came out, I looked like Jimi Hendrix, only worse. My hair was one stringy, matted, clump where not even a single strand remotely resembled a dreadlock. I burst into tears as I wrote a check to the salon for $100. I couldn't believe I paid them.

So, nearly six years later, I suddenly feel the urge to go blond. Breaking up with my boyfriend was the last straw. So many things had changed in my life, I felt like a different person. I wanted to look different. I saw a picture of Natassja Kinski on the cover of *Interview* magazine and she had this really cool blond hair, so I ripped out the picture and showed it to my friend Renee. "I want this color," I said, "and let's cut it a little, too." I had imagined a 1940s bob, just above shoulder-length, the multicolors of brilliant sand.

Renee lives in a warehouse across town, and part of her space is a salon. One chair, one hair dryer, one sink. The best part is, she stays up all night, so I can go to her place for a midnight haircut and cocktails. So I get to Renee's place around 9 P.M. (I'd just come from getting all the hair waxed off my pussy, but that's another beauty tale) but she's cutting some other babe's hair, and chatting on the phone and we don't get started until almost eleven. We pick the shade of blond I want, it's called Champagne Surprise or something, and then she lectures me on how the

bleach will feel like my head's on fire, but I should just suffer because in the end it will look great. Applying the bleach to my long hair takes forever, maybe 90 minutes. Then she puts a plastic bag on my head and I sit under the dryer. "Just for a few minutes," she says. The pain is excruciating. It's like having a swarm of bees attacking my scalp. I try to turn it into some kind of positive S/M experience, but nothing helps. The hot air starts to put me to sleep. I nod out in the chair.

When I come to, it's 1:30 A.M. Renee is on the phone in the other room. "Hey, am I done yet?" I mumble. All night long she's been on the phone consoling some insane friend of hers who is breaking up with her boyfriend. We rinse off the stuff and I sit in the chair. Suddenly I hear Renee making these sick noises, like "Uh-oh" and "Oh, God." What? What? What's going on in the back of my head? Renee tells me not to worry, but I don't believe her.

"Look, it turned out a lot lighter than I thought it would and it's really fragile. So I think we should cut it a little now, then sleep with some conditioner on it and we'll color it in the morning." The complicated problem was that Champagne Surprise contained peroxide and if my tender hair suffered another chemical war, it might all just . . . fall . . . out. There are, however, no 24 hour beauty supply stores, so Renee promised that she would race out first thing in the morning and get some other product that would work. She chopped off about a foot of my hair, then wrapped me up in a shower cap with a towel around it, so I looked like Sister Bertrille from *The Flying Nun.* By the time I got home it was nearly 4 A.M.

I woke up at eight and began watching daytime talk shows, anxiously waiting for Renee. I called my office and told them I'd be late. By noon, she

hadn't arrived and I decided, fuck it, I'm going to wear a hat to work and deal with this later. I got in the shower and started rinsing out the conditioner, when I noticed the bathtub was rapidly filling up with water.

There was a big yellow glob of something that stuck in the drain. But it wasn't until a huge clump of hair came off in my hand that I realized my hair was falling off. I started sobbing hysterically. Renee rang the bell. I answered the door naked, soaking wet and crying and screaming that my hair was falling out! She tried to downplay the situation by calmly stating, "Your hair's not falling out, it's falling off. If it was falling out, it would never grow back. There's a difference." I hate you! I hate you! I thought, barely able to breathe between sobs. The only way to stop it from falling off was to cut it off.

The rest of the day was one big soap opera. All the way across town to Renee's studio. Repeat runs to the beauty supply store. My hair didn't even feel like hair—it felt like

cotton candy, it was so overprocessed. And what didn't fall off was a horribly slutty shade of blond. I demanded that she at least bring back the color of my old hair. No problem. So you can imagine my shock when I looked into the mirror, after an application of Medium Brown Beauty, and saw that my hair was now GREEN!

"I have to get out of here before I kill someone!" I went berserk. When I got home, I searched all of my hiding places just in case there was a forgotten stash of Quaaludes or something. I had a drink. I washed my hair a million times, until it was sort of mint green, rather than dark green. I wondered what I would do about my PBS appearance the next day and if they would still film me if my hair was an unhuman shade. Then I collapsed.

As if having my hair fall off and turn green wasn't enough, I was also completely self-conscious about my ears. Ever since I was a little kid, my mother has made a big to-do about my sticky-out ears. She always made sure that for school pictures, my hair covered my ears and that I never exposed them. It was so intense that when I looked in the mirror, I only saw Alfred E. Newman. Or Dumbo. But now I was naked, and my ears stuck out into the world like

giant antennae, waiting to be made fun of. Plus, I thought, everyone will think I'm a lesbian.

I had to live with green hair for the next 24 hours until I could get an appointment at the highest-priced salon in San Francisco. I felt the whole world was staring at me. "Such a pretty girl, but those ears," they were sighing. Perhaps even more humiliating was the idea that people might think I was trying to be cool by having green hair. "God, doesn't she know that punk rock is over?" I felt so small.

But when I finally unveiled my new look to America, I was surprised by the reaction. Without fishing for them, I got compliments ranging from "Just like Madonna in the *Papa Don't Preach* video" to "Very Jean Seberg." Not one person has said, Wow, I never noticed what massive ears you have. (Although my mother's first words were, "You could buy a wig." Some things never change.) Instead, people tell me that they never noticed what pretty eyes I have. My ex tells me that he's never seen me look so good. (Is that a compliment?) And I like the way the cute butches pay attention to me.

Somebody told me that if it weren't for this hair disaster, I might never have known how cute I look with short hair. True, this beauty parlor catastrophe has seemingly ended up in my favor. And at least this time, I didn't pay a hundred bucks for it.

TRANSGRESSIVE HAIR: THE LAST FRONTIER

•

By **Susan Schnur** *from* *Lilith*

One of the biggest taboos for women is facial hair. Although it's rarely discussed and never advertised, lots of women have some sort of facial hair. Most try to rectify what they see as a problem with bleaches, tweezers, waxing, or electrolysis.

Some don't see it as a problem. Some women, like Jennifer Miller, use it to make a statement about themselves and their lifestyle choices. Jennifer Miller is a woman with a beard. The interesting thing is that in the '90s, she's certainly not alone. There are more than a handful of women like her, at the vanguard of '90s trends like gender-bending and hip, new circuses (in fact, Jennifer operates her own, Circus Amok, a traveling feminist circus).

Susan Schnur, the editor of *Lilith,* a magazine that explores feminism and Judaism, first met Jennifer at a Yiddish music camp, where Jennifer was more a figure of fascination than the famous klezmer musicians on hand. For *Lilith*'s "Jewish Hair" issue, Schnur talked to Jennifer Miller, and in this story, a clear picture of a strong woman emerges.

DAY 1: Here I am at Yiddish music camp (KlezKamp) —five days with 450 other people, extraordinary programs, so much Jewish talent, brains, attitude. Despite this atmosphere of abundance, however, everyone's fixated on this one thing: this gender-ambiguous person. Is it a male or female? This person is on- and off-stage all evening (as a microphone techie), so you can really stare.

DAY 2: I'm told her name is Jennifer. Now it seems obvious—she's a woman with a full beard. It's amazing how dominating her quiet presence is. Everybody's whispering about her. Why doesn't she shave? What's her story?

DAY 3: By today she's got people fascinated by their fascination: How is it that a little bit of hair is so damn interesting? Here we have the hottest Klezmer bands around, witty instructors, great food, and everyone's walking around: "Help me out with this HAIR thing."

DAY 4: Lunch today at a table that ends up all female. This young woman says, "There are lots of women here who would look exactly like her if they didn't remove their facial hair. Like me." (No! I would never have guessed. Now, looking close, I see: she must shave. Golly.) Then she challenges all twelve of us at the table: "If you've never bleached or removed hair from your face, raise your hand." No one's hand goes up. "See?" she says. I realize so many dark-haired women must walk around with some low-level shame. Who is this Jennifer person? None of us at this table, we decide, would ever have her courage.

DAY 5: The last day of camp. A woman mentions how attractive Jennifer is. I agree. She looks like Jesus—mournful doe eyes, gentle body carriage. Courage is so attractive. We actually don't see Jennifer's beard anymore; just this beautiful face that presents itself unapologetically, just the way it is, to the world. It's amazing what an education this face—wordlessly—has given many of us this week.

T he lessons Jennifer Miller taught me—just by being in my world for a few days, walking around like any other person—were profound. She refused to apologize for herself. It was liberating just to be around her. She's what you might call a Jew's Jew. To be a woman who likes her body the way God made it—this is treason; wanton, male, too independent.

Jennifer Miller told me her story:

"I grew up in Hartford, Connecticut, where both of my parents were college professors. I was a tomboy, very athletic, interested in juggling, clowning, gymnastics, dancing, acting—pretty much in that order. By the time I started to get a little beard hair, around age 17, I had a strong core, particularly from my mother and grandmother, that people should be who they are: true to themselves.

"My mother and grandmother were both educators, tough, dynamic women who stressed the individuality of each learner in a classroom. My mother, inheriting her mother's educational philosophy, fought the public school system in Hartford and eventually got every teacher retrained to teach in open classrooms. So the message I got was fundamentally nonconformist: it's appropriate, important, beautiful, to be who you are. Their perspectives had a lot to do with strengthening my character. What I understood was: read at your own speed, do math according to your ability, and, by extension, I guess, love your own face.

"It took ten years for my facial hair to grow in. My mother, with whom I was very close, died when I was 21 (she was 48; cancer), so she and I didn't really work out my hair thing. For years I didn't even talk to my closest friends

about my beard— it was sort of taboo. I harbored fear and insecurity; I did not blossom overnight into proud beard ownership. At first it was just a few hairs, then a few more, then more; it was not at the beginning clear that this was going to be a beard.

"Through these same years, though—I'm now 34—I was coming out as a lesbian, getting involved in issues of the 1970s: equal rights, 'the matriarchy overthrowing the patriarchy,' this whole new aesthetic of reclaiming nature and naturalness. My beard grew really slowly, so I had a long time to think and change alongside of it. By the time I created my own theater [Circus Amok, a 12-person, one-ring traveling feminist circus complete with musicians, jugglers, acrobats], I had developed a lesbian feminist ideology, and a circus image to go with it. I was growing up artistically in the East Village of New York, learning how to get away from the tyranny of gendered roles in performance.

"One day when I was 20, my grandmother made an appointment for me for electrolysis. I held this rubber rod to ground the jolts of electricity; this needle prodded my face. It felt like mutilation, a losing battle. I felt defeated. I felt like a traitor to myself, to the cause—as I was beginning to understand it. If the electrolysis was a one-time permanent removal, I would have gotten rid of the beard (it's not; you have to go back many times). Yes, there have

been times that I've shaved—to get employment, to travel with Ben and Jerry's circus, but it never really worked for me. There's a beard line that makes me feel embarrassed and nervous. People are thinking, That's a woman who wants to hide her imperfection but she can't.

"There have been painful and depressed times in relation to the beard. For example, I have a fear of going to the bathroom in a public place. I always bring someone with me so people can hear my female voice and they won't look at the beard and say, 'What are YOU doing in here!' I have to steel myself to walk in and be seen. There are times I literally don't pee. When I'm traveling outside of New York I pee in a jar in the car.

"Recently in an airport, I used the men's bathroom for the first time. I just went in—it seemed less scary than the women's room. When I came out of the stall, a man was at the sink. We looked at each other in the mirror and he didn't gasp, so I felt somewhat comfortable in there. Many public places are hard—lines in movies, stores—people have the opportunity to stare. I have to be so alert all the time. It's hard.

"My biggest difficulty is financial—there are so many jobs I can't get with a beard. I have a desire to teach like my mom and grandmother, but how can I invest in an education for myself when I could never get a teaching job with a beard? It's also very hard to go to new places, to leave New York. I've often wished things were different. In my twenties, I pretty much intellectually withdrew from the straight world, decided not to go to college, not to climb a career ladder. It was much easier to have my alternative look within an alternative community. It's different for me now: I feel able and eager to participate in all kinds of communities.

"A few years ago I worked at a Coney Island sideshow as 'Zenobia, the Bearded Lady.' It was heavy; something I thought I'd never do.

"Interestingly, coming on-stage as the bearded lady wasn't different from people staring at me anyway. But, like gay drag behavior on stage, calling yourself the bearded lady is an empowered response to being looked at. It justifies my being looked at; makes me feel safer, in control of the staring. I can express things with my own timing. I can act instead of react.

"There's also the issue of becoming what one looks like. I am so often assumed to be a male on the street, and I respond to that. For that moment, I am in fact a male. This widens my construction of my own gender. A woman with a beard is a bigger gender than a woman without a beard. So my character is affected, my interaction with society creates my gender, and I feel consequently that I'm something that's a little different from just a woman.

"Being bearded gives me lots of power. Power from feeling I have no secrets; the striving for womanly perfection is over. The power that comes from being liberated from going for anything mainstream. As much as I sometimes *wish* pluckers and shavers were at this place with me, I don't think they should do what I do unless they're ready. It's hard to do what I do unless you start when you're young, because it takes many years to grow a full beard, and you have all that time to grow and develop strategies along the way.

"Having a beard has given me cause to become radical, of course, to have courage. As I get older, I get more and more committed to the beard. Its fibers are deeply woven in with who I am. The cost of giving it up now is a cost of selfhood. I'm wearing this beard as a political act, because I have some hopes for a changed cultural future. I wear the beard because I intend to effect change with it. Therefore, on some level, I'm teaching, doing political work. I couldn't maintain this very difficult thing if I wasn't coming at it from many angles: a subversive act, a teaching tool, a lifelong conceptual art piece; it's who I am."

A Lifetime of Support

•

By **Donna Black** *from*

Hysteria

There are lots of things about pregnancy the average single guy doesn't know—and probably doesn't want to know, either. Donna Black explores some of the more painful aspects of motherhood—cracked nipples, engorged breasts—in this hilarious and disgusting piece from the eighth issue of *Hysteria,* the "Boob Issue." If there's anything *Hysteria* really knows about, it's boobs. Not just because *Hysteria* is the official humor magazine of smart women everywhere; it's also because Deborah Werksman, editor and publisher, was the founder of *The Quayle Quarterly,* the publication that kept a jaundiced eye on our biggest boob of a vice president ever. With Bill Clinton's 1992 presidential win, Werksman saw that her work in that arena was done, and the *Quayle Quarterly* transmuted into *Hysteria.*

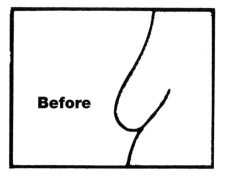

Before

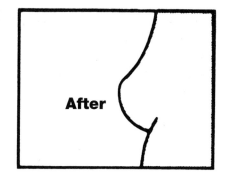

After

Even though I gave birth to one, average-size newborn, my breasts mistakenly thought I was having a litter. They began tingling in the delivery room soon after my last great push, and as I was being wheeled to the maternity floor, they started leaking huge quantities of a clear liquid later identified as colostrum. Whatever. By the time we made it to my room, I was able to ride through the door on a wave of my own making, and landed with a great splash on the bed. The triumphant first-time giver-of-life resplendent in all her motherly glory? More like one big human puddle with head, hands, and feet.

"Aren't you lucky," the nurses cooed. "Most new mothers worry about having enough of a supply for their babies. But you, well, my goodness, you have enough for everyone."

Comforting words? Terrifying words. In my post-delivery, highly emotional state, all I could picture was a horde of other highly emotional new moms frantically pushing their hungry babies at my nipples.

I was told my "regular" milk might show up in a day or two. However, my breasts began producing the "real" stuff early the following morning. I watched in disbelief as my breasts swelled and swelled and swelled. Then they got warm. Really warm. Hot. In a panic, I managed to reach way around them to push the call button. By the time the nurse arrived, they'd started to turn red and you could actually see the veins throbbing. I didn't know whether to beg the RN for help or tell her to run for cover. I was certain they were gonna blow.

The nurse just chuckled and told me my breasts were engorged (more like *enraged*, it seemed to me). She said I needed to express them. I told her I thought they were expressing themselves quite clearly. She assured me that all would be well once I had the baby nursing. On her way to get my newborn, she instructed me to manually pump out some milk so that my daughter would be able to latch on to a nipple. After pumping, I felt a little less overwhelmed. I had a nice, manageable stream from both nipples and my breasts were beginning to feel better.

Then my daughter arrived. As soon as my breasts heard her crying, those nice little streams turned into roaring rivers, cascading down my chest, down the bed, out the door . . .

So you can imagine what happened when I attempted to place my newborn's tiny, heart-shaped mouth over one of my raging faucets. She looked like one of those courageous salmon swimming upstream bravely, but hopelessly, against the current. After a second or two, she started howling and so did I. When the nurse finally calmed us both down (and dried us off), she promised that within a few days, my flow would adjust to my infant's needs and everyone would be happy.

Just as the nurse predicted, my flow did slow down and adjust to my child's needs. My daughter was quite content and would have liked nothing better than to suckle in a leisurely fashion at my breasts from dawn to dusk. Which was fine with me. That is, until my nipples went on the warpath. I never thought it possible that two such little buds of flesh could be capable of generating so much pain. When I called the doctor's office describing my raw and cracked tips, the nurse asked if I had done any nipple-toughening exercises while pregnant. Nipple-toughening exercises? The only exercise I got while *enceinte* was lifting my hand (holding some tasty, fat-filled morsel) to my mouth.

After a week or so of applying lanolin and heat after every feeding, along with walking around topless so that they could air dry (the UPS man didn't seem to mind), my nipples healed and the four of us—me, my breasts, and my newborn—finally bonded and thoroughly enjoyed our time together.

And even though we got off to a bit of a rocky start, in return for hanging in there and helping my child begin her life in the most nutritious way possible, I have promised my breasts a lifetime of support.

ASK THE GEAR QUEEN

•

By **April Miller** *from*
Fat Girl

Hey, girls, tired of flipping though fashion magazines and ogling the pencil-thin models? Proving once again that zines can fill any publishing niche, *Fat Girl,* "A Zine for Fat Dykes and the Women Who Want Them," has in the three years it's been published become a formidable force in zinedom. Its mix of lush and fleshy photo spreads, roundtables on the politics of lesbianism, sexy fiction, activist news, health updates, and how-tos appeals to a wide range of women—those who want information and resources, and those who just want to ogle the pictures and read arousing stories.

Combining a bit of both information and sexiness, April Miller, a.k.a. The Gear Queen, devotes her column in issue #4 to "packing"—that is, stuffing one's pants full of animal, vegetable, or mineral substances that make it look as if one has a set of male genitals. What woman, straight or gay, hasn't wondered how walking around with a penis in her pants would change her worldview? With the Gear Queen's tips on how to pack for maximum comfort and ease, everyone can be king for a day.

 udging by the contents of my "in" box, it appears that my readers have an interest in packing. Well, let me do my poor best to answer all the intriguing questions raised by your charming letters.

First of all, I should mention that there are at least two forms of packing: one which creates a nice bulge to show off, fondle, and rub against (soft packing) and another (hard packing), which is—in addition to all of the above uses—insertable.

Soft packing has a (probably infinite) variety of forms, but the basics are easy. Put on a close-fitting pair of undies, briefs, or a jockstrap, stuff the groin to create an appropriate bulge, and voila! You're ready to go.

Hard packing requires more in the way of equipment (namely a dildo and some form of harness), but the technique is simular to that of soft packing. Insert the dildo into the harness and put them on, then "banana curve" the dildo up to fit into a jockstrap, etc., or tilt it down to ride along your leg under boxers or jeans.

Of course, things can get a lot more complicated.

If you are packing hard, you might want to consider a smaller dick than you might ordinarily use for fucking, as larger items are harder to manage when they're stuffed down your pants leg. (They're also a lot easier to give head to, but we weren't talking about that.) However, do keep in mind that action between fat bodies sometimes requires extra length, what with the bellies (and butts) bumping. If the look of a harness ruins the mood for you, try wearing a pair of men's fly-front briefs over the harness and pulling your hard-on through the fly when you're ready for action.

Speaking of action, a lot of girls say that a snug-fitting pair of button-fly jeans make "the best harness I've ever used." Just open the fly all the way, put your dildo at the bottom of the opening with its base/balls resting on your pubes and the shaft thrusting forward, and button the jeans as far as you can. (This is a good moment to switch to a different dildo if you're into that sort of thing.) I hear that this method gives you lots of control, plus nicely targeted, er . . . stimulation from the base of the dildo.

If you are packing soft plan to experiment with the material you use for stuffing. I've heard of women using all sorts of things—from realistic medical prostheses to candy bars ('cause Snickers really satisfies). Just remember that you're looking for a combination that is secure, comfortable, and unobtrusive. You want girls to notice the bulge, not the noises it makes when you move or how it looks as it falls on the floor.

If you are looking for something more realistic than

socks, you can make your own cock and balls by carving them out of heavy-duty foam, or by following these instructions:

Cock: Take an unlubricated condom without a reservoir tip (say, Trojans in the orange box), fill it with hair goop (like Dep) until the size seems right, tie it off like a balloon, and roll and tie another condom or two over it for leak protection.

Balls: Follow the same procedure as for the cock, but make two considerably smaller balls. Don't worry about getting them to be identical sizes; balls tend to be naturally asymmetrical.

Assembly: Cut up a pair of tights and use them to cover/encase your cock and balls. (This involves sewing by hand, which, while it doesn't have to be neat, needs to be carefully done to avoid puncturing holes in the condoms.)

Since I don't usually pack I made a set, that I wore to a *Fat Girl* staff meeting, where I passed it around for opinions. It was such a hit that it didn't come home with me! (What greater recommendation could there possibly be than the fact that someone developed such a relationship with the cock-and-balls that she couldn't leave without them? I had to give it to her.)

Have fun.

A Closet Affair

●

By **Francesa Castagnoli** *from*

Princess

With row after row of cover models staring out from the newsstand on stacks of women's magazines, you'd think there wouldn't be a call for a zine that discusses fashion, hair, and music. But you'd be wrong. The typical mainstream fashion magazine is filled with watered-down writing that panders to advertisers and rarely rises above a sixth-grade reading level. That's why publications like *Princess* are becoming such a vital part of the zine community.

***Princess* covers both the kitsch angle of fashion as well as the real angle, featuring photos of street fashion and interviews with real-life designers, along with poetry, essays, and historical pieces that put today's trends in context. In addition, *Princess* sprinkles in coverage of music, food, and other topics of interest to women.**

Publisher Francesca Castagnoli reveals the hilarious and tawdry details of "A Closet Affair" herein when she compares various labels to types of men: J. Crew is the writer she'd move to the country for; Banana Republic a drunken frat boy. The moral of the story is, of course, never fall too hard for a label; you never know how many other women he's seeing on the side.

F or me clothes are like boyfriends. I either wear them out or keep them hanging around, just in case. While shopping, I listen for the flirtatious "buy me" whisper from the racks of groovy boutiques, my overstuffed drawers admit my careless affairs of catalog lust. I want it, I need it, yes, yes, yes, and then—the satisfaction of overnight delivery. Then there is the tease of haute couture, staring at me with the confidence of a pretty boy, from across the fifth floor of Saks Fifth Avenue. Overcome with desire I let the clothes seduce me. Feeling the fabric rub against my thighs, I'm foolishly ready to give all that I have, until I read the price and real-

ize I don't have that much. If you looked in my closet you'd see I'm not dating anyone right now. Each morning I consider my celibacy, and wonder how long it will last. I'd rather remain frustrated and wait for the right look than throw myself at the latest trend. Trends are like one-night stands: they seem right at the time, but afterward I feel embarrassed and trashy.

Naked, I stare at my closet fantasizing about my perfect wardrobe. It's understated and elegant, with strong lines, smart cuts, and creative patterns. It's gorgeous and hugs my shapely figure. It's sensible at the office, but smooth at the supper club. It's not terribly romantic, but it's in touch with a feminine side. I want the kind of clothes that turn heads when you walk into a party. The kind of clothes that other women want but can't ever seem to find. "Sorry, girlfriend, this jacket is an original."

In college I dated Banana Republic who turned me off real quick. Like a fraternity boy who experiments with the drug of the moment, his intellect never widened. Unfortunately Banana Republic is too busy epitomizing '90s style to get beyond the surface of things. Like the $278 rip-off leopard jacket that's brand-new but ironed to have a worn-in "feeling," he's an imitation. Banana Republic is prepackaged style promising, "Buy the new, clean, boring you here! You'll never have to use your imagination again!" Yeah, it's a shame. Banana Republic is a husband who has a wife, two children, a dog, and whose entire house is decorated from top to bottom in Pottery Barn.

I was more in love with J. Crew than Banana Republic and certainly more hurt by our breakup. J. Crew and I grew together, and I loved the cozy warmth of the weekend clothes. For me J. Crew was like a writer I'd move out to the country with. He'd need the simple pleasures of country life to work, and I, feeling so comfortable in my flannel shirts and leggings, would go wherever he'd ask. But this changed when the 1994 Christmas catalog arrived. Flipping through pages of

rugged menswear I turned a page and suddenly felt flushed. Stunned, I perused the women's holiday line. Butterflies flew in my stomach—bright, sophisticated colors in cashmere. Casually elegant wide silk pants. This was all new to me. A little flash, a little lust, and in a surprisingly low-key presentation. An austere white background with faceless wire frames. Without models, I had no one to associate the clothes with but myself. I was sure no one else would order a thing. Love is blind. My unassuming writer had just hit the New York Times Bestseller List. Now, we had the pleasures of both country and city life. I was ecstatic. I did very well that Christmas, receiving a beige woolblend jewel-collared vest, two pairs of pants, black and tan, a lovely aqua silk blouse, a dusty blue cashmere sweater, and a nice thick gray wool cardigan. I was set.

Pleased, I wore my ensembles to work, and to play—and to my surprise so did everyone else. What I thought was the swellegant lifestyle of "town and country" was really just a clean look for the "bridge and tunnel" crowd. While having lunch with a friend I spotted my vest on a

blonde, with matte pink lipstick and Payless shoes. So, my writer was not so virtuous after all. He'd sold out, with a book tour and talk shows, capped off with high-priced lecture series only for exclusive women's colleges in the South. At a party wearing my aqua silk blouse, I realized that along with the hostess who wore it in kiwi and her mother who wore it in flame, my silk blouse had caressed the shoulders of half the sorority girls in the room. I saw what these women looked like. It was not cultivated simplicity, or graceful style—it was generic, even preppy. And despite my personal twists, I looked just like them.

I felt like a styleless slut, or worse, one of the thousands of happy, smiley club kids sucking on lollipops outside unmarked warehouses in San Francisco. I might as well have been wearing a flimsy snap-up satin skirt, a tight white T-shirt, and pink glitter jellies. I needed my coat.

After a while, I passed J. Crew off as a lesson I learned. I still wore my country staples on weekends. But for my real clothes, I had a very special rendezvous planned. Ever since I entered a small shop in Florence five years ago, I had been waiting to wear the Italian-Zen ensembles. Prada was like the esteemed editor I'd meet through work. He'd be smart, witty, and strangely familiar. He'd have a

strong sense of the past and a vision of the future. He'd give me a sense of myself—telling me becoming a woman means becoming who you want to be. It doesn't mean you have to wear Chanel. It doesn't mean you have to be your mother. He'd sweep me off my feet. And I wouldn't tell a soul because this one was for keeps. The signature piece was a black nylon bag. The designs of my dreams. My Prada.

During the fall 1995 Paris shows, tragedy struck, Prada was suddenly everywhere. The *New York Times, Vogue, Allure, Elle,* and *Bazaar* all talked about Prada as the new anonymous status symbol. Announcing themselves to a whole new audience as hip-to-be-cool-haute couture, Prada ran a spread in *Details* featuring John Malkovich in a black pea coat. I was devastated. How could something I identified with as singular and unique to me become a status symbol? It was supposed to be my secret. Now everyone knew.

Seeing Prada in magazines is a bitter reminder of my break up with J. Crew. Angry, I ask myself, how is it that my taste ends up mocking me—especially when I was careful about staying away from trends? But in the '90s everything is a trend. All creative expression has been labeled, and sold—music, art, books, food, home decoration, and clothes. Nothing remains untainted by the commodificaton of style. What's worse is that I'm so envious of the women who have Prada bags, dresses, and jackets that I hardly notice the clothes, all I can do is stare at them, disgusted. It's like watching the man I have wanted and waited for my whole life settle for some shallow bitch: a character from *Beverly Hills 90210.* I can't get over that what I thought was the real me could so easily be everyone else. Today I shop slowly. Browsing has become more like inspection. I count the number of patent leather purses left in the store, three in red, two in white, and only one in black and it's in the window. If a brown boxy jacket catches my eye, I won't buy it. I'll simply visit it from time to time. Dropping in unexpectedly, I imagine catching the jacket in the hands of some shag-haired hipster. Aha! I know that rag would go for just about anybody.

Walking down little streets I've discovered new, young designers creating soft linen pants and structured gabardine jackets. I enjoy wearing these pieces, but I'm not seduced by their ensembles. In time these designers will become stars—they'll get caught up in high-profile romances with Kate Moss, make guest appearances on *House of Style,* be torn off Courtney Love at Lollapalooza, and eventually everyone will be wearing them when they're pimped down at the malls.

travel

I love reading travel books, with their exciting descriptions of overseas adventures. But to duplicate those experiences you'll need more money and time than most people accumulate in a lifetime. Reading travel essays in zines is like taking a trip *way* off the beaten path, but these folks have developed techniques for getting there and finding a place to stay that fit even the tightest budgets. Real-life travel experiences, advice on exploring unlikely destinations, and unusual ways of getting there are all examined in zines.

Zine publishers are more likely to hop a freight train than to fly nonstop across the country. The reason they do it is just as much a lust for adventure as it is for lack of money. Thankfully, they write all about it so we can join the fun. After reading all these travel zines, you're likely to get the bug yourself.

People create zines for numerous reasons, ranging anywhere from an intense devotion to a hobby to a primal need to be heard. Another important reason is that because our society is so mobile, with people traveling back and forth between home and college, across the U.S. and overseas, it's hard for friendships to survive. Publishing zines allows very mobile people to report on their travels all over the world and still keep in touch with their friends.

A whole culture has sprung up around low-cost carry-your-own-backpack tours of India, Indonesia, Asia, or Europe. It started in the '60s with hippies who wanted to see the world but didn't need to limit themselves to places with four-star hotels. Now it's almost a rite of passage to hit the youth hostels when you graduate from college. Some of the selections here fall into this world-tour backpack aesthetic, while others explore American open roads like the legendary Route 66. Either way, these stories will transport you to places you'll find exotic and compelling.

THE BEST OF ROADSIDE JOURNAL

•

By **Chuck Woodbury** *from*
Out West

The granddaddy of all travel zines has got to be *Out West.* Since 1988, Chuck Woodbury and his reluctant family have been hopping in their RV and heading off on several road trips a year. Departing from their current home base in Edmonds, Washington, they venture out looking for the strangeness that awaits them alongside our nation's roadways.

Ignoring the bland superhighways, Chuck prefers the slow route through the backroads, searching out forgotten ghost towns, weird roadside attractions, the best greasy diners, and the wackiest signs. California, Nevada, Oregon, Utah— it's the American West that Chuck is in love with. With more than thirty issues to his credit, he has developed a large and devoted group of readers who eagerly await to hear of new treasures he has discovered. Chuck has been bitten by the travel bug and has got it bad. In this piece he describes his favorite experiences, which can only be found as a backroads traveler.

Here are a few places or things I must see each year.

❧ I need to see several Cascade mountains.

❧ I need to visit and camp at the Furnace Creek oasis in Death Valley, Calif. While there, I need to buy an Eskimo Pie ice-cream bar at the general store, and then eat it outside.

❧ I must drive at least one lonely Nevada highway—U.S. 50 or 95, if possible.

❧ I need to sleep in at least a half-dozen campgrounds where I can hear coyotes howling.

❧ I need to share a cafe counter with at least six guys in cowboy hats.

❧ I need to camp in the parking lot of a Reno casino.

❧ I must have at least one battle with chipmunks over who gets to eat the last crackers in my box of Cheez-Its.

❧ I need to spend at least three nights by the ocean.

❧ I need to be in the middle of at least one violent lightning storm where I am scared out of my wits.

❧ I need to spend a minimum of one night in or just outside the desert outpost of Quartzsite, Arizona.

❧ I need to see a movie in the theater at the Riverside Casino in Laughlin, Nevada.

❧ I need to visit at least 10 pioneer museums.

❧ I need to be out of range of TV at least 40 days, and radio 7 days.

❧ I need to eat at a minimum of 15 cafes named EAT.

❧ I must eat at least one buffalo burger.

❧ I need to visit at least six Indian Trading Posts and buy at least five jackalope piggy banks.

❧ I need to find at least one jackalope postcard I've never seen before.

❧ I need to travel a Wyoming road with antelope grazing by its side.

❧ I need to spend at least three nights when the temperature drops below 20 degrees, and three days when it exceeds 100.

❧ I need to visit Zion and Yellowstone National Parks.

❧ I need to spend at least one night, but no more, in Las Vegas.

❧ I need to camp three nights in a redwood grove.

❧ I need to be snowed on at least twice.

❧ I need to visit at least five towns with populations of 5,000 or more that still don't have an enclosed shopping mall (this is getting harder every year).

❧ I must spend at least one night in a cheap motel with a Magic Fingers–equipped bed.

A Motel Idea

The Motel 6 in Medford, Oregon, charges $30.95 a night. That's for one person! I can remember when it cost $6. It wasn't that long ago. Relatively speaking, of course.

Budget travelers need a new motel chain. Here's my idea: The rooms would be a third the size of those in Motel 6—just big enough to squeeze into. There would be a twin bed, and a bathroom about the size of the tiny one in my porta-home. There would be no TV or phone.

The charge would be $10 if you furnished your own sheets, or $12 if you didn't. Couples would pay a dollar more for a double bed.

Asian culture seems to really have a hold on Americans these days. Jackie Chan's Hong Kong action flicks are becoming hugely popular; Japanese pop music is taking the alternative scene by a storm; and of course there's the food—there's *always* been the food.

Years back, a wonderful zine called *Lizzengreasy*, produced by a couple of American expatriates living in Japan, told tales of the Japanese lifestyle from an American perspective. Sadly, that zine ceased publishing back in 1992, but since that time a number of new zines have sprung up on both sides of the Pacific, capturing life in Japan, China, and Taiwan.

While primarily a music zine, *Exile Osaka* also presents wonderful tales covering all aspects of Japanese culture. Because of the dollar's sinking exchange rate while Matt was there, living as an American expatriate in Japan was difficult at times. In this piece Matt Kaufman describes some of the tricks he learned over his years in Japan.

HOW TO BE CHEAP (JAPAN STYLE)

●

By **Matt Exile** *from*
Exile Osaka

This is a rip-off of Joe Matt's excellent comic "How to Be Cheap." After I read it I thought that people might be interested in learning how to be cheap in a foreign country.

1. How to Furnish Your Apartment for Free

The most important thing to know is what day Big Garbage Day (*sodai gomi*) falls on. Since Japanese houses are rather small and don't have basements, people throw out perfectly good items all the time. You can find anything from a stereo color television to a washing machine in the *gomi* (garbage). The best thing about *sodai gomi* is that it's usually held about once a month. That means that most people throw out their stuff the night before collection. I guess that people don't want their neighbors to know what they are throwing out because I often see people bringing stuff to the site very late at night. Most people would not take stuff from the *gomi* anyway (except *gaijin*—foreigners), because secondhand merchandise, other than used clothing from the U.S., is not highly regarded in status-conscious Japan.

The funniest thing about *sodai gomi* is that people bring their unwanted goods wrapped in the original boxes, so the area looks like the dumping grounds for discarded Christmas presents. Some of the boxes even have ribbons on them! A lot of these items were never used (or opened, for that matter). There are gift-giving seasons in the summer and winter, and people pass the same gifts around from person to person.

Let's say you bought a set of towels for your boss. Half the other lackeys in the company probably bought him towels, too. He might receive enough towels to last a lifetime. So what is he going to do with all those towels? He's going to pass them on to someone else. (When I first arrived in Japan, the assistant principal from my school gave me *seven* boxes of towels.) Eventually someone is going to throw the towels in the garbage. (That's what I did.) I'm not just talking towels. There are hundreds of useful items that wind up in the *sodai gomi* unused.

Here are some of the things that I found in the *sodai*

gomi: 1) Two color televisions; 2) a VCR; 3) a microwave; 4) a cassette deck; 5) two bikes; 6) three bags filled with 300 perfectly good audiocassettes; 7) Bart and Lisa Simpson dolls; 8) an acoustic guitar. Plus loads more.

If you think I scored big, you should check out my friends Niall and Gary's pad. Their whole apartment is furnished with *gomi*. They found a CD player, bilingual television, bass guitar, and a huge Karaoke machine that has enough power to blast the roof off their apartment.

One thing to keep in mind. The more upscale the neighborhood, the better the *gomi*. You should see what people find in the garbage in the elite areas of Tokyo. But there's competition. One British guy has started a business called "Top Recycle," that sells stuff from the gomi to other *gaijin*. He has a warehouse in downtown Osaka to hold all the junk he found! Anyway, if you're thinking of going *gomi* hunting, get there early and pray that it doesn't rain. (If you're looking for cheap entertainment, stick around and watch the garbage trucks crush everything from space heaters to bicycles. More fun than the monster truck rally.)

2. How to Eat Dirt Cheap (And for Free)

A. FREE SUPERMARKET SAMPLES. Go to any of the supermarkets (Daiei, Seiyu, etc.) in your area at a certain time. (It varies from place to place.) You can try samples of sausages, spaghetti, salad, and other yummy stuff. I found that it's a good idea to act like whatever you've just tried was absolutely delicious. (I pretend to be interested in the item, put it in my shopping cart, and dump it out later when the clerk is not looking.) If you go to a couple of supermarkets, you can have a well-balanced meal absolutely free.

B. THE CITY HALL CAFETERIA. Every city has a city hall (*shiyakusho*) building that houses a cafeteria for city employees. The meals are subsidized so you can get a piping hot bowl of udon or ramen for only ¥180 ($1.60 U.S.). Fried rice is a steal at ¥250 ($2.25 U.S.). There are also set dishes available that include soup and a side dish for very little money. You have to buy tickets from a vending machine. Bring the ticket up to the counter and you're set. You'll have your food in minutes. Don't worry that you're not a city worker. Nobody cares one way or another. Who would go out of their way to eat in city hall except a cheap bastard? Most Japanese people don't really think too highly of cafeteria food, but in all fairness it's better than most of the Japanese food you can get back home.

C. SHAKEY'S ALL YOU CAN EAT HAPPY HOUR. This pizza chain has a fantastic buffet from 11 A.M.-3 P.M. Starve yourself for 2–3 days and pig out for a couple of hours. Pizza, baked potatoes, salad, and more.

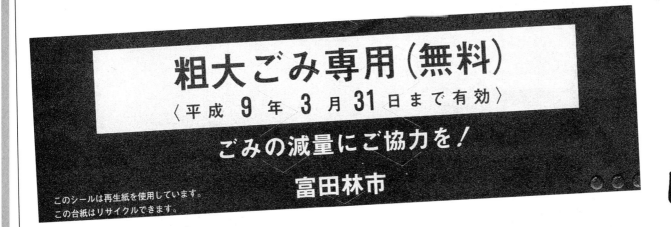

NEVER PUT ANYTHING IN YER EAR EXCEPT YER ELBOW

●

By **Marko Krabschaque** *from*
Grade D But Edible

India is another popular destination for travelers—especially for those on a budget. It's affordable, exotic, and offers a wide variety of incredible experiences. Goa, with its long-standing reputation for drugs, nudism, decadence, and free sex is a primary destination for the itinerant Western traveler. Word has it that Goa still offers plenty of *charas* (potent hashish) and techno raves that go on past dawn.

But the creators of *Grade D But Edible,* Marko Krabschaque and Ms. Chyph, bypassed the trendy Goa on their 1993 trip through Southeast Asia. It was a nine-month odyssey that took them to Vietnam, Singapore, Thailand, and India. This chapter covers their visit to Delhi, where a vagabond professional ear cleaner removed the detritus of traveling from Marko's ear.

We arrived in Delhi by air in the middle of the night and immediately jumped on a rattletrap bus owned and operated by veterans of the Indian military. The bus took us through the dark foggy streets to a place called "The Tourist Camp," which was a compound in the heart of the city surrounded by a high brick wall where you could set up a tent or rent a tin-roofed room. In the morning the fog still hung close to the ground, and an unbelievable cacophony of traffic and other noises that we could not identify came from the other side of the high walls. We had an itch to see the madness that we had heard so much about, but also a certain fear. After all, this was Delhi, a city that was legendary for its total chaos.

After breakfast we decided to venture out to the market with an Englishman we had met. We wanted to get some wool blankets since the Indian winter was radically different than the stifling heat of Bangkok where we had just been. So, the three of us stepped outside the gate and into the real world. We were immediately dumbfounded by what we saw. Madness to the umpteenth power! Every type of vehicle imaginable clogged the streets; trucks, buses, cars, bicycles, rickshaws, wagons pulled by draft animals, homemade wheelbarrows pushed by barefoot men, motorcycles; you name it, it was out there honking, spewing exhaust, and jockeying for position. "In battle there is no law!" is what I kept thinking as I watched the suicidal and homicidal vehicles swarm and convulse. And that was

just the street. The sidewalk (if you could call it that) had been transformed into rows of rigged-up livestock pens. Cows, goats, chickens, horses were all living on the side of the road, getting skinnier and shitting.

Then there were the people themselves, lots of them, carrying on the business of the day in every available space. Men crouched at the side of the road using hand tools to make wooden doors, repairing bicycles and motorized rickshaws, tending to cattle, or perhaps just squatting down to take a crap. Women cooked meals over small fires of dried cow dung; children played or worked. Their homes and businesses were housed in shanties made of clay brick, wood, and a variety of scavenged materials. Sometimes these rickety structures would be three stories high with ten people to a room. They went about their daily chores seemingly oblivious to the surging pandemonium that enveloped them.

As we walked toward the market I realized that it was not so much foggy as just plain polluted! The air was thick with dust from the road, heavily leaded diesel exhaust from the vehicles, and smoke from millions of cooking and heating fires burning everywhere in the city. It was so bad that the famous ancient architecture was nearly invisible from a few blocks away, shrouded as it was in a cloud of smog. We stumbled along, turning down the persistent offers of rickshaw wallahs, and being careful not to get creamed by an oncoming truck or bus. We had to walk in the street, because if the sidewalk was not a cow pen or an open air shop then it was a latrine. You see, these folks don't have plumbing, and they don't have a sewage system, and that means anything goes. So human shit is everywhere in India, as well as swarms of flies that feed on it. On this, our first day, all this stimuli hit us like a ton of bricks, but eventually we almost got used to it.

So we got to the market, and had a great time looking around at all the stuff and jostling about in the teeming crowds. The English guy and I scored some nice warm blankets, and then we all headed toward a park that was on our map to relax in. Ha! You do not relax in Delhi! You sink or you swim, but we were still greenhorns and the con artists and entrepreneurs who regularly worked the tourists in this park could smell our naïveté. As soon as we sat down under a tree we were approached by a little guy with thick glasses and a gray scraggly beard.

"Good day, baba, perhaps it is you who is liking a massage from magic hands?"

"No! Go away!" was my response. This may seem hostile and rude, but months on the road standing up to the badgering touts and grifters of Southeast Asia had taught me that a zero tolerance policy was the best way to get rid of these types. However, this guy was unfazed, and instead of going away he set to work massaging my neck.

"Stop it! I don't want a massage! I'm not going to give you any money!" The trouble was, it felt damn good; this guy had shown me in a few seconds of fondling that he had the touch. He had learned that if he really was good, rather than just saying so, he could snare the tourists and make a living. Still, I was adamant in my refusal. I was a hardcore shoestring backpacker and would not open my purse except to purchase absolute necessities. He wandered off saying it was my loss, and within ten minutes had a German laid out on his stomach and moaning in ecstasy a few meters away. I was impressed. It seemed these Delhi hucksters actually had something to offer, and their approach was slick and funny, so before you knew it you had fallen into their hands. Of course, I knew that when it was all over the German and the masseur would have a hot argument over the price—that was the catch.

We were approached repeatedly in the few minutes we sat there by a slew of men offering various services or products. It was then that I was approached by the master. He wore a filthy wool sweater and sported a bad haircut that showcased a few cowlicks that stuck up despite the "greasy kid stuff" slathered on his head. He grinned at me, showing a mouthful of bad teeth, with a few silver ones glinting in the sun, and a bidi cigarette hanging off his lower lip. His head wobbled from side to side in that endearing manner peculiar to Indians and he asked me where I was from.

When I told him Antarctica, he produced a small black book and flitted through the pages until he came to what he was looking for and then handed it to me. I knew what was up; this was his book of testimonials from past satisfied customers. Usually a guy that worked the tourist trade had a message of endorsement in as many languages as possible to ensure targeting a wide spectrum of foreigners.

The book was opened to a message written by an Australian: "I was skeptical at first, but now I can hear the songs of birds and the laughing of children. I don't regret doing it and neither will you!"

Doing what, I wondered. My curiosity was teased and this guy could tell. He thumbed through the book until he came upon another paragraph, written in English. I read it.

"This man is a magician! I hadn't realized how bad off I was until this saint got a hold of me. Imagine my amazement as he produced what looked like a ball of hashish from my ear!"

His ear? What the hell? At this point the guy could tell I was hooked. He smiled wider and opened a small purse that had been hanging from his shoulder. He produced a few small, stainless steel tools that looked like dental instruments and maneuvered around to my side and began to insert one of them in my ear. I jerked away.

"What the hell are you doing, man! You ain't sticking that thing in my ear!"

Can you believe it? He was a professional ear cleaner! This guy actually made a living by going around and scraping the collected crud out of people's ears! He backed off and gave me a more intense rap about his service to try to get my ruffled feathers down.

"Baba! There is no needing this fear! I am a professional and do quality cleaning. You have read what your countrymen say. It is not so healthy having so much things as this in your ears, stopping you from hearing the music of life! Come, let me have just a look . . . "

Actually, I had been thinking about how dirty my ears were and wondering if I should have them cleaned out by a doctor when I got back to the States. I was even suffering a bit of hearing loss, I thought. I considered the maxim, "Never put anything in your ear, except your elbow"—let alone some unsterile fondue fork wielded by a grinning street person! But I relented to this sweet talk, and he had a look.

"Hmm . . . Ahh yes . . . Oh my my . . . Yes, baba, this is no good. There is much nasty things in here; I must remove it for your sake. I do it and you pay me what you think it is worth. I use special instruments and special Ayurvedic cleaning water. You will be happy to hear again!"

"All right, do it!" I said.

The Englishman, who had been fighting off solicitations this whole time, looked at me as if I was a unique blend of stupid and crazy.

"You mean to say that you are honestly going to let this bloke prod about in your ears with that miniature harpoon?"

"I can't help it. This is too cool an opportunity to pass up! To have my ears cleaned on the streets of Delhi, it's the chance of a lifetime!"

He shook his head in disbelief as the guy went to work. He scraped. He whittled. He blew air in my ear canal. And every time he fished something out, he would wipe it on the sleeve of my shirt as evidence of his ability. Sizable chunks of ear booger were deftly excised by this steady-handed surgeon. It was the most amazing sensation, almost bordering on sexual pleasure, kind of like having your teeth cleaned by a skilled dental hygienist with big hair. When he had at last

extracted the final waxy nugget and smeared it on my cuff, he produced a small bottle of liquid from his purse.

"This is Ayurvedic healing medicine," he said. "It will clean out that which prevents the songs of birds from reaching your heart!"

He tilted my head to one side and poured it in. When I heard it fizzle like soda pop I knew it was just hydrogen peroxide, but still I played along. By then I was convinced that this guy not only knew what he was doing, but also had the most entertaining line of B.S. you could ask for. We agreed on a price. I wrote a strong endorsement in his book, and we left the park to get something to eat. Now the chaos of Delhi was not so intimidating, and my ears gratefully sucked in the aural pandemonium, which had doubled in volume. I knew at this point that I would love this crazy country.

THE ADVENTURES OF RICHARD
•

By **Greta S.** *from*
Mudflap

Long-distance bicycle riding, previously the exclusive domain of Spandex-clad athletes, is gaining a foothold among people who look like they'd be more comfortable on a skateboard or at a punk rock club than in the saddle. For many young zine publishers, bicycles have become their primary mode of transportation—they're inexpensive, easy to maintain, don't harm the environment, and are completely unlicensed.

In recent years we've seen a flood of new bicycle-related zines. Outspoken about their anti-car beliefs, these zines feature articles about the grind of being a bike messenger, unconventional bike accessories, fighting bicycle theft, and the monthly Critical Mass rides that are springing up all over the world: Once a month, hundreds of riders meet for Critical Mass in cities like San Francisco and Minneapolis for long meandering rides though their main streets. These immense group bike rides tend to slow down traffic and increase bike visibility—which is precisely the idea.

Many people look at *Mudflap* as the original bicycle zine. Started more than four years ago, it features photos, advice, rants, stories, and comics about bike riding. It's definitely one of my all-time favorite zines, and I'm happy to report that you can still get copies from Greta. While she often writes about her own experiences, this is a tale of her friend Richard and his pierced genitalia. Greta illustrated his story in her joyful, yet explicit, comic style.

The Adventures of RICHARD

RICHARD GOT HIS DICK PIERCED in S.F.

HE HAD A BEAUTIFUL SEXY PIERCING

THEN HE WENT ON A LONG BIKE TOUR THROUGH THE SOUTH

THROUGH ALL THE JOSTLEY RIDING, ONE OF THE LITTLE BALLS LOOSENED OFF THE POST

THIS UPSET RICHARD.

HE TRIED TO GET A NEW LITTLE BALL FED-Xed TO HIM...

...CAUSE NO STORES HAD THEM IN STOCK.

FINALLY HE MADE A TEMPORARY STUD-HOLDER WITH DUCT TAPE.

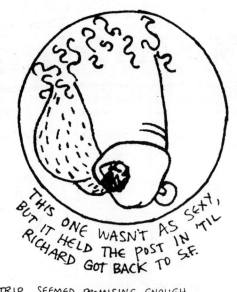

THIS ONE WASN'T AS SEXY, BUT IT HELD THE POST IN 'TIL RICHARD GOT BACK TO S.F.

THINGS WENT OKAY WITH RICHARD'S PIERCING FOR THE NEXT YEAR OR SO, THROUGH MESSENGING AND SOME ACCIDENTS EVEN. UNTIL HE WENT ON TOUR WITH CRINGER....

THE TRIP SEEMED PROMISING ENOUGH...

"SURE IS NICE OF YOU TO DRIVE US ON TOUR, RICHARD. HEY, WHAT ARE THOSE FLASHING LIGHTS?"

BUT SOON THERE WAS TROUBLE FOR RICHARD.

"YOU MEAN YOU DON'T HAVE NO LICENSE, NO REGISTRATION, NO LICENSE PLATE, NO INSURANCE NO I.D., AND YER CARRYIN' MAREEJUANA? SON, I'M GONNA HAVE TO TAKE YOU IN TO THE STATION... DAM FREAKS."

RICHARD'S JEWELRY WAS DISALLOWED IN JAIL, AND THE PIERCING HEALED OVER DURING HIS SENTENCE!

HOLY SHIT!! WE WON'T HAVE NO SATANIC IMPLEMENTS IN THIS JAIL!

THE END!

THIS STORY IS 100% TRUE.

(15)

STITCH
•

By **Aaron Cometbus** *from*

Cometbus

When people think of punk rock zines, the first that may come to mind isn't even a music zine. It's Aaron's zine *Cometbus*, which is filled with travel stories and other true tales of punk adventures. Aaron has been part of the Berkeley punk rock scene long enough to have become somewhat of a celebrity. He's written for many other zines, played in a number of bands, worked as a roadie, been mentioned in songs, and has developed a huge audience for his zine, which he sells as he travels around the country.

Cometbus is one of the original personal zines. By handwriting the text in every issue and telling us intimate details of his life, Aaron's readers feel as if they know him personally. Like other well-known zinesters, Aaron prefers anonymity over the limelight, though you might just run into him at Gilman, or some other punk rock club.

This first piece is an emotional love story about Aaron's brief encounter with a girl named Stitch. Being on the road you're certain to meet lots of people. Sometimes things can grow out of these chance encounters—more often they don't last too long.

The second selection, by Bill Daniel, chronicles his years of trying to track down the elusive freight train graffiti tagger Bozo Texino. In 1983 Bill started noticing graffiti drawn on the sides of boxcars and started taking pictures of them. This obsession led him to hopping freight trains all over the country to document the incredible phenomenon of boxcar monikers. After taking hundreds of photos and writing extensively about this phenomenon, he's now working on a film that explores this subculture.

It's one more party in one more unfamiliar town on my first cross-country road trip. Her name is Stephanie, but she says to call her Stitch. Stitch in time. Keep you in stitches. Keep you at Stitch's, as she likes to say. Stitch, rhymes with you know what. She gives me a necklace and I'm already in love with her before she shares her beer.

A week later in a different town, I find her again. She is swinging on a swingset in the park, smiling and shooting me with her fingers. We strip down to our underwear and go swimming in the lake. She wraps herself in seaweed and says she is a mermaid. I pick a dandelion and wish for her and blow off every single bit of fluff. She kisses my hand when it is time to go.

I get sick of traveling and being around so many people, so I move to a new city and am restless and lonely. I write her letters saying I have a big crush on her, which isn't exactly news. Days and trains pass and I look for her, but no such luck.

Winter comes and I head back home on the Greyhound, hoping to find a letter from her waiting for me. Hoping to find her waiting for me, but a letter will do. On the way I pass through a million miserable small towns and stop in a handful to walk around. One day like every other, I put on my overstuffed backpack that weighs a ton and walk the five-mile walk from the bus station to downtown.

I look up and there she is. It is too good to be true. Walking down the sidewalk looking at me and smiling, all sly and sneaky-like. We get two bottles of strawberry wine and end up in a Dumpster wrestling and biting and screaming and kissing in who knows what kind of stinky trash. When we emerge an hour and a half later, I can barely stand up. She asks if I'm drunk. Of course I'm drunk. Isn't she? Nope.

Oh my. I'm a little embarrassed. Also, I'm wrong about her being shy. We walk through the empty latenight streets toward her squat. Her squat is a beautiful abandoned theater with two empty bottom floors and her friends still awake on the third. They are huddled around a makeshift table eating Dumpstered bagels. We join them and share stories, water, cigarettes, and some leftover beer.

It's wonderful in there. There are murals on the walls and candles are burning everywhere. The bathroom is the roof outside. The living room is the table. The bedrooms are mattresses separated by sheets hung from the rafters. Stitch is acting aloof, so I set up camp by the table. She calls me into her room. We feel bad for keeping everyone awake.

In the morning I look like I got the worst of a fight. She still looks beautiful. I am about to miss my bus. I am about to miss her badly. She is heading to the jungles of Mexico. She says she will send me a monkey. She kisses me good-bye.

I get home. It sucks. What's new. I check my mailbox for a letter from Stitch. Weeks pass, and where my monkey is, I do not know. I lie awake at night, unable to sleep, crawling out of my skin, thinking of her.

Three months later and I'm in another new town. In a laundromat. In between broken-hearted country songs on the radio, there is a live call from Sue asking William to marry her. She is tired of waiting for him to ask. Another sad song, then William calls the station and accepts on air. The DJ asks if he can come to the wedding.

It's all very depressing. I'm in a laundromat, listening to country music, with poison ivy covering my body from head to toe. I watch my clothes go 'round and 'round in the dryer, hoping the heat kills the bugs this time. It's the seventh time I've done the goddamn treatment.

I wish Stitch would send me a letter. She is hard to forget. She gave me something to remember her by. Not a monkey, but some other animal. Scabies. I am scratching and thinking of her. Stitch, rhymes with you know what.

WHO IS BOZO TEXINO?

●

By **Bill Daniel** *from*

Cometbus

This here story begins in 1983 when I moved into a warehouse right next to the Santa Fe freight yard in Dallas, across from the state fairgrounds, next door to the Slurpee machine factory. The trains ran right past my windows all day and all night. After the first week of waking-up-on-the-tracks-in-front-of-a-charging-locomotive–style nightmares, I got used to the little diesel earthquakes. The next thing I knew I was having to go out every time to watch 'em go by because, you know what?, freight trains have graffiti on them. A very particular sort of graffiti.

Not your usual junklike sloppy bomber tags or band logos, but stuff that looked to be a full-on underground art scene, a Boxcar Graffiti Cult with hundreds of characters; cowboys, drunks, nekkid ladies . . . I figured I had discovered some kind of secret hobo society. And so I decided I would try to become a hobo myself and meet these brilliant writers and adopt their carefree lifestyle.

I began first by taking pictures of the drawings, like hundreds of them, and taking pictures of the odd places where the hoboes crashed out (called jungles). Then the day after Thanksgiving, a bunch of homeless dudes (bindle stiffs) invited me to join in the partaking of a big rusty drum of soup made of filthy Dumpster food (mulligan stew). They were friendly and cool but didn't have much to say about the graffiti (monikers). I was hoping they might know who Bozo Texino was. Bozo Texino was the graffiti I had seen the most often, and for unknown reasons it had become my mission to find the originator of that character. The one with the most absurd hat and the blankest stare.

Next I moved to Austin, and later to Galveston and Houston, always hanging close to the rail yards and empty buildings, collecting graffiti and scoping the hobo potential. One tramp-type I met in Texas City "didn't know of no Bozo Texino neither," but he did have a very folded-up Xerox of a USA railroad map, which he gave me. I studied what rail lines were still legible on that thing and pretty soon I had what you call "itchy feet."

So I did what I had to do and hopped a Southern Pacific freight and, I'm not sure how, made it to San Francisco, which seemed like a cool place so I stayed. Unfortunately nobody in S.F. had ever heard of Bozo Texino except for Nosmo King of Jak's Team. Nosmo was a hell of a well-traveled bike messenger, but his beery account of actually meeting Bozo Texino out on the rails was kinda mythic and turned out to be not really what you'd call a solid lead.

Finally a breakthrough appeared anonymously in my mailbox. "Colossus of Roads," one of the most prolific and witty boxcar writers, was revealed to be none other than Buz Blurr, a mail-art guru living in Gurdon, Arkansas. So I packed my bags with cameras and as much Super-8 sound film as I could carry, and, wearing as much clothes as I could and still manage to walk (it was cold), I high-balled it out of West Oakland on what I hoped would be a fast train headed toward Arkansas. Along the way I heard like a dozen sketchy stories of who Bozo Texino was supposed to be: a Texas hobo, a Mexican migrant worker, a conducter on the Sunset Limited, dead.

I found myself kicked off the train in Beaumont, Texas, where "The Rambler of Beaumont" signs his work from. I met a couple of switchmen there who I figured were buddies of "The Rambler," the way they happened to know a hell of a lot of stories about him, but they covered for him and wouldn't let on to me that they knew who he was. They turned out to be regular guys, though, and gave me an old newsclipping about "Herby." Herby is the granddaddy of boxcar graffiti; his famous sleeping Mexican under the palm tree is probably the number one railroad drawing, seen for more than thirty years all over the country. According to this article he was Herbert A. Meyer, retired switchman in St. Louis, Mo., who after all those years drawing under anonymous stealth finally went public. This major revelation debunked about a million "Herby" stories I'd heard. Although I could sometimes find someone to remember some pseudo-account of Bozo Texino, every cotton-pickin' tramp and pin-puller out there thinks he's met the real Herby. "Oh, yeah, in San Antonio"; "I saw him in Denver, did that dang drawing on eighty-seven cars in three minutes . . . in the rain . . ."; " . . . saw him in a whore house in Odessa"; "Aw, he's dead."

By now it'd been eight years and about 1,600 graffiti snapshots since I saw that first bunch of drawings in Dallas, and here I finally got the actual names of two of the coolest boxcar artists ever. So I got goin' again, my bindle full of film and a big roll of duct tape, and headed up toward St. Louis. On the way I stopped in Gurdon, a real old-time rail town, and found Buz Blurr (a childhood pal of punk legend, Gary Floyd, no lie!). Buz has got to be the most poetic of the boxcar graffitiers and he's an international mail-artist and archiver of all things paper. He said he had a file on Bozo, something about the history of the Bozo character, somewhere in a stack of things, here or there . . . Well it'd take a while to find it, and I had to keep moving, to St. Louis next, so I shot a bunch of "Colossus" graffiti then hit the grit.

Herbert turned out to be a funny old gent who entertained with funny old stories and he even did a few Herbys for old times' sake. He started telling something about the original Bozo Texino, but right then I ran out of sound film, and anyway I couldn't really understand what he was trying to say; he's pretty old.

Now I'm really heckin' jazzed, having met and filmed two of the true greats of rail art, but on the way back to Texas I'm realizing I still don't know jack about Bozo Texino. These days you don't see his drawings as often and they're starting to fade. No more fresh ones with crisp

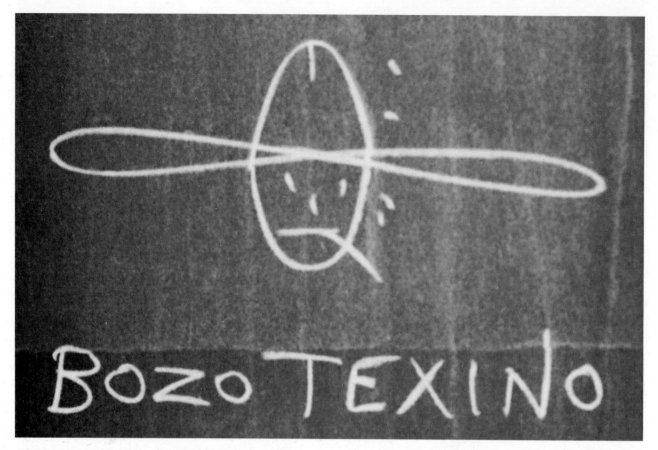

white lines. I'm guessing he's not writing anymore and wondering if he's even still alive.

I head for the Santa Fe yard in Temple, Texas, a place where he'd once been rumored to be (one rumor out of a million, that is). I'd also been told that at times the trains rolling through here could be seen with fresh Bozos on every car down the line. The first guy I meet here knows exactly what I'm talking about. He casually scribbles a pretty authentic-looking Bozo Texino right there, and for a second I wonder, could this be him? No way, he says, says he doesn't know who.

The next dude I run into is wearing this giant cowboy hat. Like in the Bozo Texino drawings. This is kinda weird too, 'cause cowboy hats have pretty much been replaced by gimme caps as the standard western headgear. So this cowpoke with the crazy hat, that kinda made an infinity shape, just like the drawing, said if I wanted to know anything about trains I should go see Mainline Mac, that he knows everything about trains. Mainline Mac was easy to find; seems everybody around here is usually hangin' around—they're never gone too long or too far.

I was fairly beat and the day was gettin' late when I landed on the front porch of Mainline's shack. We weren't

strangers for too long, but old friends, once we realized we shared a crazy obsession: Bozo Texino, and we commenced to swap railroad stories. I told him about all the wrong turns and side tracks I'd been on looking for Bozo, and we both noted that there wasn't any new graffiti out there, that whoever it is ain't writing much anymore. Then he digs out an old *Railroad Stories* magazine dated 1939. That's one of those little pulp mags like the old western dime novels. In there was an article about a Mr. J. H. McKinley, a.k.a. Bozo Texino, a MoPac engineer in Laredo, who wrote railroad stories and had a passion for writing his moniker on every boxcar he could. This was a habit he began in the '20s and made quite a name for himself all over the country. The article gave no explanation of the orgin of his handle and, of course, no clues to who might be still using that name in the 1980s.

This was as close as I was gonna get to the Holy Grail, 'cause now I was broke and had a big pile of film to process and edit. And realizing I was no hobo anyway, I arranged a drive-away car (a nice late-model Honda) and motored back to California.

If you think you know who Bozo Texino is, or if you have snapshots of any old railroad graffiti, drop me a line. I'm still looking.

work

Unfortunately, for most Americans, work consumes way more of the day than any other activity, except for maybe sleeping. And if that weren't bad enough, most people actually hate their jobs. It's not surprising then, that a lot of great, bile-filled writing comes from people who devote pages and pages of their zine to bitohing about their jobs. Working is a big drag, seriously boring, but creating a zine about your job makes the workdays fly by (especially if done on company time and using the company's Xerox machine).

Writing about work from a personal rather than a political point of view is a relatively recent development. The groundbreaking text has got to be Studs Terkel's *Working*. This book, published in 1974, features discussions and interviews with people about their jobs. Terkel captured what amounts to a composite photograph of the American workplace and inspired many people to explore their own feelings about their jobs.

In recent years we've seen an explosion of writing about work and quite a number of zines exclusively devoted to that dreaded activity. Work zines feature people complaining about their mindless jobs, ranting about their asinine bosses, or exposing the inner secrets of a faceless corporation. It's amazing what you can find in them.

Sadly, our entire economy has been transformed over the past few years. People can no longer expect lifetime employment with steadily increasing salaries. Instead, many settle for a series of temporary jobs, each offering little more than minimum wage.

Zine publishers seem to gravitate toward these low-wage temp jobs (or perhaps, jobs like these inspire people to publish zines). For all you know, that waiter bringing your food, that bike messenger delivering your urgent package, and that record-store clerk ringing up your CDs could all be zine publishers.

Here is a collection of the best work-related writing in zines. The jobs these worker/writers describe range from blue collar to professional, the writing from angry and political to elegantly descriptive. I wouldn't say their essays about work *glamorize* jobs like dishwashing, but they certainly put things in a new light.

I Am Hobart: Dishwasher as Man and Machine

•

By **Randy Russell** *from*

American Job

Man, in front of the machine—the mighty Hobart dishwasher, high art, low art, industrial stainless steel, children's toy, your best friend and worst enemy. The first and last in the food factory line. The top of the circle, the integral part of the mechanism, and the bottom of the totem pole. "We need more spoons *right now!*"

Always the first to get blamed and the last to get paid. No respect, high turnover—just waiting for a busser spot to open up or a bus to get out of town. The job of *Dishwasher:* something you could depend on if everything else failed. There was *always* an opening *some*where, according to myth—all you had to be was willing. All you had to do was *not* be able to pay for your dinner and you were automatically a dishwasher for the evening.

It meant: no money in your pocket. It meant defeat. Desperation. Romance. In the mythical land of America, The United States Of, there are three things you can do if all avenues lead to Shit Creek: Join the Navy, Turn to crime, Be a dishwasher.

So it turns out that crime is really the only thing you can depend on. It took me awhile to learn the truth about the dishwasher racket. It wasn't something I set out to discover the inside-outs of—it was just something that happened, like the bad haircut you get when you join the Marines. It all started, appropriately against my will, in grade school, my first job ever, at the school cafeteria. They had this deal where you could work on the slop line a few times a week and you'd get lunches free, so you could save your lunch money from Mom for beer and drugs.

The kitchen was fascinating, as I recall—my job was to scrape the unwanted food off the returned trays and then load the trays and silverware on racks that would run through a huge car wash–like automatic dishwasher. A Hobart, no doubt. The kitchen, especially next to the dishwasher, was balmy as Hell itself, and it didn't help that I was a frail kid who used to get sick all the time and faint. The women who worked there were just plain scary, and what I remember most of all was the overwhelming, sickeningly strong smell of black coffee. It would be over a decade before I would be able to touch a cup of coffee again without it churning my stomach, much less enjoy it.

I suppose the whole experience was supposed to prepare me for the work world somewhere down the line, but I found it to be distasteful and unnecessary. Call it common sense or greed, but I soon realized that my parents were paying for my lunches anyway, and I didn't even particularly *like* the lunches, and I was not really benefitting *personally* from all my toil. I retired from the world of work forever, I hoped, figuring I'd become a millionaire playboy. Later, in high school, when *that* goal started to seem a little unrealistic, I vowed to become a bum. The point was: not to work. Of course, that was before they invented the word *homeless*.

In 1982, a year after I had begun to drink coffee again—too much coffee—I headed west to start a new life. I stopped in Tucson, Arizona, long enough to lose the momentum necessary to make it to California, so I hit the streets in search of a dishwasher job, or any job, really. A newspaper article had said that Tucson had the fourth best economy in the country. I was naive and believed it. I found out there *were* jobs in Tucson, if you were unskilled and a student and willing to get paid nothing, or skilled and an illegal alien and willing to get paid less, or in the Air Force (and were willing to join the Air Force). The school wouldn't have me, nor would the Air Force, nor would the illegal aliens.

A couple of years later I did the student thing, after I found out that through financial aid they would *pay* for me to go to school. I also found out that low-paying jobs were readily available—jobs that weren't supposed to have anything to do with your *goals,* and in fact you weren't even expected to do a very good job, or even be there all of the time. In fact you could call in and say you couldn't make it in that day because you have to *study,* and it's, like, a legitimate excuse.

Well, I guess some of these jobs can be pretty uninspiring, having to work side by side with other pinhead students, but I got lucky—I went in, said, sign me up for *any*thing, and I got "stuck" with morning weekday dishwasher. See, I *like* getting up early, and I started at seven and worked until the dishes were done, at ten or so. The best thing about it, however, was that I worked in this huge dishroom *alone.* The students would put their trays on a conveyer belt in the dining room that led through a long tunnel back to the dishroom where I'd take care of them. There was a switch where I could turn the belt off if I was getting swamped, and I pretty much set my own pace.

The great thing about this job was how it seemed to dominate so little of my life. I'd usually wake up about five minutes before I was supposed to be at work, throw on some clothes, drive there like a maniac,

and be in the dishroom before I was even awake. It usually takes most people a while to become a human in the morning—you can sit at home for two hours reading the newspaper, eating scones—but this was better. I'd be at about 15 percent of my mental capacity for about the first hour, and by the time I got done I was feeling good and awake and ready for classes.

The other good thing was that every morning was like an all-you-can-eat buffet. I was allowed to drink all the "juice" and "coffee" I wanted from the serving line, plus they'd give me a breakfast item each day. But besides that, I had an incredible amount of untouched food coming down the conveyer belt. At first I was eating a stack of pancakes and french toast every day. Always enough donuts, and often greasy "breakfast sandwiches" of soggy toast, melted cheese, and slimy ham.

After awhile I couldn't touch the pancakes or french toast to save my life, but I always enjoyed making a huge doughy cannonball out of uneaten pancakes and then throwing the massive object as hard as I could at the trash can. Golly, what fun.

How was I to know this would be the peak in my dishwashing career? In a way I think I *did* know, or I *should've* known. I knew *nothing.*

So with that ideal in my mind, I figured I'd have dishwashing in my future—if I wanted it. Something to fall back on, like dogshit on the sidewalk. A couple of years later, I found myself at an Indian restaurant in one of my famous (in *my* mind) one-day jobs. Just because I *liked* Indian food didn't mean I'd enjoy cleaning curry stains off dishes. Plus, there was no Hobart—just a sink.

Later that year I tried my hand again—at a Holiday Inn restaurant, second shift. They gave me the whole introductory treatment, the head chef with a tall hat taking me around so everyone could make a big point about wiping their hardworking hands on their aprons before shaking my hand. The sous chef was a guy named *Dent*—he'd be my actual boss—and the other two dishwashers I was working with were crazed rednecks who came to work with three-foot-high ostrich feather cowboy hats. They told me how the "best thang" was when we had to work until four A.M. More money. The later the better. Dent told me that whenever we get off earlier than bar closing time, *everyone* meets at the bar across the street, *Cheers, Too.*

On my way to work on the fourth night—what would it be tonight? cleaning the deep fryers, or the broiler oven, or filters?—I didn't exactly make it in. I flipped out on the highway and seriously considered running my car into one of those concrete abutments. I decided that I would stay on the road, but go in a different direction.

That fall I did something I had never done before. I found a job in a town *before* moving there. I was visiting Kent, Ohio, and I kind of impulsively went out looking for jobs one morning because there was a room open in my friend's house. I found the job in twenty minutes, and I was working the next morning.

Going to work that first morning, bright and early, fear and dread running through my consciousness, I'm thinking, "What the hell am I *doing?*" I made the big walk there, with all the cars zipping by me to their jobs and the sun on the horizon.

The job turned out to be a nightmare, however. Some advice: If you get considered for a dishwashing job, check to see if the machine is a Hobart, and not a makeshift jalopy *piece of shit*. I worked eight A.M. until four P.M. with no break, struggling against my faulty technology. I kept this up five days a week for a month, and about halfway through my tenure, they hauled out the contraption and replaced it with something worse, but funnier. This new non-Hobart had an oval-shaped track that ran the dishes around like a racetrack so you could let them go through as many times as you wanted. It was nice in theory, but it was held together with bag ties and kept breaking down, and I'd have to go climbing *inside* the machine to fix it, kind of like Scotty on *Star Trek*. It also made a horrible noise, and at one point my annoyed boss and owner yelled at me, "Can't you keep that thing quiet?" I *didn't* say something like: "*You* bought the fucker!"

Yes, and then there was that wonderful day when I just couldn't bring myself to go into work. I hadn't planned it, nor was I thinking about it the night before. I decided they couldn't *pay* me to do that job, not one day more. My solution was to send them a letter and tell them about the job dreams I was having and how I feared for my mental health. Their solution was to then hire a mentally disabled person—they *told* me this when I picked up my last check —which they were happy about because they got government subsidies for hiring a mentally disabled person.

I approached my next dishwashing job with a better attitude. Another 24-hour country restaurant without a Hobart, but it was a fine dishwasher, and a pretty good setup—isolated in the back. Cleaning hillbilly vomit from the bathrooms and mopping the lobby over customers' feet was also part of the job, so I really savored the dishwashing part. The most work came after the Sunday buffet, when there were a lot of dishes *and* all the buffet pans to clean—but also the most free food. I would load up a plate high with leftovers from the buffet, lots of sausage and eggs with cheese, potatoes, and even waffles. It was not something to scoff at.

It was, I think, during this job that I kind of figured out how the restaurant thing really works. To be able to do this job you have to actually *get into it*—kind of like dancing. That's why when you work at a restaurant they encourage you to drink all the caffeinated beverages they have on hand. Coffee and cola just aren't enough to get *me* rockin' and rollin', even if I know it's for my own good. Rock 'n' roll just isn't my natural state. I don't mean to sound like a snob, but I wash dishes like Thelonious Monk plays piano. You can't work in a restaurant like Thelonious Monk.

Oh, and there was one more dishwashing job—the real anchor for my résumé. It was later that year at a 24-hour truckstop, where I got hired for a few nights a week as third-shift Hobart operator. I was delivering flowers during the day, but the thing about working two jobs is that it makes the inferior of the two seem all that much worse. And all that much easier to quit. Even though I saw some magnificent sunrises after work, my days were too filled with haziness. And even though they had a fine little Hobart, they also had a video monitor in the kitchen, presumably to keep employees from stealing steaks. I saw a few fine sights at this job, like the cook throwing up blood from an ulcer just before his shift, but mostly it was just pretty depressing. I quit before too long even though I had promised the boss I would stick around. He yelled at me the day I came in to pick up my check, and I happened to be in a rare good mood, so I yelled back at him, "Fuck you asshole!" Not very original, but it *was* in front of several waitresses and customers. A solid gold moment.

I *still* want to wash dishes. But what I want is a pleasant weekday morning, part-time but good-paying, all-you-can-eat, Hobart-rich dishwashing job. I may as well ask to be CEO of my own corporation. It is a job that just doesn't exist.

But then as you can tell by my attitude, I don't *really* want to work. I just want to hang out in the steam, eating free food, looking at art, and jotting down whatever comes into my head. And occasionally read a book.

The only form of entry-level employment left these days seems to be in the temp-worker industry. Zine publishers are certainly well represented in these ranks. While not necessarily a good thing, working as an office temp does offer several advantages to the zine publisher. Most notable is the ability to churn out a zine at one's place of enslavement/employment. Having a flexible schedule also allows plenty of downtime for a range of other projects.

WORKER RIGHTS FOR TEMPS

●

By **Keffo** *from*
Temp Slave

In 1992, Keffo put together a one-shot zine called *Temp Slave* to express his frustration with shitty jobs. The response was overwhelming and folks from all over sent in their own tales of dreadful office work, so Keffo decided to keep publishing. Five years later, *Temp Slave* is better than ever, with devoted readers all over the world. Each issue features the most incredible stories of office oppression and office rebellion. If you've ever had a crappy job (like 99 percent of the people in the country), you're sure to enjoy this zine.

In the first piece, taken from the premier issue of *Temp Slave,* Keffo describes how to take back the workplace from corporate fascists. If that doesn't work, at least you can have fun trying. Next up, Brendan Bartholomew describes the reality of having the "dream job" of working for a video game company.

TEMP SLAVE!

WORK! WORK!

ISSUE 1

A temp worker has little or no rights in the workplace. In essence, a temp worker is close to being a nonentity. Sadly, not much can be done to alleviate the situation. A temp worker can be moved from job to job within a workplace, even though the temp may have been told they would do only one kind of job. As for job security, obviously there is none.

The normal avenues for channeling job discontent are not open to temps. For example, the normal course of unionizing a workplace is out of the question for temps since almost every union will not make the effort. The avenues used in a non-union workplace are also out of the question. Most companies set up human resource departments to act as a buffer between workers and management. If a problem arises, the human resource managers are summoned to sort out the mess. But this does nothing for temps, since any complaints by a temp will most likely result in termination. Finally, getting unemployment benefits off a temp agency is like pulling teeth. Most of the time, requests for benefits are denied.

So a temp is forced to put up and shut up or get out. However, there are a few things a temp can do to gain a semblance of power in the workplace.

First, DON'T SPEED UP! SLOW DOWN! Most of the time a temp is expected to work at the rate of a full-time employee or faster. At first a temp may want to impress the fact that he or she is capable of doing the job. But once this is accomplished there is no reason for a temp to continue the pace. If you are working with a group of temps, band together and SLOW DOWN your rate of work. Slowing down your work allows your assignment to linger on. After all, why put yourself out of work? Plus, a group of temps working together cohesively puts the company on notice that people cannot be treated like slaves.

Second, NEVER rat on another temp to the bossman! Trying to put yourself above other temps is silly and ultimately hopeless. The person doing the ratting may think they are getting ahead, or think it will lead to a full-time job. But it seldom if ever does. What it does do is divide the workforce and keep people in place. To get rid of a rat, a few simple things can be done—"lose" their paperwork (make them look bad in the eyes of the bossman), chill out the rat (do not associate with the person on break time). And never volunteer to work with a rat if two people are needed for a job. In other words, make it known that the rat is not wanted within your work area.

Third, GET BACK AT THE BASTARDS! If you are being treated like shit by a company, give it right back. Many companies entrust you with sensitive information. Use this info, "lose" it, sabotage it. Learn your job well and take every advantage possible with it.

Finally, if you are ending an assignment and really want to mess up the works legally, there is a fun thing you can do. Start talking union to everyone in the workplace. This gives you the opportunity to file charges with the National Labor Relations Board (NLRB). The NLRB is a national

governmental agency set up to broker labor disputes. Under law, a worker is allowed to organize unions in the workplace. But, even with the law, workers are still fired. However, filing charges with the NLRB is a kick in the ass to a company because it forces them to deal with investigations and endless paperwork. In the best-case scenario you may win your case and receive back pay, sometimes amounting to thousands of dollars. But even if you lose, you can go away happy knowing that you were an incredible pain in the ass to the corporate hacks.

In closing, a workforce divided by petty jealousies, fear, and self-loathing is a workforce that plays into the hands of the bosses.

DON'T MAKE IT EASY FOR THEM! THEY DON'T DESERVE IT!

THANK YOU FOR CALLING SEGA

•

By **Brendan P. Bartholomew** *from*

Temp Slave

There are twelve-year-old boys who would suck your dick to have the temp assignment I just completed. For the last three months, I went behind the scenes of what most kids consider the coolest company in the world. I worked for Sega of America's Consumer Service Department. I spent eight hours a day answering the phone and getting berated by angry parents whose children's video games weren't working.

The department was staffed by about a hundred phone reps, most of whom were temporary. Our primary function was to talk people through the installation of Sega's home video game system, the Genesis. If somebody's Genesis wasn't working, we would troubleshoot it over the phone, and if that didn't work, we would have them send it in for repairs.

If you consider the demographic you're dealing with, you'll understand that this job was a prescription for misery: video-gamers tend to be losers. They have no friends. They sit in their dark little rooms with the curtains closed, playing *Mortal Kombat* while the rest of us are out there

having lives. From this demographic there is a special sub-class: those who are too stupid to connect a Genesis to a television. These are the ones I dealt with.

The stupidity of our callers was usually a function of age: I often found myself talking to ten-year-olds who could barely tie their shoelaces, but somehow had mustered the brainpower to dial our 800-number. Kids are passionate about the industry. They would sometimes ask me, "How do you get a job at Sega?" I worked for the company that had created *Sonic the Hedgehog* and *Altered Beast*. In their eyes, I was the luckiest guy in the world. I was part of the inner circle, and they wanted to talk to me for an hour.

Our callers' passion for video games had a dark side. It was damned easy for them to become irate. Adolescent boys would call just to harass us: "Why do you guys make such crappy games, man? I think Nintendo really kicked your ass with *Donkey Kong Country*. You guys don't have anything to compare with that game! I've got over a thousand dollars invested in Sega products, and all you give us is crap! I think Sega fuckin' sucks, man." Blah, blah, blah. Like I care.

I felt like saying, "Listen, you little punk, let me get you alone in a jail cell for two minutes and I'll beat you until blood comes out of your ears." But I couldn't say that, because our calls were randomly monitored.

Once a week, my supervisor would listen in on two of my calls and then grade my performance. He used a score-card of Standards and Expectations, which was a list of the things we were supposed to do and say in every call. "Thank you for calling Sega" was supposed to be the first thing a customer heard when we answered the phone, and the last thing they heard before we hung up.

Before we ended a call, we were also expected to say, "Is there anything else I can help you with?" This is not a good thing if you've got an idiot on the line who just called to chat or, worse yet, a complainer. That offer of additional assistance could turn what should have been a five-minute call into a twenty-five-minute ordeal. "Oh, yeah, actually there *is* something else. Can you tell me why it's so hard to get through to you people? I've been trying to call since Christmas, and the lines are always busy, and when I finally did get through, I had to wait on hold for twenty minutes . . . " Blah, blah, blah.

You didn't want a call to stretch on like that, because a computer kept track of your average length on calls. If you weren't careful, you'd get a voice message from your boss saying something like, "Hi, I was just looking at your stats for this week, and you did well on the monitoring scores, but you really need to work on reducing your talk time."

The worst thing about the job was that it was an endless grind. Day after day, you had to listen to one irate parent after another, all with the same complaint. Because the complaints were totally predictable, you would find yourself having the same exact conversation over and over:

"We sent away for the free game promotion over three months ago, and it still hasn't arrived! I've got a very impatient five-year-old who asks me where his game is every day. I've called you people twice already, and both times you've assured me it's been shipped, and I'd like to know where it is . . . " Blah, blah, blah. I listened to that complaint hundreds of times.

If the customers weren't getting what they wanted, they would fly off the handle. The stupider people would threaten legal action: "The store told me I could get a free game if I bought the Sega, and now you're telling me I bought the wrong system? This is bullshit, and if you don't do something to make me happy, I'm going to the State Attorney General and the Better Business Bureau!" There's somebody with a keen understanding of our legal system. One bitch threatened to take her story to "some big radio station." Yeah, right. I'm sure the news director will devote at least an hour of airtime to your complaint.

In almost every case, Sega had done nothing wrong. The more baseless the customer's complaint, the more likely they were to scream, ask to speak with my supervisor, or claim they were going to the authorities.

It was grueling to take this abuse, and I dealt with it by using my favorite stress relievers: sabotage and theft! Here's a brief overview of my activities:

Masturbating at work: The computer kept track of every minute you were logged on to the phone system. You were expected to be logged on for a minimum of seven hours and fifteen minutes a day. This made it especially thrilling to run into the bathroom and furiously pump my erection, knowing my time was limited. Having beat off in a wide variety of work environments, I've mastered the art of the quick jerk. I could usually have a satisfying fantasy and reach orgasm within two or three minutes.

Drinking on the job: One day, during lunch, I decided to get bottles of orange juice and load them up with vodka. I gave one to the guy I shared my cubicle with, and we were pleasantly buzzed for the rest of the afternoon.

Antagonizing customers: In spite of the possibility that the call was being monitored, sometimes I just had to make these people unhappy: "You want to talk to a manager? Well, I hate to say it, but my manager's not gonna tell you anything different from what I'm telling you. There's just no way Sega's going to do what you're asking . . . "

Free subscriptions: If a customer was irate, we could set them up with a free subscription to *Sega Visions,* the company's magazine. This subscription normally costs $14.95. Needless to say, every friend I have now has this magazine coming to their house.

Adding customers to my Shit List: The Shit List is something I've been compiling for several years. Having worked in the service industry all my life, I've been abused by all sorts of customers. I've often had access to my customer's phone numbers, addresses, and credit card numbers. If somebody was very nasty to me, I would record said information, with the intention of tormenting them until they die.

The easiest way of doing this is to fill out those little postage-paid magazine subscription cards and check the box marked "Bill me later." The customer then gets magazines they didn't order and bills they weren't expecting. For this very reason, the raunchier porno magazines don't have "Bill me later" cards, but *Playboy* and *Penthouse* do. Some of those subscription cards even give you the option of sending gift subscriptions to other people. This makes it possible to have one asshole customer get billed for magazines being sent to some other asshole he's never even met.

Of course, subscription cards are for amateurs. The next level is credit card fraud: You call a mail-order catalog and, posing as your customer, use his credit card to have crap sent to his house. I do feel sorry for the phone rep from the catalog who will eventually have to deal with someone screaming and yelling because merchandise he never

ordered is arriving at his house and being charged to his credit card.

Mail order catalogs are happy to send gift orders, so, as with the subscription cards, you can have one schmuck sending products to some other shithead he's never met. If you're lucky enough to know the name of your customer's wife, you can have him send her expensive flowers or other presents. Most catalog companies will include a gift card that says, "From your adoring husband," or whatever. Imagine the predicament of your asshole customer when he comes home from work to find his wife creaming all over herself, thanking him for the beautiful jewelry. He can't very well say, "I didn't send you that!"

A word of caution: credit card fraud is serious business. If you get caught, the authorities will bury your ass in a hole so deep, you'll never get out.

Misuse of company mail: We were provided with all the envelopes we could use, because customers were always requesting instruction manuals, promotional materials, and game-play hints. Nobody thought anything of it if I sent out twenty large envelopes a day. Naturally, I felt the need to steal things from the office and mail them to my friends. All of my friends. Every day.

Sega knew we were a bunch of temp scum. They made sure there was hardly anything in the office we could steal, so I had to get creative. I would send people confidential documents, memos on how to dispose of confidential doc-uments, memos on awful, hidden flaws that had surfaced in our products, and so forth.

In my desperation to steal something, *anything,* I stole packets of tea from the employee kitchen. Sega also provided packets of instant soup, so I sent a lot of those out as well. Toward the end of my assignment, it occurred to me to snoop through the emergency medical kit. It was a cornucopia of over-the-counter pain killers and PMS medications, as well as lewd rubber gloves! Needless to say, I stuffed countless envelopes with these things.

I wanted to find new and interesting items to put in the daily care packages from Sega, but there just wasn't much for me to pilfer. I started bringing garbage from home and mailing it; ten-year-old copies of *People,* dirty cartoons, unknown pills, used Kleenex, I didn't care. I just had to send shit!

So there it is. Life at Sega. You'll notice I spent a lot of time complaining about my customers, and not much time talking about Sega's faults. As temp jobs go, Sega wasn't all bad: I got eight bucks an hour, forty hours a week. I could park my ass in my cubicle all day without seeing the boss, so shaving and showering were optional. We could play all the latest games in the lunchroom, and our immediate supervisors were cool. So why was I dishonest and subversive? Well, I've been sabotaging employers for so long, it's become second nature. It's in my blood. I couldn't stop if I wanted to.

WEEKEND WARRIOR: WORKING PART-TIME AS A SOLDIER

•

By **John A. Marmysz** *from*
Twilight of the Idols

Another consequence of our pitiful job market is the huge number of unemployed folks seeking financial refuge in U.S. military service. It doesn't offer nearly as many slackful opportunities as office temping or dishwashing, but the Army Reserves does offer experience and training that may lead to a real career. And while there's little call for demolition expertise in civilian life, plenty of jobs require pointless standing around, cleaning up after other people, and mindlessly following orders.

John Marmysz, a self-proclaimed nihilist and scholar of Nietzsche, published *Twilight of the Idols* from 1991 to 1993. Each issue featured a hodgepodge of bizarre fiction, hidden histories, experimental poetry, and tips for constructing explosives. In this story he describes what joining the Army Reserves is like and what you can expect to gain from the experience.

**M**any of the things that I do, I do part-time. I'm a part-time student earning minimum wage at a part-time job. I also do freelance gardening work part-time in order to augment my income, which is so small that it only allows me to buy groceries part of the time. With a preexisting lifestyle like this, it seemed like I would be ideally suited to becoming a part-time soldier.

I joined the Army Reserves because I was under the impression that a certain recruiter was telling me the truth when he said, "You'll be building bridges and then blowing them up every day!" He assured me that U.S. Army Combat Engineer School was the place to receive the most incredible, hands-on training in explosives available anywhere. I didn't know it at the time, but unlike Procter & Gamble, the government can't be sued for false advertising. To be fair, however, my recruiter didn't know that I was lying when I claimed not to advocate the violent overthrow of the U.S. government. I guess that makes us even.

Before you can take your place alongside other "part-time soldiers" you must go through four months of full-time training. I was sent to Fort Leonard Wood, Missouri, also known as "Fort Lost in the Woods, Misery." My training there took place at a time when the Army was trying to revamp its image. It no longer wanted to be the last resort for criminals to find respectability, but a place where already respectable citizens could "be all that they could be." Consequently, a number of official policy changes were implemented to create an environment in which the "American Citizen" could be sculpted into the "American Warrior" as seen through the eyes of middle-class America. To this end it was ruled that a fighter for capitalism should not smoke, swear, or overeat. In addition, he should get enough sleep to stay mentally alert, enough counseling to stay emotionally stable, and enough fiber in his diet to stay regular. Needless to say, the actual implementation of these directives fell far short of the ideal.

For example, rather than building and blowing up bridges, the most valuable skill I learned in training was how to smoke a cigarette undetected. I had plenty of instructors for this task, as everyone from the Drill Sergeants to the other soldiers were eager to share their techniques; the Drills because they didn't want to go through the trouble of processing paperwork in order to punish someone for such a minor infraction (most of the Drills were, themselves, chain-smokers), and the other soldiers because everyone felt more at ease if they were breaking the same rules as everyone else.

Smoking cigarettes was like many things in Basic Training. Officially no one condoned it, but in the routine of day-to-day life it was a common occurrence. The important thing about forbidden activities was not to get caught. Beneath all of the military rhetoric espousing discipline and order-following there lay a subtext saying that what you got away with was to the credit of your personal ingenuity. It should come as no surprise then that the soldiers who were held in the highest esteem by the Drill Sergeants were also those who were the best at avoiding detection while engaged in rule-breaking behavior.

A case in point was a certain fellow who was put in charge of our platoon. I remember one night, just as I was getting off guard duty, seeing him stumble down the barracks hallway, lean face-first into the wall, and proceed to urinate on the floor. It turns out that this disciplined centurion had snuck a bottle of booze in and was more than just sleepy and disoriented. The next morning the puddle was gone and "Mr. Platoon Leader" was still at the front of our formation. To some this may have seemed unfair, but in actuality the personal characteristics that make a good rule-breaker also make a good soldier. Ironically, those who have enough self-confidence, bravado, and nerve to piss in the barracks hallway at 0200 hours may also be the ones who possess the pluck to lead men into battle. (The behavior of many politicians might also be explained thusly.)

Every red-blooded American who joins the Army is there because he wants to play with cool "toys." Forget all of the patriotic hype and macho posturing. That's just a cover for the less honorable motivations that compel young men to give up their civilian freedoms to be yelled at, berated, and abused by oversized, foul-mouthed sergeants who dress like militant park rangers. The fact is that you join the military in order to shoot guns, drive big vehicles in places where it would be otherwise illegal, and to blow things up. Combat Engineer School gives you the opportunity to do all of these things. The only problem is that it is in extremely small doses.

Out of four months of training at Leonard Wood we had four days of demolitions instruction. Once I got to my reserve unit and had been there for four years, the number of days spent on demo totaled exactly zero. Somewhere, it seems, my recruiter had received faulty information about the supposed comprehensiveness of this training. Regardless, what hands-on training we did get was big fun. The instruction was mostly about how to detonate C-4 (composition 4) and TNT (trinitrotoluene) electrically and non-electrically. The payoff to the hours of preparation is, of course, the moment when the explosives go off and a weird mixture of fear, excitement, and exhilaration pulses through you. The amount of energy released from those little blocks of C-4, which look as harmless as bars of Ivory soap, is enough controlled chaos to provoke jubilance in the heart of any "normal" human being. Sure, there were a couple of guys in our platoon who didn't want to handle any of the explosives, but I didn't trust them. They were obviously unnatural examples of manhood.

I have touched the hand of God (or whatever supreme, divine force you like—Buddha, Allah, Yahweh, the God-

dess, Bob) three times in my Army career. The first was when we detonated the C-4 and TNT. The second was the first time I fired the M-60 machine gun. The third occurred once I had been at my reserve unit for a couple of years. This last religious experience was the result of firing the 90-mm recoilless rifle.

The 90 is a tube about five feet long that fires shells that are as long as your forearm and as big around as those bolognas you see hanging from the ceilings in meat markets. The projectile itself is a shaped demolitions charge that explodes when it hits its target. It is primarily used as an anti-tank weapon, though I've read that American forces used them extensively in Panama to blow holes in the sides of buildings. When used against a tank, the shaped charge hits the target and burns a hole through the armor, spraying molten metal into the crew compartment. The soldiers inside either abandon ship or get electrocuted.

When you pull the trigger on this weapon, everything stops. Your body becomes pleasantly numb, you're slightly disoriented, and you can't remember what day it is. This is a direct result of the tremendous concussion that rocks your world when the round goes off. You see nothing but smoke and dust for a couple of seconds but, incredibly, there is no recoil due to the fact that a jet of flame shoots to the rear and counterbalances the force going forward. Like an especially deadly fart, everyone avoids this back-blast area and its unpleasant potential.

Funny enough, the least exciting thing about firing the 90 is actually hitting your target. Sure there's an explosion upon impact, but it is nothing like the visceral, bone-jarring thunder of simply pulling the trigger. As with many adventures, accomplishing the intended goal is less fun than the things you do to get there.

Now, I don't want you to get the wrong impression. Most of the time you're on duty in the Reserves is spent standing around, cleaning up after other people, standing around some more, digging holes, standing around, putting up and taking down tents, and standing around. For this the hourly wage works out to somewhere around 17 cents (another example of how the government need not adhere to the laws it makes for others). But the U.S. can't even afford this. Our unit, along with many others around the nation, is slated for closure by the end of the year. This development will cause just enough of a financial strain on me that I'll have to go looking for another job. I wonder if there are many part-time openings in the civilian sector for someone with demolitions experience on his résumé?

Having shitty jobs is like a rite of passage; that is, unless you do it your entire life. Digging ditches, laying down railroad tracks, driving forklifts, unloading ships. Whether you think they're good or bad, some kinds of jobs seem to be vanishing off the face of the earth.

In 1979, David Greenberger started working as the recreational director for the Duplex Nursing Home, a care facility for the aged. To keep their minds occupied and elastic, he started asking the elderly residents questions about everything from pop music to advice for children. He published their unusual responses in a zine he dubbed *The Duplex Planet.* Times have changed, the original Duplex Nursing home closed, but David continues his work in several Boston-area nursing homes and elder-care centers in New York State. Sometimes confusingly funny, other times surprisingly insightful, these stories and comments show the complex relationship between old age and wisdom.

These selections were taken from issue #127, where David asked the crew "What's the worst job you ever had." If there's one thing you can learn from reading this, it is that times may change but work has always sucked.

THE DUPLEX PLANET

The worst job I ever had
was putting a piece of tape
on each of these covers.

127

JOHN **J**OYCE: The worst job, let me see . . . (whistles). I was in a position where I had to pick some lousy jobs, some second-rate jobs. Let's see . . . an onion picker up at Bridgewater. That was a lousy job. And picking up stones, fixing up the land so they can plant. That was lousy. I suppose therapeutically they thought it was good for me. I was young, I was full of water and vinegar—I don't cuss, you know what I mean.

And working on the railroad as a gandy dancer was a lousy job. It's a job that the native town men do. They call in men from the town to overhaul the railroad and set up camp for 'em.

But at the time I never looked at them as lousy. I never had a job problem. I had a lot of good jobs, too, you know. Bellhop, medical worker, nurse's assistant. Salesman in my own way—you know, door-to-door.

One part of the job was lousy: when it would rain on the railroad, you'd never get out of it. You're not to get out of the rain until they blow the whistle. You get paid for it, of course. And if the rain'd slow down to what they'd call spittin', they'd still have you working.

EVERETT **B**OSWORTH: Pick and shovel, I guess. I did it

six months, I guess. You've got to hold your back all the time. Good pay, but you're breakin' your back.

WILLIAM "**F**ERGIE" **F**ERGUSON: The worst job is the best job: taking care of children. I love taking care of children. And the children all love me, because I play with them. I mean, I see that they are entertained.

JOHN **F**AY: Diggin' graves, Mount Hope Cemetery. I did it for about a year. One thing though, Dave, nobody would talk back, no matter what you said! That's before they had those big machines. We did it by diggin' by hand.

ETHEL **S**WEET: Driving a forklift during the war. It was dangerous. I remember all the tent poles came down and if I hadn't'a had that thing on top I'd'a been dead. The army used to use those tents and we worked in the warehouse. The women had to do the men's jobs and I was stackin' those tent poles and I was puttin' 'em up and if you just didn't get 'em right, you know, I mean just that much off they would tip and they would come down. If it wasn't for the cage over top of me it would've killed me.

DBG: How long did you have that job?

ETHEL: Oh, about six months. It was just to relieve the boys who was at war. It was 4-Fs or women. At the forklift you met a lot of nice people, nice girls, and everything

[W O R K] 153

else, but it was hard work, it wasn't funny. It's a good thing when you're young, 'cause those things ain't easy to drive, takes a lot of muscles.

MILDRED MAKOFSKI: I never had any bad jobs. Maybe I was lucky, I always worked in offices because I liked to work there and enjoyed it. What I considered work was when I was a kid and I used to have to pick peas and beans and so on. By the time I got through picking them, why then I had to go in the kitchen and help my mother wash and cut and can them. And that was a lot of work! As soon as I got home from school I had to get in my work clothes and help my mother. I considered that work.

HERBERT WILSON: Sittin' down.

DBG: Sittin' down? That's not so bad.

HERBERT: (whispers) On account of I got *hemm-roids*.

GEORGE VROOMAN: In what sense? In employment?

DBG: Yes, the job you had that was the worst one.

GEORGE: Cleaning the back house, in the country, on my uncle's farm.

DBG: What was in it?

GEORGE: Manure! (laughs)

JOHN FALLON: Workin' for the First National. Twenty-five cents an hour for forty hours, fifty hours. Grocery store. I waited on people and loaded the shelves. The pay was the bad part, the work wasn't bad, you met a lot of people. I got a better job and quit. I got into the General Electric in Lynn. They paid twenty-eight and then went up to thirty and thirty-five.

BILL SEARS: Cabinet making. You have to lift cases—you'd catch your fingers. I broke a case—it slipped off the truck and I got fired. Max Star was the boss and the owner; he fired me. I think that was unfair. He should have just forgot about it; it was an accident. Got paid twelve dollars a week. The Boston Showcase Company was the name of it, at Roxbury Crossing. That's about all.

ARTHUR LABRACK: I shouldn't have been a damn fool and gone into the army like I did. Look at me now—look at the condition I'm in. I should have stayed home and minded my father and mother. I was a chauffeur, I drove a truck for a chair factory. I had a professional chauffeur's license. One time I stopped by a hydrant and got pinched. I

said to myself, "There goes my license." I said I had to speed up to get there. I thought they were doing that just to get me, but they let me go—I kept my license, I speeded up.

ED VESHECCO: Oh! One time I had to dig out a septic tank, me and another fellow. The guy that hired us told us it would take one day, but it took two, and that was really the worst part of it. It was pretty bad the first day—we had high boots on and everything, but stuff was getting over the tops of 'em and dribbling down to our feet. That was bad, but the worst part was going home, getting all scrubbed clean and knowing I had to go back the next day and get shit all over me again! Which I did! (laughs) The worst!

ABE SURGECOFF: Well, I want to tell you something. I went into the service and they gave me twenty-one dollars a month and I couldn't afford that, and I had to take some money from other sources. I couldn't bank it because the rate is small—they wanted fifty or sixty dollars a month. And, ah, we didn't like our chow. They had KP. I almost got into doing it, but I didn't have to do it—I excused myself from doing it.

Well, I'll tell you something. I worked in the kitchen and that paid twenty-one dollars, too. And, ah, I was with the chronical soldiers, chronical persons. Then afterwards they gave me his clothes—it was a fellow that didn't need to put on the clothes. The lieutenant and the major told me you can't wear no booties. Do you know what that is? It's high boots. Then they, after a while, gave me leggings—legging shoes.

We had to take care of the latrine. And we had to call out the soldiers from their bunks for review. Everybody got juiced up and got punished for it. I wasn't drinking. I drank water and coffee and salad. And tea.

Now, I want to tell you something. We were restricted to the barracks for account of the medicine they gave me put everybody into quarantine. There was an epidemic of double pneumonia. You had to wait outside the infirmary for them to take care of you when I had a high tempera-ture. This guy, well, he went out and got punished for it. He was caught by the MPs and they had a court trial with him. They had to be separated in the barracks during the court trial. It turned out favorable and not favorable, because the general—or it could have been a lieutenant—they executed the trial—you have a right to pick a lieu-tenant or a general. And since they took care of it, it could be called either good behavior or bad behavior. If it's bad behavior you get locked up. And if it's good behavior you're allowed free. It goes on more, but I'll give you some more next time.

TALES FROM THE SCRYPT
•
By **Kim Perkins** *from*
Probable Cause

Some people have found dreaded jobs like dishwasher or waiter to be their ticket to freedom. Others have found out how easily so-called dream jobs, like getting paid to play video games or to read books all the time, can turn into a nightmare. Kim Perkins found that to be the case when she took a job as submissions editor for a major book publishing house. Getting paid to read books may sound ideal, but when you're getting paid *per book,* and practically no book you're getting paid for is even worth reading —well, that's another thing entirely. In a past issue of *Probable Cause,* Kim Perkins described what it was like to face every day with a slush pile of unpublishable manuscripts that rarely offer up the slightest morsel of wisdom. It was a dreadful job that almost destroyed her ability to enjoy reading.

Described as "a literary review," *Probable Cause* was hardly your typical literary journal. It was almost an anti-literary journal, especially considering the tagline "No bad poetry or your money back." Though no longer being published, *Probable Cause* featured insightful articles that explored the world of contemporary literature from a somewhat cynical attitude. Each issue featured historical research, modern cultural analyses, and insightful interviews with leading authors.

With the list of publishing houses that accept unsolicited manuscripts growing shorter and shorter, it is almost impossible for first-time authors to break into publishing. But hey, look at the bright side: according to Kim, Random House bought two slush manuscripts over the past twenty years—they're probably about ready for their third.

For several years I was the submissions editor for a major New York publishing house. Though the title got me invited to many cocktail parties, the work itself was less than glamorous. I was a decoy, hired to divert the attention of hopeful writers away from the real source of power. While the senior editors lunched with the likes of Stephen King, T. C. Boyle, and Mary Higgins Clark, I sat in the Ukrainian coffee shop across the street, combing through a vast pile of unsolicited manuscripts—commonly known as the slush pile—in search of something publishable. During my career I read hundreds of murder mysteries, thrillers, "women's" novels, self-help books, genre romances, screenplays, cookbooks, sex manuals, and (I calculated it once) 26,000 children's books.

Not one of these was ever published.

Plenty of people make money reading books. It's considered a very junior job, and all editors start out that way, facing the slush pile with orders to find something worth saving.

I found plenty that was worth saving. It just wasn't what the editors had in mind. The stories were, for the

Earn Money Reading Books!
$30,000/year
Income Potential.

most part, ill-conceived and inexpertly written. But the people who wrote them were priceless.

Though I tried to adopt the editors' tastes, I found myself enjoying the "bad" stories more than the good ones. They certainly were more original. There was "The Doomsday Nine," "a post-nuclear war baseball story," and "The Booger Book," an explicit encyclopedia of every third-grade boy's favorite subject. If we could have overcome our grown-up prejudices, it probably would have made a mint.

It may not be entirely ethical, but I began saving copies

of my favorite unpublishable stories. This passage comes from the children's story "A Friend for Axe." It's ostensibly about Bob, Mrs. Hubbard's new handyman, and the fine way he handles the farm implements, but you get the feeling that the author had Bob's skill with a different tool in mind: "Axe stiffened for the collision of steel and wood and slipped in to make the split. Bob was all Axe could ever have asked for. His grip was firm, over and over again: chunk up, strong swing, downward thrust, split." Move over, Jackie Collins.

Most depressing were the people who spent more time on marketing than on writing. A huge proportion of the cover letters began, "With all the talk about family values," or recycling, or the president's distaste for broccoli, or whatever was the news that month. But one writer took shameless marketing to new heights. One day the *Wall Street Journal* ran a front-page article on the children's book slush pile, in which an editor at another house sneered at some stories that didn't make it, including "Seymour, the Ice Cube Who Wanted to Be a Cowboy" and another, less noteworthy story. I don't remember the story, but I do remember the call from a woman who said we should buy her story because it made the front page of the *Wall Street Journal.*

Sometimes I found stories that were almost publishable. I wrote up little reports and talked them up to various editors, who would always return them in a week with excuses that sounded as lame to me as they must have to the authors. Other stories weren't good enough to be published, but showed that the authors had some talent. These authors I was allowed to encourage, but was cautioned that too much encouragement would make them follow me around like a lost dog, calling me up all the time and sending me more and more unpublishable manuscripts.

That's not quite what happened with Doug Johnson,

but he did cause me some embarrassment. The story he sent me was not finished enough for my company, but I had scrawled some rather extravagant praise on the bottom of his rejection letter, comparing his brand of humor to some of the biggest names on our list. Naturally enough, he wrote back, dropping all these names and mine, and the letter fell into a more senior editor's hands. I was rebuked for giving him more encouragement than he deserved, for the editor expected to be inundated with dreck as a result, and I walked away wondering if my brain had gone so fizzy from reading wretched stories that a semi-passable work would look like gold to me.

As it turns out, I was in good company. Senior editors at Holt and Atheneum were feeding Johnson praise at the same time. When I ran across him again he had three books out with major houses, all selling well and receiving good reviews in important journals. When we spoke, he said he had called the company to find me, not to pitch me manuscripts but to thank me for the early encouragement.

Karen Ackerman was another success story. I never had any personal contact with her, but I rejected a story of hers nearly every month. This year, she won the Caldecott Award.

Sometimes success with a publisher isn't so sweet. One woman's extremely amateurish manuscript came in with a copy of an "acceptance letter" from a well-known vanity publisher as a testimony to her story's literary merit. Everyone I showed it to was appalled. The letter was designed to flatter the would-be author into paying the company thousands of dollars in return for publishing and promotion.

The turgid pitch, supposedly containing excerpts from reader's reports, tried the same ultra-general flim-flammery as a newspaper astrology column: "The author is to be commended for respecting the budding intelligence

of small children, for she draws the reader into an enjoyable experience. (Our editor will correct minor errors in spelling and punctuation.)" It went on to glamorize the packaging process ("printed monochromatically on quality paper with ample margins and stylized typography") and fan the author's hopes for fortune and fame ("bookstores will be contacted and reading copies rushed to major distributors for larger orders; personal interviews and autograph parties will be arranged wherever possible").

I have seen the shoddy books and cattle-call ads the company produces, and for all the respect and acumen you are supposedly buying, it would be cheaper and just as effective to get yourself a ditto machine and tape your manuscripts to lampposts. So we got together and wrote to her, warning her that vanity presses were a big rip-off, but—sorry!—the story was not right for our list, either.

Reading six hours a day, especially when the prose is taxingly clumsy, takes a huge toll on your brain. But there are ways of saving brainpower, such as speed reading and reducing the workload. Since I was paid by the piece, to avoid sacrificing income I made a rule of reading only until I was sure I didn't want to buy it. Which makes a person rather uncharitable, because when dismissing a story brings you that much closer to rollerblading, liking a story means you have to finish the book, write a report, and follow up before you can rest your weary brain. Certainly one would prefer to think oneself as nobler than that, especially when one is so vital to the process of discovering genius, but continued immersion in stories like "Drummy Drumstick and the Mean Fruities of Playland" dampens one's hopes of finding any. If the coin comes up tails 10,000 times in a row, it's hard to have faith that the next time it will come up heads.

My mind was closing, and the bad habits were leaking into my personal reading, too. "I feel like a teacher of magic who no longer has the pleasure of being deceived," I whined to my diary, demonstrating the unpleasant effect all that purple prose was having on my writing style. I knew it was time to quit when I speed-read part of *Finnegans Wake* in a bookstore and sneered to a friend that it was vastly overrated.

Good-bye, slush pile. I felt bad that I had no grand achievements to take with me. But I did get something good to keep: my favorite children's story of all time, "The Story of Wilhelmina, the Suicidal Worm." It came in the first packet of stories I ever reviewed. I thought they were all going to be like this, so I didn't bother to make a copy or record the names, much less praise the author (one Dorothy of Pennsylvania), so what follows is my paraphrase:

Francis, an elf, was in love with Wilhelmina, a worm. But all was not well; Wilhelmina was perpetually depressed, suffering from an irrational fear of whales. Francis, wishing to cheer her up, sought out Mythius, the God of All Things, to ask if he might grant her Eternal Life, which Francis figured ought to pull her out of the doldrums. Replied Mythius, "Did you ask her if she wants Eternal Life?" Francis admitted he hadn't, so he and Mythius went off to look for her. But Wilhelmina was missing. They searched high and low, but no Wilhelmina. Finally, they found her, broken in two by the side of the road—misery had made her throw herself under the wheels of a passing truck. Seeing the elf's distress, Mythius rejuvenated the worm's lower half. When Wilhelmina returned to life, she had no memory of her torment, since all her troubles had resided in her head. And so, Wilhelmina and Francis lived happily ever after.

Love, psychosis death, redemption: what a story. I've told it countless times in the six years I've known it, and rarely has it failed to delight. So, unlike most unpublished manuscripts, Dorothy's story did not go gently into that good night—I would bet it has spread as much joy as many a published book. And isn't the sharing of pleasure the root of the craving to read, the urge to write?

Of course, Dorothy might not see it that way. She might be holding out for a contract.

The big houses, 20 or so New York–based conglomerates, publish 75 percent of the 25,000 or so new trade books coming out every year, and it's been estimated that agents provide 95 percent of the material these houses put into print.

Editors like working with agents. A good agent will have plenty of editorial acumen, tell you whether a potential author is a sweetie pie or a major lunatic, weigh changes in the industry, and take you out to lunch at the Union Square Cafe.

The slush pile doesn't do that. That's why editors hate the slush pile.

food

While there's a smorgasbord of magazines on the newsstand about food, small-circulation food zines are a rare delicacy. These occasional publications are difficult to find and offer a unique perspective, more akin to your mother's home kitchen than that of Martha Stewart.

If you know where to look, you might come across a cornucopia of food-oriented newsletters, but many of these are boring affairs offering plenty of recipes, but none of the personality and character associated with zines. Some of them might even be published by large food corporations, with every recipe requiring a dollop of their brand of hot sauce, mayonnaise, or salsa.

Most food zines explore topics that are just a bit more down-to-earth than those found in magazines like *Gourmet* and offer a little more whimsy than most mass-produced food newsletters.

People write from a more personal perspective, so you'll find things like childhood memories of eating, tales of successful kitchen experiments, and tips for eating well on a tight budget.

Another key difference from the glossy mass-market food magazines is the type of recipes you'll find in zines. Instead of impossible-to-make desserts, food zines offer recipes for dishes that are healthy, familiar, and easy enough for a mere mortal to prepare.

THE SETH FRIEDMAN METHOD

•

By R. Seth Friedman from

Food for Thought

Back in 1990, when Mike Gunderloy was still publishing *Factsheet Five*, I started up my first zine, intending to carve out my niche on the zine landscape. Inspired by the many personal zines I read and my friends' praise for my cooking, I started up a zine that told tales of my life, acted as a forum for my political rants, and featured my own recipes.

This personal/political/food zine was not my first literary endeavor, but it did represent a sort of turning point for me. It was a couple of years later, about the same time that I published my third (and final) issue of *Food for Thought*, that I decided to restart *Factsheet Five*. In 1992, I published my first issue of *Factsheet Five*, which featured a story (and recipe) slated for inclusion in the never-finished fourth issue of *Food for Thought*.

While the piece included here is a little dated (written in 1991, it's one of the oldest pieces in this book), it reveals a lot about your not-so-humble editor and his attitudes about life. It was taken from the second issue of *Food for Thought* and contains a recipe that was perfected during my extended period of unemployment. I haven't prepared this dish in a while, and I don't think I would necessarily recommend it now, but it's amusing for me to see how much my style of cooking has changed over the years.

I hope you enjoy this piece. It was created during the downsizing of the 1990s that left thousands without jobs. Now the economy seems to be improving. Many of those who lost their jobs have found new ones—of course, for much less money than they were probably previously making. I hope this essay will better prepare you if you find yourself in a similar situation. I can now say with full assuredness, "Losing my job back in 1991 was the best thing that ever happened to me."

The '80s are completely over. The recession is in full swing. Corporate profits are down, wages are being cut, and many people, myself included, have lost their jobs. Most people would probably be devastated by losing their jobs. This is seen, time and time again, in the movies and on TV. A person loses his job, his home, his family. It's all very sad, but I'm still unsure how people really respond to losing their jobs. I'm sure it's difficult. Most people don't have much in savings and they owe tremendous amounts of money on their car, their home, and credit cards. For many people, the loss of their jobs would ruin their lives.

There are other reasons people fear the loss of their jobs. Too many to get into here—and I still owe you a recipe. People always say that they wouldn't know what to do with themselves if they lost their jobs. Some people's biggest fear is that of boredom. It's probably sufficient to simply point out all those people who win the lottery and still keep their jobs as janitors.

I was talking to my friend Bob, and we agreed that we are both happier when we're unemployed, broke, and hungry. We now have (or had, in my case) all those responsibilities that go along with high-paying jobs. The only things the money seemed to provide was an ability to buy things and to eat dinner in fancy restaurants. In actuality, there isn't a whole hell of a lot that I want to buy, and besides, I can make great meals at home for just pennies a serving. (Well, maybe a couple of bucks a serving.) If you sit patient and read the rest of the story, I'll tell you how to do it, too.

Initially, after losing my job (fired, terminated, canned, booted) I felt a sense of loss and rejection. It's difficult not to feel this way. I'm not sure why—I *hated* that fuckin' job and was dying to leave. Most of those negative feelings were relieved after I applied for unemployment and realized I would be getting $1,040 a month for doing *squat*.

I think being fired was the best thing that could happen to me. I got out of my miserable job, and I'm still getting a decent income. My friend Joyce is jealous of my being fired. She hates her job and wants to leave it. She is currently going to school, and if she was fired, she would have more time for her studies and still have a decent income. Of course, it runs out after six months, and I'll probably get a new job, but I'll worry about that when the time comes. An important thing to remember is that your standard of living changes drastically when you lose your job. I was spending more than a thousand dollars a month on miscellaneous things like CDs, beer, and eating in restaurants. Most of my expenses have been significantly reduced, or completely eliminated since then. I don't buy any books, CDs, or other stuff anymore (well, almost). I used to eat out almost every night, now it's only once a week. My commuting and dry cleaning expenses were completely eliminated, too.

I often tell people "Having to choose between having lots of money to buy stuff, but being required to work hard to get it, is a very difficult decision." They think the only reason for living is to make money and buy stuff. Others, like my brother David, think the only reason is to make money and keep it.

Some people think that I shouldn't be wasting my time. They say time is precious and should be seized. I wholeheartedly agree. Unfortunately, I feel like I've wasted the past few years working. The only things I have to show for it are some money and a résumé. Not the most important things to me.

Lots of interesting things have happened to me since I lost my job. My life has become much more about living. I write letters to friends, clean my apartment, and do my own laundry. I shop for food, take it home, cook it, and then eat it. I talk to my friends on the phone, but unfortunately they are always too busy to see me. They still have jobs.

People in New York are always too busy. They work constantly, and when they aren't working, they're entertaining clients or going out with the guys from work. People are so busy they need to hire other people to run their lives for them. They hire people to shop, cook, clean, and run errands. They forget that life is about living. That life is about cooking food, drinking wine, joking with friends, dancing to music, and fucking. Couples in New York have to make an appointment to fuck.

Lots of changes have also occurred in my mental state. I feel as if I've reclaimed my dreams. Whenever I worked, I would always dream about my job. It got so bad that I wouldn't dream about the office and people, but the ideas and processes involved in performing my job. Since I worked with computers, I would dream about them, not in the physical sense, but conceptually. For a while, though, I was going crazy. Now I once again have dreams that are about people and places that I loved in the past and I hope will love in the future. I used to shut out my dreams and try to forget them right away. Now I look forward to them and savor them.

I don't use an alarm clock anymore. No, I don't sleep all day. I go to sleep around 1 A.M. and usually get up around 8:30. Sleeping should be controlled by your body, not some plastic box made in Japan.

Insomnia, high blood pressure, stress management, ulcers, and heart attacks—I have trouble remembering what these things meant. So many people I know have work-related health problems. They all have several things in common: they "love" their jobs, they make *mega* bucks, and they work about *seventy* hours a week. My friends are always telling me how much they love their work. They may love their work, but it doesn't love them.

So now I start the day by reading the paper, then I clean the apartment a bit. Then I do some writing, answer some correspondence, take care of the zine business. Later on, I usually do some food shopping before making dinner. I once read a statistic that said people, on the average, spend several hours a week on a single weekly shopping trip. That completely shocked me. I go food shopping practically *every day*. I don't get very much, usually some fresh bread, pasta, cheese, or veggies. Bread is the most important staple in my diet. I love fresh bread, and I can't stand eating it if it's more than a day old. I can't understand how people can go food shopping only once a week, unless they eat dinner only once a week.

Of course, with the privilege of time to prepare proper meals comes the responsibility of preparing economical meals. When I was in college, everyone ate cheap. This was because everyone was broke. Since becoming unemployed, I've had to dig into the past and come up with some economical cooking ideas from my college days.

Beans are a really great food item. They're quite delicious, nutritious, and (best of all) inexpensive. Many people say they don't like beans, but I think the main reason they're so unpopular is because they're considered low-class peasant food. This is unfortunate. You don't have to be broke to enjoy them, but it sure helps.

Jalapeno peppers are a great complement to beans. They add color, texture, and flavor—and they don't have to be too hot and spicy. The heat in the peppers can easily be controlled or removed altogether. Start

by carefully removing the seeds from inside the pepper (don't forget to wash your hands after handling the seeds). Then by simply roasting, browning, or frying, the heat content can be reduced to any level desired. The high heat will remove the stuff that makes them hot.

You can serve these beans a hundred different ways. Serve them with chips as a dip. Smear 'em on chips and top with cheese and jalapenos, bake, and serve as nachos. Put some on bread with tomato sauce, salsa, and cheese, and bake to make a Mexican pizza. Put some in a soft corn tortilla, along with some cheese, roll it up. Then top with sauce and cheese and bake it to make delicious enchiladas.

Remember to make a big batch, because it keeps well and can easily be reheated in a microwave. Whatever you want it call it: "Chili," "Bean Dip," "Refried Beans," or my favorite, "Bean Stuff," I'm sure you'll love this versatile and delicious dish.

Bean Stuff

2 cans cooked red beans—about 3 cups
1 large onion—diced
2 jalapeno peppers—medium sized, sliced
4 cloves garlic—chopped
1 tablespoon ground cumin powder
1 tablespoon garam masala curry powder
1 tablespoon dried basil (or 2 tablespoons fresh)
1 teaspoon dried parsley (or 2 tablespoons fresh)
1 teaspoon dried oregano
³/₄ cup tomato sauce
¹/₂ cup water
1 teaspoon soy sauce or dark miso
1 teaspoon sesame oil
2 tablespoons oil for frying—safflower, peanut, or corn

Drain and rinse the beans and put them in a large bowl. Mash them using a potato masher or fork. Don't use a blender, because it's best for them to remain slightly lumpy. Take a large pot and fry the onions and jalapenos in the oil. Continue frying until the onions are tan and the peppers give off a bitter smell. This means that they are cooking and have lost some of their heat. Remove from stove, and then add the tomato sauce, spices, water, and soy sauce or miso. Return to a low heat and simmer, covered, for about 20 minutes. Then add the mashed beans and sesame oil, and slowly blend together. Continue cooking for another 5 to 10 minutes, occasionally stirring so that the beans don't stick to the bottom and burn. It's okay to add some water to thin out the beans, or leave uncovered to thicken them up. Serve with chips, rice, cheese, jalapenos, avocado—any way you want. They'll be delicious.

I LIVE FOR OLIVES

•

By **Jill Cornfield** *from*

Cooking on the Edge

Olives are peculiar things. Some people love 'em, some people hate 'em, but nearly everyone is crazy for the wonderful oil that that can be squeezed out of them. Olive trees are among the earliest known cultivated trees in the world. Primarily grown in the Mediterranean areas of France, Italy, Greece, and Israel, olives are also harvested in many parts of the U.S. It's relatively easy to prepare fresh olives you pick yourself, but most folks would prefer choosing from the more than twenty varieties available in stores.

As mentioned earlier, zines are about passion —and if there's one thing people get passionate about, it's food. Different foods bring out different passions in people, and Jill Cornfield, publisher of *Cooking on the Edge,* is passionate about olives. She's often written about olives in her zine, including the insight that generally women love 'em while men hate 'em. This time she reveals her evolving relationship with the olive spread, tapenade.

Salty food bad for you? Nonsense. Just look at the gallons of water you gulp after eating Greek olives. That's got to more than balance out the sodium boost.

Goodness only knows why tapenade has escaped this olive-lover's notice for so long, but now I'm in love. First had it at a friend's party, where she served up a little dish of it. Even though it has anchovies in it, and I don't like anchovies, I liked this. In fact, I may now like anchovies.

Both M.F.K. Fisher and Elizabeth David note that tapenade tastes as old as time, like something the Romans would have eaten. ("An ancient powerful flavor," says Elizabeth David in *French Provincial Cooking.)* But tastes can be deceiving: tapenade is a nineteenth-century creation, although probably based on an older existing sauce, she points out.

There are a few variable ingredients—mustard, tuna fish, brandy, or cognac—but what you really need for tapenade is olives, anchovies, and capers. Dijon mustard seems to temper the fishiness of the anchovies and tuna. Cognac adds a very sharp edge to the tapenade. I felt no need to add it after my first experiment with it.

In my opinion garlic is essential, even though some people (even venerable people—Elizabeth David among them) leave it out. Some people add raw egg yolks. I think that's unnecessary. Even if the tapenade weren't fattening enough, there's that salmonella deal to contend with.

I think tuna fish is a pointless addition. But anchovies, which I've been trying really hard to like, without much success, are key. Even if you think you don't like them, try tapenade with them. I use the oil-packed fillets you can buy in nearly any grocery store.

Lulu Peyraud, in *Lulu's Provencal Table,* by Richard Olney, has a very simple tapenade flavored with savory leaves (preferably fresh, but the author and chef grudgingly let you use dry). I'm probably still not making it exactly right, because they specify salt anchovies, a pinch of salt (which seems ridiculous in the face of those other salty ingredients), and a pinch of cayenne (which seems like a great touch, except that I just moved and haven't found my bottle of cayenne).

The amount of olive oil varies, naturally. I recommend following a recipe you like just a couple of times, so you get a feel for what tapenade is supposed to be, and how you like it. Then you can tailor your own, going up or down the olive oil scale, using less or more anchovy and so on.

It's fun to make tapenade by hand, without the food processor. In some ways it's easier: the capers tend to escape the blades and end up intact in the tapenade. But that's okay, too. It's really, really hard to make bad tapenade. Going the low-tech route requires some kind of mortar and pestle. I use a rock I bought in Mexico, and since I didn't feel like dragging back the mortar that went with it (since it weighed about 10 pounds), I just use a sturdy mixing bowl. Those ingredients will come together as you pound them. The first time's the hardest. A nice thing about tapenade: it stretches a few olives into a generous serving for a number of people. Sort of an "Olive Helper."

Eat tapenade on any kind of bland cracker. Little slices of baguette or cold sliced boiled potato are sublime substrates.

When you get home from work, pour yourself a glass of something. I recommend Lillet, a French aperitif. It's wise to cut its sweetness with a bit of orange rind. Arrange crackers or even a slice of whole wheat bread, cut into fingers, and a little dish of tapenade on a pretty tray. Sit where you can watch the sunset—a perfect backdrop for a perfect hors d'oeuvre.

Some food quote I read long ago pointed out the distinction between an epicure and a gourmet. Rather than fancy dishes with lots of fuss and bother, the true epicure is the one who appreciates the simplicity of a few olives and a crust of bread. I think the true epicure would insist on those olives being made into tapenade.

If you like, you can add something to the following tapenade: a few drops of cognac, a couple of dabs of mustard, a squeeze of lemon juice. But this is your basic tapenade, with only the essentials, and it's fabulous.

Basic Tapenade

1 cup olives
2 tablespoons capers
2 cloves garlic
2 anchovy fillets
1 tablespoon olive oil
Dash of black pepper

1. In food processor, pulse a few times till the olives, capers, garlic, and anchovies are roughly crushed, but not completely pureed.
2. Add the olive oil and pepper and pulse just once or twice more.

Martha Stewart is a one-woman cultural revolution. Through her successful TV shows, magazines, books, newspaper columns, and other flotsam, she creates an image of home life that could only be accomplished if you have as much money and as many servants as she does. Her image of perfection is so appealing that she's developed a cult following that verges on religious devotion.

GIVING THANKS FOR WHAT YOU DON'T HAVE

●

By **Dan Goldberg** *from*
Curmudgeon's Home Companion

While this might bode well for the folks at Time Warner, most folks just struggle to keep their milk from going sour, the dirty dishes from piling too high in the sink. We all enjoy a bit of fantasy now and then, but it's a portrait of real life that you'll most likely find in zines.

The Curmudgeon's Home Companion is like many other food newsletters. Each monthly issue features a bounty of recipes and useful cooking tips. What makes it stand out from the crowd is Dan Goldberg and his cynical attitude toward picky eaters, health Nazis, pretentious restaurants, and the sobriety movement. In addition to all his advice, Dan also includes cantankerous rants that blast away at the frustrations of modern living.

Holidays are a time of great stress for most people. Thanksgiving and Christmas top the list with their unpleasant family reunions and general hysteria about food. Everyone talks about how much they *love* the holidays, but privately most people probably dread it all.

In November '93, Dan composed this personal confession that reveals his feelings about Thanksgiving. No Martha Stewart pumpkin soufflé, no extended families holding hands in unity, just messy kitchens and family squabbles. The only thing to be thankful for is when the whole thing is finally over.

No matter how good a cook you are, magazine photos of perfect golden-brown turkeys, crimson cranberries, and yellow-orange yams put a real-life Thanksgiving to shame. Just look at the pictures. There's no wine spilled on the damask tablecloth, no gravy on the rim of the serving bowls. There aren't even any dirty pots. The stove that produced this feast is spotless, unsullied by so much as a single grease spot, and the kitchen is bigger than my whole house.

The people in the pictures are as perfect as the food. Nobody in the pictures is fat, ugly, handicapped, or drunk. Nobody has a cranberry-sauce stain down the front of her pants. The children, toddlers to teens, are happy and remarkably well-mannered. There are no cross words. The cook doesn't even need to wear an apron, unless it's planned as part of his outfit.

What Thanksgiving means in real life is rather different. It means fending off invitations from relatives who got me to their house one year and served a frozen turkey that had cooked up into something as woody as a lumberyard and as dry as Betty Ford, and bragged about how much money they saved by using the cheapest brand of packaged stuffing while I tried to gag down a polite amount of a freezer-burned supermarket pie. It means coming up with an excuse not to go to the house of another relative whose idea of Thanksgiving entertaining is buying "lite" frozen turkey dinners and letting everyone nuke his own.

It means doing the whole meal myself, so at least it will taste good, using nearly every pot in the kitchen, and then having my wife and children refuse to help clean up because the mess is all my fault. It means providing recipes, moral support, and a 24-hour telephone hotline so that the guests who insist they must make something because they feel guilty about sponging off us year after year don't bring the kind of slop they normally cook for themselves.

It means making twice too much food for the crowd we've invited and then panicking and whipping up another 200,000 calories just in case. It means eating until I feel like I'm going to be sick, then going for a walk and coming back for more.

It means having the kids home for a five-day weekend long before we've recovered from the three-day Veterans Day holiday the week before and the four-day parent-teacher-conference no-school weekend the week before that. It means renting enough video games and videotapes to keep the kids in a stupor so they won't trash the house right in front of our glazed eyes while we sit paralyzed by the pressure from within.

It means sitting across the table from people I often think I'd only be truly pleased to see in a coffin. It means yet another futile attempt at tuning out the ceaseless prattle of brain-dead relatives. It means watching one member of the family run out of the room weeping over some ancient injustice inflicted on her before half the people at the table were born.

At times like this I like to imagine how our table would look if Norman Rockwell tried to paint it. (Something like a Francis Bacon, is my guess.) I also like to wonder what the original Pilgrims would make of the way we live now.

I'm not talking about the Jacuzzis, the video equipment, or the car telephones, but the food. While they made do with corn and turkey, we load our tables year-round with arugula, salmon, radicchio, kiwis, and God knows what. Even their wildest fantasies about food probably weren't as abundant and varied.

And what would the Pilgrims think if they could see all the melodrama that goes with this annual homage to them? My guess is that they'd be thankful they had so little. When you're not sure your meager supplies of corn are going to last for the winter, you don't spend much time hemorrhaging over whom Mom nursed longer forty-five years ago.

FIRST DINNER PARTIES, OR ENTERTAINING WITHOUT A NET

•

By **Catherine S. Vodrey** *from*

Convivium

The transition from college life to the "real world" is often a traumatic one. Not something you take in stride, it's a gradual change involving moving off the college campus, getting a job, and finding your own place to live. When I say gradual, I mean it—I have some friends who are still making the transition, ten years later.

For some people, the most difficult step in the process is getting a job; for others it's learning how to feed yourself. Some people leave home, graduate college, get their own apartment—all without ever learning to cook.

That wasn't Catherine's problem. As she reveals in this piece reprinted from her zine *Convivium,* she knew the basics of cooking, but was a bit *too* enthusiastic. Fresh out of college, she organized an elaborate dinner party for her friends. She bit off more than she could chew when she decided to roast a huge turkey.

Some people love to entertain. Others view it as the grimmest of tasks—the social equivalent of filling out an organ donor card. Depending on which view you subscribe to, I am either the most deluded of creatures or the happiest, because I enjoy having people over and cooking for them. My parents entertained frequently when I was growing up, and I guess I come by this predilection through their influence. I was unable to indulge it, however, until I had my own place—probably the most basic of essentials for embarking on the fevered life of the inveterate party-giver.

Shortly after I moved into my first post-college apartment, I was possessed with a desire to entertain my friends, many of whom were still living in college dormitory rooms with cheerless views and bad heating. As I had taken my apartment in the fall, I thought that a holiday party would be fitting. I would have over a month to plan, and the idea of having my first real dinner party during the year's most festive time appealed to me.

In keeping with the spirit of the party, I decided to serve a turkey. There would be side dishes, too, and drinks and some extravagant dessert, but the turkey is what will remain forever fixed in my mind. It was the first turkey I had ever attempted to cook on my own. My mother assured me that turkeys were the easiest things in the world to cook, and that people were only put off by them because of their size. Because my mother is a wonderful cook and because she is, well, my mother, I took her advice.

I began to shop for the party a week in advance. As I wandered through the grocery store like a lamb to the slaughter, I saw that only fresh turkeys were available. I had a vague memory of having heard from someone I trusted that you should cook a fresh turkey within twenty-four hours of buying it. Since several days yawned before me, I opted to wait and buy my turkey the very day of the party.

The party morning dawned crisp and bright. I set out for the grocery store in the afternoon with a song in my heart. I rounded the bend to the meat section, when what to my wondering eyes should appear but a Siberian expanse of frozen turkeys. Dread filled my heart as I read the defrosting directions on the packaging. I was lost! My menu would consist of a few lonely side dishes and some obscene dessert, lolling like a hussy on the barren table! My reputation as a hostess would be dashed to pieces before I had even established it! Numb, I picked up a turkey anyway and walked to the check-out line as to the gallows.

This bird was frozen through. Hope and youthful enthusiasm not completely deadened, I poked it a few times in the car on my way home, hoping to find some give beneath my fingers. When I got home, I reread the directions for thawing. Even the erroneously named "quick thaw" method would take hours, and involved filling and draining the sink with cool water at strict half-hour intervals.

With nothing on my mind but the salvation of my party's main course, I decided that *running* water might be more efficient at the job than simply allowing the turkey to wallow in a sink bath. I was fortunate enough to live in a building with terrific water pressure, so I put the turkey into the shower and turned on the water—warm, not cool, thereby encouraging the breeding of salmonella but assuredly saving my party.

This plan felt more active to me than the packaging's cautious recommendations, but it was not enough to make a noticeable difference in the turkey's texture. When I prodded it after about twenty minutes, it was still roughly the consistency of a slab of granite. There was only one course of action left to me, and I took it. I turned the water up to a comfortable bathing temperature, and the bird and I took a shower together—it in its plastic cloak, and I in shorts and a T-shirt. I had no pride; I had a dinner party staring me in the face, and I was hell-bent on serving that turkey.

I cradled it in my arms, rolling it back and forth, letting the water pound each side. About a million hours later, there seemed to be a substantial softening in the bird's texture. I rinsed it one last time, laid it on the bath mat and proceeded to finish my toilette.

My next step was to call a local fish and meat market to ask for advice on how to cook the bird at lightning speed (I did not, at the time, own a microwave). I babbled to the man who answered the telephone that I didn't have the four hours the package dictated. He said, "You got any tin foil there?"

"Somewhere around here."

"Crank the oven on up to 500 degrees, wrap the bird in loose foil, and roast the hell out of it for a couple of hours." He then told me to remove the foil for the last half-hour of cooking time to allow the turkey to brown, and let me go only after a dire warning about undercooked meat and poisoned dinner guests.

I am happy to say that this kind gentleman's advice worked, and that my guests and I feasted on the turkey by candlelight that evening. No one called me up the next day complaining of stomach pains, but it was a long time before I cooked another turkey.

**One of the strangest zines out there has got
to be** *Religion of the Month Club.* **So far 21
issues have been published, and each one has
obsessively explored a unique and different
subject. Past issues have reported on such
irreverent subjects as Holes, Shit, Dog, and
Marx-Lennon.** *Religion of the Month Club* **isn't
really about religion; that is, unless you define
religion simply as a devotional obsession—in
that case the title is perfect. The key to**
Religion of the Month Club **is how completely it
tackles each subject.**

**This piece is borrowed from their self-
proclaimed "Chicken" issue. Like prior editions,
this one explores every aspect of the subject
imaginable. In it you'll find lists of famous cartoon chickens, chickens that appeared in
movies, mentions of chickens in music, chicken
jokes, the bizarre cult of Colonel Sanders, and,
of course, lots of chicken recipes.**

**What tastes like chicken? I wouldn't know,
I've been a vegetarian for more than fifteen
years. (Though lots of folks
tell me that the fake chicken
—made from wheat gluten
and tofu—at my favorite
Chinese restaurant tastes**
exactly **like chicken.)**

And what about those famous words *"Tastes just like chicken"*? Who in the hell first uttered such an atrocious abomination? Whoever it was, must have been out of their gourd. For example, let's take a look at some of the foods (many of which are very tasty in their own right) that are compared to chicken. First we'll start off with some of the more obvious culinary delights and then we'll get into some of the more absurd.

1. *Duck.* No, I'm sorry, duck is much too gamy and greasy to be compared with its kinder, gentler cousin.

2. *Turkey.* While some people consider turkeys to be nothing more than really big, ugly chickens, the fact of the matter is that they act different, they smell different, and most important they TASTE different. I have been given a blind taste test on a few occasions to prove this very point and have unerringly picked out my favorite fowl, that is, the chicken, every time.

3. *Cornish game hen.* This is the one that gives even my finely tuned palate the most trouble. Let it suffice to say that if any other creature on this spinning ball of rock can be said to taste very close to chicken, this is the one.

4. *Pigeon.* Give me a break!

5. *Penguin.* I have to honestly say that I haven't tried this one yet.

6. *Whale.* Disgusting what some people will say to get you to believe it's OK to eat these gentle leviathans.

7. *Tuna.* I haven't been able to figure this one out myself!

8. *Rattlesnake.* Having eaten this particular delicacy I've got to say it has a very distinctive flavor, and while it is faintly reminiscent of chicken, I know for a fact that if somebody mixed up my order of fried chicken for an order of fried rattler I'd most assuredly know the difference.

9. *Steak.* NOT! Chicken fried or otherwise! *(The editor promises to never ever, allow use of the word "not" in such a manner again. We apologize for any inconvenience.)*

10. *Alligator.* From what I understand this particular critter tastes more like beef than chicken.

11. *Rabbit.* While it looks a little like chicken, when it's cooked it has a flavor that's all its own.

12. *Dog.* I don't think so!

13. *Cat.* Who knows? Not me, that's for sure! The only

way I'd eat a cat is if I was starving or it tried to eat me first. *(The editor thought about making some kind of comment about eating pussy, but decided to ignore the obvious.)*

14. *Horse.* Same as alligator.

15. *Squid.* Taste like octopus, cuttlefish, and other such critters.

16. *Shark.* I can't believe this one either! There is no way that a shark tastes anything like chicken. It's big, red slabs of fishy-tasting stuff.

17. *Buffalo and Beefalo.?*

18. *Bear.* Not as far as I know.

19. *Antelope, Deer, Elk, and others of this family.* Tastes like gamy beef.

20. *Pork.* With something as obviously different from chicken in aroma, consistency and texture, it's beyond comprehension that pig can be confused with chicken in the taste department!

21. *Squirrel.* Gamy, greasy and much tougher than chicken.

22. *Skunk.* Odorous to the point of nausea.

23. *Automobile parts.* If anyone has successfully consumed automobile parts, you're one up on me! As far as their tasting like chicken, most probably not.

24. *Elephant dick.* NO!

25. *Atoms.* Too small to taste or tell.

There are many other consumables that have been compared to the fine taste of chicken, but space and time considerations (not to be confused with the space-time continuum, but again I digress) force us to leave these out for possible inclusion in another edition of this magazine.

TOAST MODERNISM

•

By **Paul Lukas** *from*

Beer Frame

Paul Lukas's *Beer Frame* is by far one of the most popular zines out there. Propelled by his regular columns, Paul Lukas earned a veritable legion of devoted fans.

Most zines fill their pages with reviews of CDs from generous record companies; others take the high road and review books; almost every zine helps the community by reviewing other zines. Paul Lukas employs the grand tradition of reviewing, but adapts it to his own style by reviewing many common (and some not-so-common) products that have sprung forth from our vast consumer landscape.

He's got an incredible eye for uncovering the most unusual consumer products (and sometimes uncovering unusual aspects of very common products). His more memorable finds include kraut juice, described as smelling like a "cross between a malfunctioning septic tank and an overcrowded poultry farm." He also uncovered the final tally of the votes for the new M&M color. Blue tallied 54 percent, with purple getting 32 percent, and red 10 percent. Of course, no one realized that blue was added at the expense of replacing the tan M&Ms.

Recently he came across Pepperidge Farm's line of specially formulated "toasting breads." It's such a bizarre concept that only Paul Lukas could appropriately analyze what this means for the future of American society. Try this bread yourself, but don't eat it cold.

 our morning rituals may involve coffee, but mine center on toast. I don't know who first thought of heating a slice of bread until it got all brown and crispy (*Webster's* dates "toast" to the fifteenth century), but it sure was a fine idea. I just *love* toast—white toast, rye toast, raisin toast, wheat toast, toasted English muffins, toasted bagels—whatever. As a friend of mine once said—and I'm jealous not to have said it first—bread is just raw toast.

So you can understand how excited I was when Pepperidge Farm recently unveiled their Toasting Bread line. Imagine—bread specifically made for toasting! This sounded like the greatest thing since sli— uh, right. Still,

toast is a very personal matter—one person's almost-burnt is another's just-right, and you may discard the heel slice while I savor it most of all. Which factors would Pepperidge Farm consider when devising a toast-tailored loaf?

The main factor, as it turns out, is heft. A slice of Toasting Bread is much thicker than your average slice, one result of which is that there are only 10 Toasting Bread slices to a pound loaf, compared to 18 slices in a loaf of conventional Pepperidge Farm white. Or, to take a more cynical view, at the typical rate of two slices per breakfast, Toasting Bread will have you running back to the store for another loaf four days sooner.

Pepperidge Farm Corporate Communications Vice President Edie Anderson says it's a bit more complex than that, however. "Toasting Bread is a specially formulated product," she explained, "not just another bread sliced thick." Anderson said the firm's market research shows toast consumers are hankering for precisely what Toasting Bread offers: a thicker, denser slice that gets crunchier on the outside while staying squishy on the inside. When I asked if consumers were also allowed to use Toasting Bread for, say, making a sandwich, she said, "Absolutely—we don't mind at all." But in a moment of surprising candor, she later admitted that untoasted Toasting Bread "really doesn't have as full a flavor" as regular bread. She had fewer reservations when I asked if Toasting Bread was suitable for feeding to ducks.

Pepperidge Farm has been selling a 15-slice toasting version of their white bread since about 1970. But as one of their fact sheets puts it, the new Toasting Bread represents their big push "to compete for more of the breakfast eating occasion." The three initial varieties—white, wheat, and seven-grain—were test-marketed in the summer of 1995 and launched nationally later that year, and have now been joined by raisin-oat and cinnamon. The package wrapper and the firm's coupon advertising both attempt to liken the product to English muffins (which according to the fact sheet constitute a $381 million business and, as Anderson pointed out, "are used almost exclusively in toasted form"), but that isn't even a fair fight—Toasting Bread doesn't have enough textural variety to justify the comparison.

That said, Toasting Bread does make a decent batch of toast. I sometimes find it a bit *too* thick—two slices feel like more of an entrée than an appetizer—but the extra density is great for dunking, if you're so inclined. Try as I might to focus on this product's practical utility, however, I keep coming back to the larger implications. Specifically, what does it mean when manufacturers begin marketing this sort of extreme compartmentalization of function? As another acquaintance of mine remarked when she first heard of Toasting Bread, what'll they think of next—Sniffing Glue? (Pepperidge Farm, Inc., Norwalk, CT 06856.)

DESPERATION SNACKS

•

By **Mark Owens** *from*
Peaches & Herbicide

The great thing about zines by punks is that they're rarely only about music. Zines like *Peaches & Herbicide* are more about the whole punk lifestyle, with articles that run the gamut from travel and political rants to how-tos, pop culture, and food.

In Mark Owens's "Desperation Snacks," from issue #4 of *Peaches & Herbicide,* kids with empty larders but full imaginations make do with what they have. The results are less than appealing, but certainly amusing.

All of us have had a craving for something special at one time or another, only to go to the kitchen pantry and find that one critical ingredient is missing. Then, still intent on satisfying that hunger, we substitute the next closest thing, often using the most harebrained logic. Usually, the result is some rancid, inedible brew that just gets thrown away. What follows is a list of actual desperation snacks as related to me by family and friends.

In grade school, my roommate Charles had a fiending for grape Kool-Aid, but when looking for the sugar he found none. Instead he substituted the next best mixable sweeteners, honey and powdered sugar. Needless to say, powdered sugar and honey don't dissolve like our old friend sugar, and the mixture that resulted was closer to cough syrup than the cool refreshing beverage he longed for.

Another friend, Marshall, told me that once he developed an urgent need for chocolate pudding but found that he was out of milk. Ingeniously, he mixed up a batch of protein health shake using cold water and some month-old shake powder, reasoning that one milky-like substance was as good as another and the instant pudding wouldn't know the difference. The result, however, was a watery, far-from-pudding paste that tasted a lot like balsa wood.

My best friend used to come home from school during the summers dying for something sweet and cool, like fruit sherbet. The next best thing, he decided, was good old orange juice concentrate straight out of the can. Although the concentrate packed quite a wallop, he actually developed a taste for it while it slowly ate a hole through his stomach lining.

I myself used to have quite a fondness for Noodle Roni Fettucine Alfredo, which requires both $1/4$ cup milk and a

half stick of butter or margarine. Well, one day I was all ready for my Roni when I found out that we were out of margarine. Since the water and milk were already boiling (and my hunger was peaking) I acted fast, grabbing a large spoonful of Skippy Crunchy Peanut Butter and plopping it into the water. "Peanut Butter is a kind of butter," I thought. "It's sort of oily like butter; it should work fine." I was sadly mistaken, however. Peanut butter does not react well with dairy products, resulting in a lumpy-sweet noodle and sauce blend that was very unkind to the tongue.

fringe

What defines the fringes of society? Who's to argue that one particular essay represents an extreme viewpoint, while another is deemed "normal"? Some might say that zines themselves, that *all zines,* represent the fringes of society.

While I'm not in any position to define what's normal, some zines I come across seem a bit *too* emotional, explore ideas that are *way* off the beaten track, represent viewpoints that are *far* from any reasonable position on the political spectrum. It's these zines that we categorize as fringe.

Included here are several essays that you're unlikely to find anywhere else but in zines. Hardly more than a sampling of what's out there, we consciously avoided the more controversial subjects like Holocaust revisionism, white supremacy, Christian militia, or government conspiracies. These subjects and more can all be uncovered in zines.

When exploring the more extreme publications a few words of warning are in order: You may not agree with what some people have to say— especially their ideas about racial superiority or an imminent apocalypse. Some of the writing may be hard to read, especially the more convoluted theories. And finally, you may not want to give out your home address to some of these folks. Sometimes it's good to maintain a sense of privacy.

PLACES TO SHOOT, THINGS TO SHOOT

•

By **Hollister Kopp** *from*
Gun Fag Manifesto

The American militia movement has been getting a lot of attention these days. Thanks to the media-fueled frenzy, people are deathly afraid of gun-toting, fertilizer-hauling militiamen. Years back, before the words "Oklahoma City" conjured up anything more sinister than Rodgers and Hammerstein, self-proclaimed "gun fags" like Hollister Kopp fetishized guns for the sheer joy of it. Buying, trading, collecting, firing, and writing poetic tributes to their favorite semi-autos, these gun fags may or may not have particular political theories, but they're certainly more interested in Smith & Wesson than Bill & Hillary.

Hollister is interested in guns—not music or books or comics. So in his zine *Gun Fag Manifesto* he gets down and dirty and features comprehensive reviews of his favorite firearms. Of course, 52 pages of gun reviews might get kinda boring after a while (at least to *some* people), so along with all that is a smorgasbord of highly opinionated articles. Past issues have included such enlightening articles as an overview of the many different types of ammo and a tribute to the "Tank Guy" (the guy who stole a tank and went on a 22-minute joyride flattening 50 cars in San Diego). I'm most impressed by his in-your-face street language that doesn't pull any punches.

Are people like Mr. Kopp dangerous? Only if you cross them. You're more likely to get hit with a stray bullet in East L.A. than by Mr. Kopp, who does his shooting in the vast, desolate California desert. As he explains here, "Supervised ranges are for those who feel the need to be supervised." On second thought, it might be best to stay away from Mr. Kopp altogether; that is, unless you're another gun fag.

There was a time not so long ago, a healthier time, when man and gun went and did as they damned well pleased. A fella could step out onto his back porch and dispatch a pesky varmint with his trusty old "side b' side" or venture into the woods for weeks at a time, returning home with a harvest of deer, elk, and bear. We no longer live in a healthy time, and that varmint out by the back porch is not likely to be of the four-legged variety. But we still need to keep our shooting skills finely honed, and unfortunately we can't shoot like free men anymore. Here are a few guidelines to keep in mind:

Supervised ranges are for those who feel the need to be supervised. True gun fags, being men of *freedom*, do not fit into the category. We need to be where the deer and the antelope play (or at least to where *something* plays—scoring a hit on a moving target is much more challenging and satisfying than poking holes in paper). And add to this the sad fact that established ranges never allow us to exercise our constitutional right to DRINK BEER.

OUTDOOR RANGES. Just a mile or so up the road from the hallowed spot where that well-known punk got his ass whipped by the L.A.P.D.'s Foothill Division (they should have just shot the son of a bitch) is the Angeles Crest Shooting Range. They charge ten bucks to get in, with a $1 discount for NRA members. The place is all right if standing shoulder to shoulder with a bunch of armpit-smelling ragheads firing cheesy little .25 autos is something you consider fun. I personally am not allowed back into that range, since they kicked me out for drinking beer. Can you believe that shit? They probably even supported the Brady Bill! Fuckin' pansies!

INDOOR RANGES. They're stuffy, they smell bad, and they're always full of non-English-speaking immigrants who have no business handling guns in the first place. Avoid them.

Save your money. There are plenty of places—even outside the city—where you can fire at will all day long without suffering through annoying "safety" rules. FUCK

RULES! Of course, it's a sad fact that experienced shooters generally don't drink and shoot, so for safety's sake, I recommend shooting with experienced drinkers.

Just start driving north or east out of L.A., and after about an hour and a half look for a place to pull off the road. You should set up in a place out of earshot, and not visible from the road; a lot of family types get nervous at the sight of gun fags with beer, and they're liable to call the cops or, worse, the fuckin' Sierra Club. Not that any *smart* cop or bunny-hugging Bolshevik is likely to approach a dozen or so drunks under a hail of roaring gunfire, but they like to report our activities, which eventually leads to legislation, and we certainly do not need any more of *that!*

TARGETS. These can range anywhere from the previous night's beer cans to your ex-girlfriend's car. One of my favorite targets makes some people nervous, but you can't beat it for ballistics observation: a human corpse. If you know anyone who works for the city or county in any law-enforcement capacity, it's pretty easy to claim a John Doe from the morgue; the coroners are more than happy to get rid of them. Be sure to bring a shovel, because when you're finished with the target you'll have to bury it deep enough to where the coyotes can't get at it. When some do-good hiker spots a coyote gnawing on an arm, he's bound to report it, and again, this is something we do not need.

AMMO. Bring plenty, and don't waste your money on the expensive stuff. It's surprising how fast you can burn up a thousand rounds, even if you're only firing revolvers.

FIRST AID KIT. Will do you no good. In case of an accident, the above-referenced shovel will be all you'll need. Hospitals are required by law to report gunshot wounds to the police, so it's best to not deal with them at all. It should be understood by all parties involved that if a guy acquires lead, he ain't coming back.

Happy shooting!

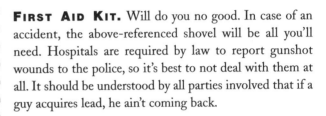

For over a decade, *2600: The Hacker Quarterly* has been presenting information that the U.S. Justice Department, the FBI, IBM, and The Telephone Company would like to keep bottled up. It's grown to become one of the most widely read fringe zines, with detailed instructions on everything from making free phone calls to descrambling cable TV to constructing computer viruses. These days I'm not exactly sure who reads *2600*, as the entire hacker mystique has been so blown out of proportion by the media. I'm sure the zine's thousands of readers probably include plenty of high-priced computer and telephone security specialists who are forced to subscribe to it to stay abreast of new developments in hacking techniques.

While *2600* has been publishing for more than ten years, it wasn't the first long-running hacker zine. In the early '70s, as an offshoot of the Yippie movement, "Al Bell" started the newsletter *TAP* (or *Technical Assistance Program*). This publication continued for about ten years, exploring the inner workings of telephone systems, telex switches, and computer operations. As a political tactic, phone-service theft ensured that Yippie advocates would have ready access to long-distance telephone communication, despite the Yippies' chronic lack of organization, discipline, money, or even a steady home address.

The zine *2600* was started by Emmanuel Goldstein back in 1984, just after the demise of *TAP.* The name was borrowed from the 2600 Hz tone generated by the legendary "blue boxes" that enabled people to make free long-distance phone calls. While blue boxes and other techniques established by the earliest phone "phreaks" have been made largely ineffective by modern computerized switching systems, *2600* continues to stay in step with technology, keeping everyone on their toes.

SHOPPER'S GUIDE TO COCOTS
•
By **Count Zero** *from*
2600

So you're walking down the street and you see a pay phone. Gotta make an important call, so you dig into your pocket to get a dime to make the call. Picking up the handset, you suddenly notice that the pay phone wants a *quarter* for a regular local call! What the hell, and *where* did this synthesized voice come from?

COCOT is an acronym for Customer Owned Coin Operated Telephone. In other words, a COCOT is a phone *owned* or *rented* by a *paying customer* (most likely, a hotel or donut shop). A COCOT is *not* a normal pay phone. The telco (telephone company) doesn't own it, and the actual phone line is usually a normal customer loop line (unlike pay phones, where the phone line is a "special" pay phone loop, allowing the use of "coin tones" to indicate money dropped in). A COCOT may *look* and *smell* like a telco payphone, but it is *not*.

Why do COCOTs exist? Simple. Money! A customer-owned pay phone is money in the bank! You pay *more* for local calls, and long distance is typically handled by sleazy carriers that offer expensive, bad service. The owner/renter of the COCOT opens the coinbox and keeps the money! Also, a particularly *sleazy* quality of a COCOT is that it *does not receive incoming calls.* This, of course, is because of money. If people are calling *in* to a COCOT, the COCOT is not making money calling out.

Where is a good place to look for COCOTS? Outside donut shops, restaurants, bars, clubs, and outside/inside hotels. How do I figure out if I have found a COCOT? Simple. A COCOT will have *no telco logos* on it. It may look just like a telco phone, chrome with blue stickers and all that. Also, a COCOT typically charges *more* for a local call than a regular telco payphone. A COCOT will most often have a synthesized voice that asks you to "please deposit 25 cents."

When does the phun begin? Soon. First, you must understand that the COCOT is a mimic. Essentially, it wants you to think that it's just a plain ol' pay phone. Pick up the handset. Hear that dial tone? Hah! That dial tone is fake, synthesized by the innards of the COCOT. Remember, a COCOT runs off a normal customer loop. Unlike a telco payphone where you must deposit money to generate tones that are read by the central office, the security of a COCOT depends solely on the phone itself. It's as if you took your own phone and put a sign on it saying, "Please put 25 cents in this jar for every call you make." COCOTS are not naive. They won't let you near the regular dial tone until you fork over the cash-ola. Or so they *think!*

See, the Achilles heel of the COCOT is that all pay phones *must let you make 1-800 calls for free!* It's not just a fact; it's the law. Now pick up the handset and place a 1-800 call. Any 1-800 number will do. When they answer at the other end, just sit there. Do nothing. Wait for them to hang up the phone. Here's an example:

Dial 1-800-LOAN-YES.

[Ring, Ring] . . . [Click] "Hello, you wanna buy some money? Hello? HELLO?!" [Click]

(You will now hear some static and probably a strange "waffling" noise, like chh, chh, chh, chh, chh.)

[Click] DIAL TONE!

Now what have we got here? A dial tone? Yes, you guessed it, the dial tone you now hear is the regular *unrestricted* dial tone of the COCOT's customer loop.

So what? So I got an "unrestricted dial tone." Big deal!

Meathead! With an *unrestricted* dial tone, all you need to do is place a call via DTMF tones (the tones a telephone Touch-Tone keypad generates). Now, try dialing a number with the COCOT's keypad. *Whoa!* Waitasec, no sound! This is a typical lame attempt at protection by the COCOT. Just whip out your Radio Shack pocket tone dialer and try calling a number, *any* number. Place it just as if you were calling from a home phone. Call a 1-900 sex line. Call Guam. You are *free* and the COCOT's customer loop is being billed!

Note: Some COCOTs are more sophisticated at protecting themselves. Some will *reset* when they hear the dial tone. To get around this, make a loud hissing sound with your mouth into the mouthpiece after the 1-800 number hangs up. Get your tone dialer ready near the mouthpiece.

When you hear the dial tone, quickly dial the first digit of the number you want to call. If you hiss loudly enough, you *may* be able to mask the sound of the dial tone and prevent the COCOT from resetting. Once you dial the first digit of the number you are calling, the dial tone will disappear (naturally). You can stop hissing like an idiot now. Finish dialing your *free* phone call. Also, some COCOTs actually disable the handset after a call hangs up (in other words, you can't send DTMF tones through the mouthpiece). Oh well, better luck next time.

However *most* of the COCOTs I have run across *only* disable the DTMF keypad. So all you need is a pocket dialer to circumvent this!

Other things to know: Sure, you can't call a COCOT, but it *does* have a number. To find out the COCOT's number, call one of the ANI services (Automated Number Identifier) that tell you the number you're dialing from (the numbers keep changing but they are frequently printed in the zine *2600*). Now try calling the COCOT from another phone. You will hear one of two things: 1) synthesized voice: "Thank you" [DTMF tones] [Click] [hang up] or 2) weird computer carrier.

A COCOT's number is *only* used by the company that built or sold the COCOT. By calling up a COCOT, a tech can monitor its functioning, etc. In case number 1, you must enter a password and then you'll get into a voice menu driven program that'll let you do "maintenance" stuff with the COCOT. In case number 2, you are hooked to the COCOT's modem (Yes, a *modem* in a pay phone). Likewise, if you can figure out the communications settings, you'll be into the COCOT's maintenance routines.

COCOT Etiquette: Now remember, you are making free phone calls but *someone* has to pay for them and that's the *owner*. The COCOT's customer loop is billed for the calls, and if the owner sees a big difference in the profits, they'll know something is up. So the rule is *don't abuse them!* Don't call a 1-900 number and stay on the line for twelve hours! If a COCOT is abused severely, an owner will eventually lose money on the damn thing! And that means bye-bye COCOT. Also, remember that a record of all long-distance calls is made to the COCOT's customer loop and COCOT companies will sometimes investigate "billing discrepancies."

COCOTs are a great resource if we use them wisely, like our environment. We've gotta be careful not to plunder them. Make a few long-distance calls and then leave that particular COCOT alone for a while. Chances are your bills will be "absorbed" by the profit margin of the owner and probably ignored, but the smaller the owner's

profit margin gets, the more likely suspicions will be aroused.

As for a tone dialer, don't leave home without one! A true phreak always has a DTMF tone dialer at hand along with a red box! My personal favorite is the *combo box* (red box plus DTMF). Take a Radio Shack 33-memory pocket dialer. Open up the back. Remove the little 3.579 MHz crystal (looks like a metal cylinder). Unsolder it. Solder on a couple of thin insulated wires where the crystal was attached. Thread the wires through the "vents" in the back. Get a hold of a 6.5536 MHz crystal (89 cents thru Fry's Electronics, 415-770-3763). Go out and get some quick-drying epoxy and a Radio Shack mini-toggle switch (cat. #275-626). Close the tone dialer, with the two wires sticking out the back. Screw it up tight. Now, attach the crystals and wires to the switch.

Epoxy this gizmo to the side of the tone dialer. Use a *lot* of epoxy, as you must make the switch/crystals essentially embedded in epoxy resin. Basically, you've altered the device so you can select between two crystals to generate the timing for the tone dialer. Now you can easily switch between the two crystal types. The small crystal will generate ordinary DTMF tones. By flicking the switch, you generate *higher* tones. Using the memory function of the tone dialer, save five stars in the P1 location. Now dial the P1 location using the *big* crystal. Sure sounds like the tones for a quarter, doesn't it! Carry this around with you. It will always come in handy with both telco pay phones *and* COCOTs. No phreak should be without one!

Information is power . . . *share it!* And drink massive amounts of Jolt Cola. Trust me, it's good for you. Keep the faith, and never stop searching for new frontiers.

JAPAN'S SPEED CULTURE

●

By **Jim Hogshire** *from*

Pills-a-Go-Go

"Just say no," D.A.R.E., Partnership for a Drug-free America—anti-drug messages seem to be pouring out of every nozzle in our media landscape. Yet more than 12 million Americans continue to use illegal drugs on a regular basis. Stranger still is that the so-called war against drugs is being spearheaded by a president who openly admits trying marijuana.

At the same time that this anti-drug hysteria is sweeping the nation, prescription and over-the-counter drug manufacturing companies are reporting record profits. Increasing numbers of people are taking a plethora of drugs for every minor ache and pain in their bodies. I have nothing against drugs, legal or illegal, but is there really a large difference between a person taking a Percocet or Vicodin simply to feel better and a person who takes one as a doctor-prescribed remedy?

Jim Hogshire is a true fan of pills. He publishes one of the most interesting, humorous, and uniquely informative newsletters around. Within the pages of *Pills-a-Go-Go,* he reports on the hottest new drugs, lawsuits against drug manufacturers, pills recently awarded over-the-counter status, and news on the latest FDA crackdowns.

Here, he reveals the secrets of *eiyo,* Japan's energy boosters.

The Japanese drive to business success has created a culture for a curious kind of "tonic" drink, called *eiyo.* Considered more than a soft drink and not quite a pharmaceutical, *eiyo* drinks occupy a special niche in the Japanese marketplace. More than a fourth of all pharmaceuticals sold in Japan are eiyo drinks. Typically, tonic drinks are slugged down by slave/businessmen who have to work more than 100 hours a week and still manage to avoid a peculiar kind of Japanese fate, *karoshi,* or "being worked to death." But the energy elixers are also consumed by cramming students, hangover sufferers, and presumably, partyers who need just one more ounce of strength to bop till they drop.

Named things like "Real Gold" (made and marketed by Coca-Cola) and "I Am King," the drinks come in small brown bottles, each containing 50 to 100 ml of a special mixture of essential ingredients. While nearly all the tonic drinks have healthy doses of caffeine, ephedrine, and nicotine (gets the old heart moving), each includes its own characteristic power ingredients. Various amino acids, ginseng, royal jelly, powdered deer antler, and viper extract are just some of the crucial ingredients found in *eiyo* drinks.

The first tonic drink was introduced in Japan in 1962 when a daring company abandoned pill-form nutritional supplements to market "Lipovitan D." It remains the leading *eiyo* drink in Japan, where the market is saturated and has begun to expand to other parts of Asia. Thais, for instance, drink more than 100,000 bottles of Lipovitan D a year and the company is aiming to take over Indonesia and Taiwan.

Eiyo drinks are tightly bound to ideas of endurance, success, and courage. They promise bursts of "fight" and the ability to "fight" for 24 hours straight. Some drinks are associated with blue-collar workers while others are targeted at white collar salarymen.

In fact, the drinking of the mostly lemon-flavored shots of adrenaline boosters has taken on subtle, ritualistic meaning to the Japanese. This cartoon depicts the abject shame of a balding salaryman as two coworkers remark that their colleague has never received a gift of Arinam V from the big boss. One of the pencil-pushers brags that he's gotten a bottle from the boss two times already, putting him far above the "C-class salaryman" who has been ignored.

For the boss to give a bottle of crude speed to an underling is a sign of approval, that the boss considers him a valuable employee.

VENOM: POISON OR PANACEA?

•

By **Michael Crosby** *from*
Eye

For me, the joy of zines is their unfettered spontaneity. It's fun to just sit down and ramble on about anything that's on your mind. Without any editors, publishers, or advertisers to worry about, zinesters can just open up their mind and let their creative juices flow. This style of writing has brought us some of the most compelling personal stories and thought-provoking political rants.

But that's not what everyone is looking for in a zine. Some folks want well-researched essays with footnotes and references. They want factual investigations without the blandness of newspapers or the oppressiveness of academic journals. These people would love reading *Eye.* Since 1993, the publisher L. Crosby has been researching, compiling, and printing the most compelling (and well-researched) articles I've seen in any zine. The best part is that it's a zine through-and-through—no pretentious academia, just healthy, meaty articles that explore history and culture, with just a touch of conspiracy theory.

Have you ever licked a toad? This piece explores alternative medicine (the medicinal uses of toad venom) and efforts to make it illegal.

On January 3, 1994, narcotics forces in Northern California arrested Bob and Connie Shepard at their home in Calaveras County for possession of four Colorado River toads from Arizona. Authorities seized all four toads—Hans, Franz, Peter, and Brian. The toxin secreted by the toad—bufotenine—is listed as a controlled substance with the California Department of Justice, and it's a misdemeanor to possess these toads in California as of March 1, 1994. Bob Shepard was accused of squeezing the venom from toad glands, drying it, and smoking it to achieve a brief trip from the 5-MeO-DMT contained in the venom. Shepard described the experience to police as "electrons jumping orbitally in my molecules."

"When certain toads are squeezed," said *Fortean Times* magazine, "they emit a bubble of venom from behind their eyes. This must not be licked as it makes humans very ill. Modern toadies have learned, from indigenous Americans, to smoke it dry in a pipe. . . . In the '50s, the Pentagon and the CIA used bufotenine . . . in experiments to develop brainwashing agents."

At the April 1994 "Gathering of the Minds: A South-ern California Psychedelic Conference," according to the *Village Voice,* Ram Dass described his amphibian trip: "I turned into a very large, black woman. I was surrounded by beings who were children—all suffering, hungry, frightened, sick. I found myself opening my arms to draw them all into myself. At the same time I was both gagging on it all and in absolute ecstasy."

Toad venom received 15 column-inches of fame in the *New York Times Magazine,*" said the *Voice,* "with a moral that could be summarized as: Don't do it; it's scary stuff that transports you directly into a void where there's nothing to buy."

On the other hand, Jim DeKorne, author of *Psychedelic Shamanism,* could be heard extolling the virtues of DMT. According to the *Voice,* when asked if one hallucinates on it, DeKorne replied, "No, it's more like a ten-minute orgasm with electricity shooting out of your fingers."

Hallucinogen, Medicine, or Poison?

Venomous plants and animals abound. Some are deadly, but others, though toxic, may have benevolent uses. However, the funds needed to analyze and isolate useful alkaloids are lacking—and some species are nearing extinction—

meaning that some miraculous venoms may never make it to the lab.

According to *Frogs & Toads of the World* by Chris Mattison, many species of frogs and toads rely on glandular secretions to deter prey: "The most important of these is the secretion of toxic or distasteful substances from the skin, an ability shared by many species from a wide range of families. Most frogs are covered with a coating of slimy mucus anyway, and this is often sufficient to prevent their capture, but many also secrete substances known collectively as batrachotoxins, a high concentration of which can be lethal if it enters the bloodstream." Frogs play an important role in many cultures, and venom has been used by indigenous peoples for thousands of years. Indians in Peru and Brazil, such as the Matses, still rely on poisonous frog venoms to tip their arrows and increase awareness while hunting.

The Deadly Poison Dart Frog

The Colombian poison dart frog *(Phyllobates terribilis)* was first described in 1978, and yields the most poison. Its only predators are a frog-eating snake thought to be immune to the toxin and the Choco Indians, who use its poison to tip their darts.

Some frogs are so poisonous that it's deadly to touch them with bare hands, yet many secretions are praised by natives for the shamanic powers they evoke. Nietzsche once wrote, "A little poison for pleasant dreams, and a lot of poison for a pleasant death." The South Americans' expertise is crucial in distinguishing deadly venoms from those with hallucinogenic properties. Knowing the dosage, which will intoxicate to the brink of death is the secret of the ritual.

Frogs consume their own animas; perhaps explaining why so many cultures respect frogs for their nearness to life and the spiritual world. A frog's skin is possibly its most fascinating feature. Its permeability allows frogs to probably absorb as many environmental chemicals as they secrete—explaining why frogs raised artificially don't produce the same chemicals as their wilderness counterparts. Steinhart explains in *Audubon*: "Frogs are probably so chemically complex because they are open to the world. . . . Both water and air pass through their skins. . . . [And] with the water and air come all kinds of soluble molecules."

Peter Gorman was the first to report venom's use as a hallucinogen by South America natives. His research took him throughout Peru gathering artifacts for the American Museum of Natural History (AMNH) from the Matses, a small Peruvian tribe in the deep jungles near the Brazilian border.

Sapo Experiences

Gorman recently returned to Peru to collect specimens of the dow-kiet! frog. This species produces the toxin of interest to the AMNH and the Fidia Research Institute for the Neurosciences in Rome. The mysterious venom secreted by the dow-kiet! is called sapo by the Matses. Gorman's previous experience with sapo proved nonconclusive, since he didn't actually see the rare dow-kiet!, so he returned to the remote forest hoping to find a specimen that could be studied in a lab.

It is said that the Matses know the jungle's secrets, and sapo is one of them. On his third trip to the Amazon in 1986, Gorman met a Matses man named Pablo. It was under Pablo's supervision that he first tried sapo. Gorman recounts Pablo producing a small piece of split bamboo that "was covered with what looked like a thick coat of aging varnish. 'Sapo,' [Pablo] repeated, scraping a little of the material from the stick and mixing it with saliva. When he was finished, it had the consistency and color of green mustard. Then he pulled a smoldering twig from the fire, grabbed my left wrist, and burned the inside of my forearm." He scraped away the burned skin, then dabbed a little of the sapo onto the exposed areas. "Instantly my body began to heat up. In seconds I was burning from the inside and regretted allowing him to give me a medicine I knew nothing about. I began to sweat. My blood began to race. My heart pounded. I became acutely aware of every vein and artery in my body and could feel them opening to allow for the fantastic pulse of my blood. My stomach cramped and I vomited violently. I lost control of my bodily functions and began to urinate and defecate. I fell to the ground. Then, unexpectedly, I found myself growling and moving about on all fours. I felt as though animals were passing through me, trying to express themselves through my body. It was a fantastic feeling, but it passed quickly, and I could think of nothing but the rushing of my blood, a sensation so intense that I thought my heart would burst. The rushing got faster and faster. I was in agony. I gasped for breath. Slowly, the pounding became steady and rhythmic, and when it finally subsided altogether, I was overcome with exhaustion. I slept where I was."

After waking, Gorman says that his senses were more acute. "During the next few days, my feeling of strength didn't diminish; I could go whole days without being hungry or thirsty and move through the jungle for hours without tiring. Every sense I possessed was heightened and in tune with the environment, as though the sapo put the rhythm of the jungle into my blood." Gorman reports that sapo was used among hunters to sharpen the senses and increase stamina during long hunts when carrying food and water was difficult. In large doses, it could make a Matses hunter "invisible" to poor-sighted, acute-smelling jungle animals by temporarily eliminating their human odor. As a medicine, sapo had multiple uses as well. Gorman explains that "in sparing doses applied to the inside of the wrist, it could establish whether a woman was pregnant or not. And during the later stages of pregnancy, it was used to establish the sex and health of a fetus. Interpreting the information relied on an investigation of the urine a woman discharged following the application of the medicine. Cloudiness or other discoloration of the urine and the presence or absence of specks of blood were all evidently indicators of the fetus's condition. In cases where an unhealthy fetus was discovered, a large dose of sapo applied to the vaginal area was used as an abortive."

Returning to New York, Gorman reported his experience with sapo to the AMNH. But it took him two more trips to Peru before finally securing a sample of a dow-kiet! frog for analysis. It was on his sixth trip that Gorman found Pablo at San Juan and went with him to collect dow-kiet! specimens. "I told him two were enough, and he came into the camp, a frog in each hand. He gave one of them to me. It was beautiful. A little smaller than my palm, it had an extraordinary electric-green back, a lightly spotted white underside, and deep black eyes. It grasped my fingers tightly, and in seconds I could feel my blood begin to heat up as the sapo it was secreting began to seep into the small cuts that covered my hands."

One dow-kiet! died during transit, but the other returned to the United States with Gorman. Samples of its secretion generated scientific interest in sapo. Vittorio Erspamer, a pharmacologist, wrote Gorman that if it could be shown that one of those frogs was already in use by humans, it would be an important scientific breakthrough.

Poison as Medicine

From the overgrown Amazon to the overread West, science has studied and tested frog venom from various species and believe its isolated alkaloids have medical value. According to *Audubon*, "at least 26 different venom constituents exist," including a powerful anesthetic called cinobufage, and the hallucinogen bufotenin.

After sending a sample of sapo and a photo of a dow-kiet! to Erspamer in Rome, Gorman received word that he identified the dow-kiet! as a rare arboreal tree frog. "The sapo," Erspamer said, "is a sort of fantastic chemical cocktail with potential medical applications." According to *Omni*, Erspamer believed that no other amphibian skin could compete with it since up to 7 percent of sapo's weight is in potently active peptides, easily absorbed through burned, inflamed areas of the skin.

The effects of sapo can be attributed to isolated alkaloids in the venom, explaining the reactions Gorman experienced in Peru: a violent purging effect of salivary glands, tear ducts, intestines, and bowels; dilation of blood vessels, intense rushing of the blood, and a drop in blood pressure; feeling of satiety; heightened sensory perception; and increased stamina. Sapo was also reported to increase physical strength, enhance resistance to hunger and thirst, produce an analgesic effect, and increase the capacity to face stressful situations. Side effects observed in volunteers were nausea, vomiting, facial flush, heart palpitations, changes in blood pressure, sweating, abdominal discomfort, and urge for defecation.

Sapo's peptides also have medical potential as digestive aids to assist cancer treatment patients, and possible use as anti-inflammatories, blood-pressure regulators, and as pituitary gland stimulators. Erspamer also suggested that two peptides in sapo could facilitate access to the brain's membranes. By administering medicines straight to a specific brain area, researchers could better contribute to treatments for AIDS, Alzheimer's, and other disorders.

The New Morphine?

In addition, Deltorphin and dermorphin, two other peptides found in sapo, are similar to the opiates found in morphine, and are considerably stronger. Amazingly, the development of tolerance would be considerably lower and withdrawal less severe than to opiates. In the *Journal of the American Chemical Society*, John W. Daly and his colleagues described the structure of the alkaloid epibatidine found in the secretions of a frog species related to the dow-kiet!. Daly explained that epibatidine numbs more effectively than morphine. According to *Science*, epibatidine, when tested on mice, "proved to be 200 times as effective as morphine in blocking pain." What's more, the chemical seemed to work in a completely different way from morphine and other opiates—its painkilling power was undiminished even when administered along with an opiate blocker.

The implements of epibatidine research are far-reaching. "Preliminary animal studies by researchers at the Warner-Lambert Company have hinted that those receptors . . . could offer a target for treating depression, stroke, seizures, and cognitive loss in ailments such as Alzheimer's disease," says *Science*. "'It represents what appears to be a new class of pharmacological mediator,' remarks biochemist Michael Zasloff, who founded Magainin Pharmaceuticals, Inc. to develop drug leads from the vast, barely catalogued library of animal chemical defenses."

And it's not only one particular frog species that could be valuable medicinally. Recently, a wonder antibiotic first found in the secretions of an African clawed frog was developed by Magainin Pharmaceuticals. The substance was coined Magainin-2, and, according to *Popular Science*, "In preliminary tests, one of Zasloff's magainins destroyed skin cancer cells, but left normal cells intact. This stands in contrast to today's chemotherapy treatments, which also ravage healthy cells."

Zasloff's company has "chemically synthesized more than 2,000 variants of the frog's magainin," says *Popular Science*. One form of magainin being focused on is a cream for treating impetigo—a serious skin infection that usually afflicts children—and also for diabetic foot ulcers that can lead to amputation. Further down the line are possible remedies for eye wounds, ovarian cancer, skin cancer, stomach infections, and a mouthwash.

The Vanishing Frog

But if you want to find a frog's back to lick, you'd better move fast. "While thousands of golden toads were found in Costa Rica's Monteverde Forest Reserve in the early '80s, only two have been found in recent years," reports *Audubon*. "The stomach-breeding frog of Australia has not been seen in the wild since 1981. There are steep declines in Rocky Mountain populations. There are die-offs and disappearances in Peru, Colombia, Panama, Puerto Rico, and Nova Scotia." It is imperative that frog species be researched and recorded before extinction ensues and scientific inquiry is made impossible.

Only one out of every five drugs that reach advanced stages of testing are ultimately approved for sale by the Food and Drug Administration. But how many undiscovered, animal alkaloids hold medical importance? Because of the difficulty in reproducing the alkaloids in labs and the scarcity of the species that produce batrachotoxins, research on venoms hasn't progressed like that on synthetic substances.

Expense seems to be the greatest deterrent. Years of research are expensive, and drug companies would rather finance substances that can be researched and synthesized cheaply and quickly. Until enough is known about the amines from venomous creatures, most finance will be reserved for inadequate researching rather than marketing and producing an effective pharmaceutical product.

But venom research could be of life-saving importance. Strains of bacteria that are the cause of tuberculosis and gonorrhea have become resistant to virtually all known antibiotics. Moreover, traditional medicines have never worked well against many ailments such as certain skin infections, viruses, and cancers. But when animal antibiotics were tested, they proved to kill bacteria, protozoa, fungi, and yeast infections, and may be our only defense against certain mutated strains of deadly bacteria.

Even though batrachotoxins may yield more medicinal alkaloids than easily researched synthetics, effectiveness is still governed by cost. But if lives can be helped, why should the lack of finance for research stand in the way? Scientists should study these unique species while they're still around to be studied.

Bibliography

Amato, Ivan. "From 'Hunter Magic,' a Pharmacopeia?" *Science*, November 20, 1992, p. 1306.

Bradley, David. "Frog Venom Cocktail Yields a One-handed Painkiller." *Science*, August 27, 1993, p. 1117.

Brody, Jane E. "Personal Health." *New York Times*, September 8, 1993, p. C12.

"Toking the Toad." *Fortean Times*, issue 75, p. 8.

Gehr, Richard. "Notes From a Psychedelic Revival Meeting." *Village Voice*, July 5, 1994, pp. 25–28.

Gorman, Peter. "Making Magic." *Omni*, July 1993, pp. 64–67+.

Langreth, Robert. "The Frog Treatment." *Popular Science*, August 1993, pp. 58–59+.

Mattison, Chris. *Frogs and Toads of the World*. New York: Facts on File, Inc., 1987.

Pennisi, Elizabeth. "Pharming Frogs." *Science News*, July 18, 1992, pp. 40–42.

Steinhart, Peter. "When a Great Frog Swallowed the Moon." *Audubon*, September 1991, pp. 20–24.

CHOO CHOO CRASH BANG

●

By **John Marr** *from*
Murder Can Be Fun

Murder Can Be Fun
#17 ——————— $2.⁰⁰

Wanna play, Buster?
NAUGHTY CHILDREN

Every Christmas Day, living rooms across America provide the stage for a heartwarming Rockwellian drama. The presents have been opened. The room is a happily confused welter of loose ribbons, crumpled wrapping paper, and empty boxes, punctuated with all manner of shiny new toys. A radiantly cheerful fire crackles in the fireplace. The air is filled with the sounds of juvenile glee.

But one discordant note sounds in the midst of this merriment. For one boy, Christmas has not turned out to be all he hoped. The pile of bright and shiny presents before him lacks one crucial item. Bravely, he feigns satisfaction, little knowing he is but an unwitting player in a greater drama.

Then, as if by magic, Father produces one final present: a large, flat box. The mopey lad comes alive in a sudden burst of Christmas morning enthusiasm. His eyes glowing, he frenetically tears off the wrapping paper and all but destroys the box in his haste to open it, even though he knows exactly what is inside. It's an HO-scale model train. His Christmas is now complete. The afternoon is spent in an idyllic father/son project of assembling the tracks. By dinnertime, Junior is adeptly running his own railroad— coupling and uncoupling cars, operating the switches, and skillfully guiding the train over the yards of track winding throughout the living room.

And, sure as death and taxes, before bedtime Junior stages his first model train wreck.

Fortunately for American railroads, most children are content staging head-on collisions between scale models of the Cannonball Express and the 20th-Century Limited. But for a small, hard-core group, mayhem at 1/87 scale is only a pale imitation of the real thing. These baby-faced train wreckers prefer playing with real rolling stock.

Even the casual student of railroad history knows that these youngsters have fought their long-running war with a bitterness exceeding that of the legendary railroad strikes. Their antics have liberally strewn the tracks of America with shattered railcars and mangled bodies, with casualties heavy on both sides. As one veteran railroad detective put it, "Ask any railroad police officer what his principal worry is and there is little doubt that his reply will be juveniles." Give American youth a free hand and rail traffic would grind to a thundering halt.

Even fragmentary statistics—and railroads prefer to keep them as fragmentary as possible—tell a grim story. Reportedly over 75 percent of all cases of track tampering, signal resetting, and barricade building are traced to children. The plight of the Long Island Railroad in 1931 offered a rare glimpse of the railyard as playground. Out of desperation, officials mounted a publicity campaign aimed at school principals and clergymen to help curb "mischievous and malicious practices" of local kids on railroad property. The railroad had already arrested 326 boys in the first four months of the year. The crimes read like a laundry list of dedicated saboteurs. Equipment was stolen or vandalized. Rocks were thrown and guns fired at passing trains. Some enterprising lads put stolen lanterns to use, waving locomotives to unscheduled, potentially lethal stops. But the hands-down favorite was piling debris on the tracks. In those few short months, track workers and railroad police removed iron rods and tire rims from the electric third rail, and boards, auto parts, rocks, and at least one small building from the tracks proper. And this was no Depression-era aberration. In the '40s and '50s, around 80 kids under 14 were killed, and a good many more maimed, each year on railroad property. It's a safe bet they weren't all taking a shortcut to the library.

Probably the most widespread, yet least reported phase of this long-running conflict can be summed up in a simple phrase: trains make great moving targets. At times, it seems as if passenger trains could proceed through certain areas only if accompanied by a shower of stones, punctuated with the occasional bullet.

Newspaper accounts of this brand of juvenile deviltry are few and far between; railroads like to keep the incidents quiet to prevent a rash of copycat attacks. Typical incidents include one in the Bronx in 1934, when a trio of boys, none older than 10, enlivened the evening commute by pegging some 13 trains within an hour, injuring 23 passengers. And in 1947 in nearby Queens, five more young lads were apprehended following a similar spate of broken windows and injured passengers. It's not unusual for lines caught in a "stoning" fad to report a thousand broken windows and a hundred injuries in a year. And shootings, while rare, are far more lethal. In August 1953, a 13-year-old-boy taking a few pot shots with his friends down by the tracks managed to kill a brakeman.

But stoning and shooting at trains are just small potatoes, kid stuff, if you will. They offer only momentary thrills. Real kicks, as any enterprising young vandal can tell you, come from real train wrecks. Imagine 20 tons of locomotive suddenly torn as if by magic from the rails. Behind it, the cars scatter about like ninepins. Wood, metal, and glass are smashed together in an entangled mass. The roar of the crash gives way to the ominous hiss of steam. And that boom—could it be a boiler explosion? Any child witnessing this horrific spectacle can have but one reaction: Cool!

Children have not been implicated in any of the major malicious derailments of this century. This has not been for a lack of effort on their part. It takes technical knowledge, hard work, and careful choice of location to cause a major derailment. Time and time again, children have demonstrated no shortage of these first two qualities of the successful train wrecker. They may have never caused a major

wreck, but the little fellows have been behind a startling amount of trackside mayhem and carnage.

One is struck by the effort these young vandals put in. It's difficult to decide what shocks their parents more: the fact that the apple of their eye has callously destroyed thousands of dollars of property, possibly maiming or killing a few innocent people in the process, or the fact that their son, who reacts to a request to take out the garbage as if it was banishment to a Nazi labor camp, has just voluntarily spent hours hauling hundred of pounds of debris uphill to pile on the tracks.

Perhaps the most elegant and least labor-intensive means of wreaking havoc along the rails is simply to reset the switches. Imagine the look on the engineer's face when his train, traveling at full speed, takes a sudden, unexpected detour onto a siding. That's a Kodak moment in anyone's book.

Switch tampering is easier said than done. Railroads routinely keep them locked and only distribute the keys to authorized personnel. Most switches also trigger a signal when they are thrown to warn an alert engineer and remove the essential element of surprise. But the system isn't foolproof and children are no fools. When all goes well, the results are truly sublime. The express train hurtles along the main track. Suddenly, it's as if a giant hand brutally pushes it aside. Within seconds, locomotives and cars are flying akimbo, possibly colliding with other trains on adjacent track. It ends with rolling stock turned to piles of mangled wreckage—all from the clever manipulation of a few levers.

Kids of all ages have gotten into the act. Police investigating a minor yard derailment in Washington in the '50s were surprised when the only person they could place near the mis-set switch (which had been accidentally left unlocked) was a four-year-old boy. But they were stunned when said preschooler demonstrated just how he'd thrown the switch to cause the wreck.

But switch setting is generally the work of older, wiser naughty children. One of the most memorable wrecks of this type was the work of William G., the son of a sharecropper. At 15, he was perhaps a trifle old for "naughty child" status, but he was still in seventh grade.

One day in 1950 outside Holland, Missouri, the barefoot lad carefully set the stage to reenact a scene he'd seen in a recent movie about the Dalton Gang. Armed with a hacksaw, he sawed through a switch lock and reset the switch for the siding near his father's farm. To avoid any last-minute braking by the engineer, he also smashed the signal light so the switch looked as if it was still set for the main track. As the next train wasn't due over the line until early the next

PITTSBURGH, PA. 1926: Ernest B., 11, and his 7-year-old sister confessed to derailing an express train near their house. Their motives? They wanted to "see the train jump the tracks."

NEWARK, NJ, 1930: After a summer's worth of experimentation with stones and boards, three 11-year-old boys and a 13-year-old wired spikes to the rails on the edge of a 40-foot-high trestle and hid in the bushes to watch the fun. As an added precaution, they drew salt pork across their trail to confuse any bloodhounds. These kids were serious.

To their chagrin, a slow-moving switch engine hit the spikes first. The engineer managed to remove the spikes and back onto a siding before their target, the 2:22 express, came along and hurtled safely across the trestle. As happens so often, they were a little too loose-lipped around school about their efforts "to make a wreck" and word reached the police.

MORGANTON, NC, 1931 *(4 INJURED):* A 6-year-old boy put a large rock on the tracks, derailing a Southern Railway passenger train. None of the passengers were injured seriously. For punishment, he was inexplicably sentenced to have his tonsils removed. The *New York Times* noted "Presumably the judge is a believer in the character-restoring effects of necessary surgery."

BAYONNE, NJ, 1942 *($50,000 DAMAGES):* A Reading Railroad express hit a pile of bricks at 60 mph. The locomotive and two baggage cars derailed and a mile of track was destroyed. Police caught two boys, ages 11 and 12, throwing rocks at buildings nearby, who copped to putting "a couple of bricks" on the tracks.

HIGHLAND, NY, 1943 *($123,000 DAMAGES):* Two boys, aged 14 and 9, put a large rock on the tracks near a switch, derailing a freight train. And they picked a train that could cause a lot of damage; 24 tank cars carrying gasoline, oil, and other flammable liquids caught fire. The flames destroyed not only the train, but three nearby houses.

MILLTOWN, WI, 1948 *(21 INJURED):* Three 11-year-old boys piled stones on the tracks outside town, derailing a passenger train.

BLOOMFIELD, IN, 1951 *(THREE KILLED):* While "just playing," a 10-year-old boy jammed a 10-inch bolt into a switch. The obstacle derailed a locomotive; three trainmen, trapped in the cab, were scalded to death by steam from the ruptured boiler.

GREER, SC, 1955 *(TWO KILLED):* A group of boys aged 12–14, broke open a switch and reset it for a dead-end siding. A freight train came along, crashed through the stops at the end of the siding and fell 15 feet down an embankment. A tank car landed on top of the engine, crushing the cab and killing both members of the crew.

POMPTON PLAINS, NJ, 1960 *(TWO KILLED):* A 12-year-old boy, with the help of a 7-year-old playmate, broke open a switch with a baseball bat and reset it for the siding. They wrecked the next freight, killing two crew members.

morning, he walked back home and went to bed. He later claimed he never intended to derail the train. He just wanted it to veer onto the siding and veer back onto the main line as some kind of a big joke. Ha! Ha! William was safely in bed when the *Memphian*, the crack Memphis-to-St. Louis express, thundered by at 2:30 A.M. It took the switch at 57 mph. The results were no joke. The locomotive and the tender were torn from the tracks, tumbling onto their sides and dragging two baggage cars with them. Two passenger cars also derailed. The locomotive was so badly smashed it took rescuers four hours to free the body of the engineer, the wreck's lone fatality. The fireman had been seriously scalded by the steam but was thrown clear and survived. Twelve passengers also suffered minor injuries. It

didn't take too long to catch William. This had been a long-term project of his. Other farmers spotted him the previous week, trying to break open the lock without a hacksaw.

A less elegant, more labor-intensive, and far more popular way to keep trains from running on time is simply to pile junk on the tracks; the more, the better. Rare is the train track without a plentiful supply of stones, rocks, spike, and other industrial debris conveniently located nearby. A little sweat, some elbow grease, and a bit of luck, and any boy can be his own train wrecker.

This was how one of the most dramatic and successful examples of juvenile train wrecking happened. The scene was the small town of Walton, Indiana; the year, 1947. One day after school, Jack S., 12, and his 11-year-old pal

Lysle G. amused themselves by riding their bikes around the village. By dusk, a light snow began to fall. The boys were bored; one can only do so much riding around a village with a population of barely 700. When Jack said, "Let's go over and wreck a train," his suggestion fell on receptive ears.

The lads rode over the tracks. They started by putting a plank on the tracks. They stepped back to admire their handiwork. It didn't look like much. So they added a few steel fence posts. Better, but still not good enough. Nearby was a roll of wire fencing weighing almost 200 pounds. They laboriously dragged it 20 feet uphill to add to their rapidly growing barrier. After heaving it on top of the plank and posts, they stepped back with a sigh of satisfaction. Now, that was a good, substantial barrier. They'd like to see a train get by that one.

But slowly, reality set in. They realized that they'd just piled several hundred pounds of junk on the tracks. And as soon as a train hit all that stuff, they'd be in a whole lot of trouble. So they reacted the way naughty children do when they lose their nerve: they went home.

That is how the young train wreckers missed the biggest show ever to play Walton. An hour later, a passenger train hit the barrier. The train stayed on the tracks—at first. But the wire was hopelessly ensnared in the locomotive's front wheels. It pushed the roll of wire along until the wire snagged a switch in the center of town. This jerked the front of the locomotive from the rails, sending it careening along the track bed and tearing up 2,000 feet of track before the rear wheels finally left the rails. The engine, now free of the tracks, spun around and fell over. It dragged six other cars with it. They crashed into a grain elevator and freight cars on nearby sidings. When the wreckage was finally cleared, the toll stood at four dead (the fireman and three passengers) and 23 passengers injured.

It didn't take the police very long to crack this one. The following week, they hauled Jack in for a few burglaries pulled the weekend before the train wreck. But they had a pretty good idea that his naughtiness went beyond a few B&Es. Nonchalantly, in the middle of a bunch of questions about the break-ins, they asked him, "Say, did you put the wire on the track before or after dark?" Jack blundered straight into the trap. He innocently answered, "Why, it was after dark." The cat now out of the bag, he quickly told the whole story. Lysle quickly joined his pal in the clink.

At first, some people doubted that such little fellows could drag all that junk up onto the tracks. So, for the benefit of the police and the papers, the boys staged a reenactment. As the cops filmed and the scribes scribbled, they demonstrated exactly how, grunting and heaving, they'd hauled that heavy roll of fencing up onto the tracks. To the amazement of spectators, it took them only 15 minutes. And they had just as much fun the second time around. As one reporter described the scene, "At times, they smiled and appeared to be enjoying the 'play,' apparently not fully aware of its tragic implications."

Sadly, the halcyon days of juvenile train wrecking have passed. The roar of locomotives has been replaced by the thunder of trucks in the nation's transit industry. Tracks have been abandoned and train traffic reduced, even as a network of heavily traveled freeways has spread across the land. The bulk of thrill-seeking youngsters have been carefully removed from urban cores to remote suburbs zealously zoned to keep railroads out. For many deprived children today, the Christmas Night model train wrecks will be as close as they will ever come to the real thing. The decline of American railroads has had one fringe benefit for workers and passengers: no longer are the shiny rails the tracks of temptation.

TIM'S TRUE TALES OF HORROR AND GORE

•

By **Tim Hartman** from
Hungry Freaks

Nothing is more "out there" than real life. Sometimes it's fun, other times dull, and on rare occasions, more cruel than any imagined hell. Zines are about describing life as it really is, and in *Hungry Freaks* Tim Hartman is trying to do just that.

In "Tim's True Tales of Horror and Gore" we read the horrifying particulars of what happens when the human body gets torn up in a massive motorcycle accident. Every time I read this story I'm shocked by how painfully traumatic life can sometimes be. This is a brutal tale, but one that happens every day. Sure, you see it on the television news, but they always leave out the true costs. Zines bring it on home—in all its gory detail.

August 10, 1982, is a day I will never forget. I'm reminded of this fateful day every waking hour of my life. I was 14 years old, on vacation for the summer, touring America with my dad on a '77 Honda Goldwing. After a brief stopover at my aunt's house in West Virginia, we were back on the road, headed north toward the Shenandoah Valley. The road was long and I spent most of the time gazing at the picturesque countryside. The blue sky, the sun, and the sprawling cornfields are blurred in my memory, like looking at a Van Gogh without your glasses on. But the burning memory of what happened next is as clear as crystal.

It was around 10 A.M. when an old farmer in a Dodge station wagon backed out of his service road and onto the highway. I wasn't even looking up, I just heard my dad shout, "Oh shit, you dumb ass!" as the motorcycle careened into the wagon at a gut-wrenching fifty-five miles per hour. We hit the trunk of the wagon sideways, and my left leg was momentarily pressed flat between the bike and the wagon's bumper. But all I felt was a quick slap below my knee as I was instantaneously catapulted fifteen feet into the air, so high that I could see over the tops of the cornfields.

Oh God! I'll never forget that second I spent flying through the air at fifty-five miles per, head first, knowing I was going to land on asphalt. Sure, I had a helmet on, but big fuckin' deal, man! I knew this shit was gonna hurt . . . bad! I was airborne for about twenty-five feet before Mother Earth suckled me back to her hard, paved bosom. Landing belly-flop style, I was immediately somersaulting down the road, like Wile E. Coyote after being tripped by the Roadrunner. The first impact splintered my left rib cage from the sternum at the costal cartilage, and forced the jagged ends through my left lung, collapsing it and almost cutting it in half. During the next few tumbles I was blessed with a shattered clavicle, a compound fracture of my left femur, a dislocated knee (right leg), and several broken carpal and tarsal bones.

I rolled for a total of sixty-four feet, and it seemed like forever. I remember wanting to stop so badly, but I couldn't. I just kept on rolling out of control. I finally bounced off the road and landed with a splat, face down in the gravel. I lay there dazed for a minute, just grateful that I had stopped. My entire body was numb, and for a second I thought I was actually OK. Then I started coughing uncontrollably as blood poured out of my mouth from my dissected lung. When I saw that shit I really started getting scared. I tried to push myself up off my stomach, but my pulverized wrists couldn't hold my weight and I toppled back to the ground, landing face first in my own blood and vomit.

Rolling onto my side, I was finally able to sit up. That's when I saw my mangled left leg for the first time. My foot was twisted around three or four times and the shoe was missing. My entire calf from ankle to knee was already swelling out of the tears in my jeans and was oozing blood from every pore. The more immediate problem was the blood gushing from my compounded femur, which was staring me right in the face, pink marrow and all. My crimson vitality was spurting from the shattered limb like water from a broken sprinkler head. I knew it wouldn't be long till I bled to death. I was already in an island in the sea of my own gore.

I looked around for my dad and saw him about sixty feet back up the road, struggling to get out from under the bike. I was just starting to black out when I felt somebody grab me from behind and slowly lower me back onto the ground. All I really remember seeing was an orange Caterpillar tractor cap on the head of a blurry figure that was telling me "You're going to be OK, just lay back and relax." It was a passing truck driver whom, to this day, I never had the chance to thank.

He tied his bandanna around my leg and told me he had to go radio an ambulance, but to just relax because he wasn't going to leave. It was to this total stranger's comforting words that I was finally blessed with unconsciousness. While I was out an ambulance came and took my dad and me to the nearest hospital, which was in Arcanum, some thirty miles away. They were pretty much just a country hospital and didn't have enough equipment to deal with someone as fucked up as I was. So they just stabilized my vitals and I was chopper-lifted to Dayton, Ohio. My father wasn't as thrashed as I was so he had to stay and get treated at Andy Griffith General. He had only suffered a broken leg and some contusions of assorted intensities.

I awoke the next morning to a most unsettling sight. I was surrounded by nuns! In all honesty, I thought I was dead! Actually, I was very close to it. I was in the Good Samaritan Catholic Hospital, and it took a dozen doctors sixteen hours (all night) to put my ass back together. My left leg was hamburger from the knee down. My tibia and fibula were crushed into thirty-seven pieces and all my ankle and metatarsal bones were dislocated from being squished flat. The leg was so puffed up and swollen when I was brought in that the doctors didn't even notice that half of my calf muscle was missing! It was back out in the boondocks, stuck to the bumper of that Dodge. I'm sure there was nothing left but a grease mark, but still, come on, you guys! Parts is parts!

Oh well. I guess they were too busy putting the rest of me back together. They drained a pint and a half of blood out of my severed lung and then somehow managed to put it back together (at least I think they did, I still can't breathe too deeply!). Then they had to open up my leg to try and put the puzzle back together. All the arteries and tendons were grated up and mangled from the jagged bits of pulverized bone that were now randomly located throughout the leg.

They managed to get the tibia and fibula back into shape with the help of eight steel rods and about four dozen screws. Unfortunately, the arteries weren't that easy. They were so riddled with little tiny holes and bone splinters that all the blood leaked out before it could travel down to my foot. I had sixteen doctors doing nothing but artery reconstruction and it still took sixteen hours! After they had all finished I was given a full-body cast so all my other injuries could heal. It took ten pints of blood to bring me back up to the "full" mark. And after surgery I had a continuous morphine drip added to my IV to keep me resting peacefully.

But I sure as hell wouldn't call it peacefully! The tripped-out dreams I was having were just way too weird! When you're only fourteen and you're high on morphine you see some pretty crazy shit—distorted Escher-esque playgrounds and classrooms; being tied down and surrounded by strange adults who are poking and prodding at me like I'm some guinea pig; hurling out of control down impossible steep hills on my skateboard; and, of course, flying through the air, unable to stop, always changing dreams right before I hit the ground.

On the third day I was rudely awakened from my morphine stupor by the sharp sting of a hypo full of adrenaline. When I was completely awake a doctor and a priest told me that during the night my new arteries had collapsed and were now unrepairable. I was hemorrhaging internally again, and they were afraid I might be developing gangrene. So the decision was made to take the leg off. When they told me that I would most certainly die if it wasn't removed, the decision was a simple one. I didn't dwell on the consequences at all, or act all melodramatic about it. I just said, "If that's what you have to do, do it." My childhood ended at that moment. I was instantly drafted into adulthood.

I was taken to pre-op where they began to remove the body cast from around my leg. They cut the cast up high on my thigh, and I asked my doctor, "Do you have to take the whole thing?" "No, no," he reassured me, "we just need to sterilize the area and make some room to work." He paused, then calmly added, "We're going to be cutting just below the knee."

MAN, that was creepy to hear! I was becoming more nervous and started having second thoughts about how my life would never be the same. I began to sweat uncontrollably.

However, once they peeled the cast off I knew the leg had to go. My nostrils were assaulted by the pungent stench of death. My foot had indeed become gangrenous, and several of the nurses and assistants recoiled in horror at the sight of the putrefied and fetid appendage. I was purple from the knee down, with splotches of black fading to solid black at my toes. It was starting to rapidly swell from the instant the cast was removed. "I think it's time to put him out," were the last words I heard as I was silently swept back into Morpheus's darkest and most forgotten pit.

I found myself in what appeared to be a barn—high vaulted ceiling, hayloft, and dusty air all in a reddish burgundy duotone. My skin tightened and I could feel the sweat evaporate on my forehead. The floor beneath my feet began to undulate. Then, whoosh, a searing pain wrenched my body as the shrieking exploded into shape and form. The spectral images passed through my terrified body, causing unimaginable pain. Upon exiting, they would circle above me, murmuring, singing, and laughing.

They flew toward me again and entered me with such force that I was thrown back, back into the abyss where pain and sanity have no meaning, a place where I sought refuge from the reality my earthbound body existed in, the reality of losing my leg. It's a reality I am reminded of every waking hour of the day, from the time I left intensive care to the time I spent in the drug rehab wing (to bring me down from my morphine addiction) to the time in physical therapy where I first learned to walk on my prosthetic leg.

Yes, August 10, 1982 is a day I will never forget, for I am reminded of it each day I wake up and put on my left leg. Life is never easy, and I accept this challenge with calm determination. I don't need anyone's pity, and I'm not bitter about it. My brother was originally supposed to go on that fateful ride, but I wouldn't wish this hellish fate on anyone else. If these are the cards I've been dealt in life, so be it.

how to get zines

Getting zines is easy. Publishers want you to read their zines—all you have to do is let them know you're interested. Zine publishing isn't a business—there are no prepaid postcards to drop in the mail, you don't get any bonus prizes for subscribing, credit cards aren't accepted, you can't simply say "bill me later."

Zines are created by regular people, just like yourself, who put them together in their spare time. They want you to read their zines, but they also would like you to help pay for the printing costs and postage.

The cost is usually minimal, just a few bucks and/or a couple of stamps. The most important thing to keep in mind is that most publishers don't have special bank accounts set up for their zines. Heck, many publishers don't have any bank accounts at all. So rule number one is this: **PLEASE SEND CASH.**

I know how everyone tells you not to send cash through the mail, but here we're just talkin' about a few bucks. If you're ordering a $20 subscription from someone, then a check might be a good idea, but for a buck or two, c'mon. It's very frustrating to return a stack of $1 checks because they're made out to your zine title. Take it from someone who knows, I've rarely had problems with cash but I've had massive problems with inaccurate checks.

In general, cash is preferable to money orders, which are preferable to checks. If you send cash, please wrap it carefully. Sending coins really sucks, though. If the price listed isn't a round number, then round it up to the nearest buck; or send a bunch of stamps; postage is expensive these days.

If you do send checks, please make the checks payable to the person who publishes the zine, not the zine title. If there's a publishing company listed, then the checks should be made out to it. Got it? And don't forget to tell them you read about their zine in this here book.

Many zine publishers print small quantities, so you may not be able to get the exact issue you want. If you really want a particular issue, please state it clearly in your request, otherwise, simply request the most recent or the next issue. Neatly print your name and address on your letter, or enclose a card with your payment. Envelopes often get lost, and return addresses along with them. Stapling the cash to the letter isn't a bad idea, either. Another important thing to keep in mind is **ZINE PUBLISHERS LIKE TO GET MAIL.**

If you order a zine because of something you read in here, please tell them what article it was that you liked. If you read something in here you found positively offensive and insulting, complain to them about it. Zine publishers want you to read their zine, but they'd love it even more if you told them what you thought. Publishing zines is a hard, lonely business and even a simple note of thanks will make someone's day. Send a letter, a postcard, a cartoon, a photo of your dog, or a copy of your zine. Which brings us to rule number three: **TRADING ZINES IS USUALLY PREFERABLE TO SELLING THEM.**

Many zine publishers are willing to exchange their zine for yours. And if you don't publish one, whatcha waitin' for? Most zine publishers trade for similarly priced, similarly sized, and similarly oriented zines. Music zinesters like to read music zines, while riot grrrls like to get other riot grrrl zines. When sending your zine for trade it's a really good idea to include a letter specifically stating that you'd like to trade zines and if you want to trade single copies or full subscriptions.

WHAT IF YOU DON'T GET YOURS? Don't be discouraged if you don't hear from them within a week. Zine publishing usually takes a backseat to most people's day jobs. More often than not, the reason you haven't heard from them right away is because your letter is on the bottom of a pile. Just be patient—wait a month or so before writing nasty letters.

Zine publishers are more often transient students than stable homeowners, so mail often gets lost. No one is getting rich publishing zines and people don't start zines just to rip off unsuspecting readers. It's quite possible that one out of five zine requests will go completely unanswered. Most likely, that publisher has no money to reprint their zine and spent your two bucks on some rice and beans. Think of it as a donation to a needy cause.

Following is contact and ordering information for all the zines mentioned in this volume. Also included is a selection of the most noteworthy zines, all come highly recommended and most offer a full selection of back issues.

2600 *The Hacker Quarterly*
The long-running guide to computer and telephone hacking secrets. $6.25 each; $21 for 4 issues.
Emmanuel Goldstein, 2600 Enterprises Inc., PO Box 752, Middle Island, NY 11953-0752
Email: info@2600.com—URL: http://www.2600.com/

8-Track Mind
Information for the obsessive 8-track tape collector. $2 each; $8 for 4 issues.
Russ Forster, PO Box 90, East Detroit, MI 48021-0090
URL: http://pobox.com/~abbot/8track/

American Job
True-life stories about people's less-than-glamorous jobs. $1.50.
Randy Russell, T.B.S. Publication, PO Box 2284, Portland, OR 97208-2284

ANSWER Me!
The controversial, but well-produced zine exploring the extremes of human behavior. $5.
Jim & Debbie Goad, Goad to Hell Enterprises, PO Box 31009, Portland, OR 97231
Email: Goad2Hell@aol.com

babysue
Very funny, but tasteless short stories and comics. $3 each; $12 for 4 issues.
S. Fievet, PO Box 8989, Atlanta, GA 30306-8989
Email: babysue@babysue.com—URL: http://www.babysue.com

The Baffler
The Journal That Blunts the Cutting Edge
An intelligent exploration into commerce and industry from a youthful, anti-capitalist aesthetic. $5 each; $16 for 4 issues.
The Baffler, PO Box 378293, Chicago, IL 60637

Batteries Not Included
A fanzine for fans of erotic X-rated videos. $3.
Richard Freeman, 130 W. Limestone Street, Yellow Springs, OH 45387

Beer Frame
A humorous look at the freakish products of consumerism. Current issues, $3; back issues; $4.
Paul Lukas, 160 St. Johns Place, Brooklyn, NY 11217
Email: krazykat@pipeline.com

Black Sheets
Kinky—Queer—Intelligent—Irreverent
A personal sex zine that covers the broad range of sexual expression. $6 each; $20 for 4 issues.
Bill Brent, Black Books, PO Box 31155-FA, San Francisco, CA 94131-0155
Email: BlackB@ios.com—URL: http://www.queernet.org/BlackBooks/

Boycott Quarterly
The complete guide to ongoing boycotts with extensive information about economic democracy. $5 each; $20 for 4 issues.
The Boycott Quarterly, PO Box 30727, Seattle, WA 98103-0727
Email: boycottguy@aol.com—URL: http://www.speakeasy.org/boycottq

Bust
A hip, women's oriented publication that isn't afraid of anything. $3 each; $12 for 4 issues.
Celina Hex & Betty Boob, Bust, PO Box 319, Ansonia Station, New York, NY 10023
Email: bust@aol.com—URL: http://www.BUST.com

Chemical Imbalance
An intelligent music zine that also explores cutting-edge literature and art. $4.95.
Mike McGonigal, PO Box 11435, Chattanooga, TN 37401

Chum
A Chicago-based humor publication that pokes fun at pop cultural icons. $3.
Darrin Sullivan, Chum Publishing, PO Box 148390, Chicago, IL 60614-8390
Email: chummag@aol.com

Cometbus
Aaron's long-running personal travel zine. $2.50; $4 for 2 issues.
BBT, PO Box 4279, Berkeley, CA 94704

Convivium
A Decidedly Unstuffy Food and Cooking Letter
A lighthearted food zine with personal stories and lots of recipes. $4 each; $23 for 6 issues.
Catherine S. Vodrey, Convivium, PO Box 835, East Liverpool, OH 43920-5835

Cooking on the Edge
Thoughtful stories and plenty of recipes for the curious cook. $3 each; $18 for 6 issues.
Jill Cornfield, 25 East 86th Street, 6-G, New York, NY 10028

Crank
Aggressive rants and harsh satire, all put together with a striking design. $3 each; $12 for 4 issues.
Jeff Koyen, PO Box 633, Prince Street Station, New York, NY 10012
Email: crank@inch.com—URL: http://www.crank.com

Crap Hound
A Picture Book for Discussion and Activity
An overwhelming compendium of bizarre imagery that was inspired by clip art books. $5.
Sean Tejaratchi, PO Box 40373, Portland, OR 97240-0373

Crawdaddy
The long-running, intelligent guide to rock music. $4 each; $12 for 4 issues.
Paul Williams, Crawdaddy, PO Box 231155, Encinitas, CA 92023

Cupsize
A lively zine which covers riot grrrl politics and bisexuality. $2.
Sasha and Emelye, PO Box 4326, Stony Brook, NY 11790-4326
Email: taneedha@suffolk.lib.ny.us

Curmudgeon's Home Companion
Dan Goldberg's Monthly Guide to Reality and Good Food
A serious food newsletter that reflects Dan Goldberg's cantankerous attitude. $3 each; $18 for 12 issues.
The Curmudgeon's Home Companion, PO Box 3312, Yountville, CA 94599
Email: MeanQzine@aol.com

Danger!
Well-written histories of pop-cultural oddities. $3.
Dan Kelly, PO Box 148161, Chicago, IL 60614
Email: DangerMag@aol.com

DIS
Southeastern Culture Quarterly
A thoughtful look at dead celebrities, vintage cartoons, and political analysis. (No longer being published.) $5.
Kim MacQueen, 922 8th Avenue, #3-B, Brooklyn, NY 11215
Email: macqueen@inx.net

The Disability Rag & Resource
An inspiring publication for the unabashed disabled person and anyone interested in human rights. $3.95 each; $17.50 for 6 issues.
The Disability Rag, PO Box 145, Louisville, KY 40201
Email: therag@ntr.net

Diseased Pariah News
A hard-hitting zine that mixes biting satire and rage against political indifference—created by people with AIDS and HIV. $3 each; $10 for 4 issues.
Diseased Pariah News, PO Box 30564, Oakland, CA 94604

DishWasher
Personal tales of low-budget travel and washing dishes in all 50 states. $1.
Pete, PO Box 8213, Portland, OR 97207-8213

Duplex Planet
Off-the-wall interviews and commentary from the semi-inspired elderly residents of nursing homes. $2.50 each; $12 for 6 issues.
David Greenberger, PO Box 1230, Saratoga Springs, NY 12866
Email: duplanet@global2000.net

Ersatz
A very hip overview of New York lifestyle and literature. $2.
S. S. Pratt, 441 West 37th Street, 2d Floor, New York, NY 10018-4015
Email: ersatz@echonyc.com

Evil®
The Newsletter for True Crime Book Fanatics
Reviews of true crime book and reports on serial killers. $1.50 + 2 stamps each; $8 for 6 issues.
Dan Kelly, PO Box 148161, Chicago, IL 60614-8161
Email: dangermag@aol.com

Exile Osaka
Japan Underground Bizarro World
Reports on what's happening in Japan from the perspective of a U.S. expatriate. $3.
Matt Kaufman, 3115 Brighton 6th Street, Apt. 6B, Brooklyn, NY 11235
Email: exileosaka@aol.com

Eye

Lengthy explorations into fringe medicine, unexplained phenomenon, pop culture flotsam, and conspiracy theory. $3.95 each; $9.95 for 4 issues.

Lisa Crosby, *EYE* magazine, 301 South Elm Street, Suite 405, Greensboro, NC 27401-2636

Email: eye@nr.infi.net—URL: http://www.infi.net/~eye

Factsheet Five

Indispensable as the best source of reviews and information about zines. $4 each; $20 for 6 issues.

Factsheet Five, PO Box 170099, San Francisco, CA 94117

Email: seth@factsheet5.com
URL: http://www.factsheet5.com

Farm Pulp

A wonderful mix of original writing and reprints, put together with an exciting, playful design. $3 each; $10 for 6 issues.

Greg Hischak, 217 NW 70th Street, Seattle, WA 98117-4845

Fat Girl

A zine for fat dykes and the women who want them

Political commentary and erotica that breaks the mold of the skinny waif look. $5 each; $20 for 4 issues.

Fat Girl, 2215-R Market Street, Suite 197, San Francisco, CA 94114

Email: airborne@sirius.com—URL: http://www.fatso.com/fatgirl/

Fifth Estate

One of America's longest-running alternative/anarchist newspapers. $2 each; $8 for 4 issues.

Fifth Estate, 4632 Second Avenue, Detroit, MI 48201

Food for Thought

A personal look at politics and food. (No longer being published.)

R. Seth Friedman, PO Box 170099, San Francisco, CA 94117

Email: f5seth@sirius.com

The Freakie Magnet

A compelling zine for collectors of breakfast cereal boxes and premiums. $5 each; $20 for 4 issues.

Kevin Meisner, 92B North Bedford Street, Arlington, VA 22201

Email: kmeisner@erols.com

Girlfrenzy

Comics and Music

A compendium of comics created by women cartoonists and discussions about riot grrrl music. $4 each; $10 for 5 issues.

Erica Smith, PO Box 148, Hove, East Sussex, BN3 3DQ, U.K.

Girlhero

A comic compendium featuring the ongoing story of Bottlecap the riveter. $3.

Megan Kelso, High Drive Publications, 4505 University Way N.E., #536, Seattle, WA 98105

Grade D But Edible

Comics, travel tales, and political commentary. $2.50.

Marko Krabschaque, 307 Hayworth Street, Knoxville, TN 37920

Gulp

A mini collection of wacky comics, single-page fiction, and never-dull poems. $3.

Andy Stevens, 21 Main Street, Binghamton, NY 13905-3127

Email: snevs@aol.com

Gun Fag Manifesto

Entertainment for the Armed Sociopath

The zine for gun collectors who buy guns to go out and shoot stuff with. $4 cash.

Hollister Kopp, Gun Fag Manifesto, PO Box 982, Culver City, CA 90232

Happyland

Tales of Times Square in all its decadent glory. (No longer being published.)

Selwyn Harris, 137 Emerson Place, Brooklyn, NY 11215

Hermenaut

Sophisticated analysis of pop culture mixed with a bit of philosophy. $3 each; $10 for 4 issues.

Joshua Glenn, PO Box 731, Williamstown, MA 02167

Email: editors@hermenaut.com—URL: http://www.birdhouse.org/words/hermenaut/

Hip Mama

The Parenting Zine

A feisty zine for single parents that explores the difficulties and joys of raising children in the '90s. $3.95 each; $15 for 4 issues.

Ariel Gore, HipMama, PO Box 9097, Oakland, CA 94613

Email: hipmama@aol.com—URL: http://www.hipmama.com

Hip-Hop Housewife

For Homemakers with Attitude

A delightful zine, full of observations on kids and lots of humorous essays. $1 each; $19.95 for 12 issues.

Fran Pelzman Liscio, TLR Publishing Corp., 19 Bellegrove Drive, Upper Montclair, NJ 07043

Hitch

The Journal of Pop Culture Absurdity

Well-written, well-edited, humorous attacks on stupid celebrities and cultural absurdities. $3.50 each; $20 for 6 issues.

Rod M. Lott, PO Box 23621, Oklahoma City, OK 73123-2621

Email: rlott@aol.com—URL: http://www.ionet.net/~twilken/hitched.shtml

Holy Titclamps

A personal examination of gay culture, lifestyle, and history. $3 cash each; $10 for 4 issues.

Larry-bob, PO Box 590488, San Francisco, CA 94159-0488

Email: larrybob@io.com—URL: http://www.io.com/~larrybob/

How Perfectly Goddamn Delightful It All Is, to Be Sure

A frighteningly honest account of sexual encounters and bitter feelings. (No longer being published.)

Sky Ryan, PO Box 1242, Sherwood, OR 97140

Hungry Freaks

A varied exploration into everything from film monsters to car culture to radical politics. $3.95.

Sebastian Goodrich, PO Box 20835, Oakland, CA 94602

Email: Hungryfrks@aol.com

Hysteria

Women, Humor, and Social Change

Feminist theory mixed with plenty of humor. (No longer being published.)

Deborah Werksman, Hysteria, Box 8581, Bridgeport, CT 06605

Email: hysteria@bridgeport.com—URL: http://www.bridgeport.com/hysteria/

It's a Wonderful Lifestyle

A Seventies Flashback

A loving deconstruction of the fads, lifestyles, products, and people of the 1970s. $4.

Candi Strecker, PO Box 515, Brisbane, CA 94005-0515

Email: strecker@sirius.com

Lies

Record reviews, short stories, and political commentary, all wrapped up in a nice, neat package. $3 each; $12 for 6 issues.

Matt Worley, 1112 San Pedro NE, #154, Albuquerque, NM 87110

Email: okeefine@aol.com—URL: http://cent.com/abetting/

Lilith

The Independent Jewish Women's Magazine

A glossy magazine which explores feminism and Judaism, and the nexus where the two meet. $5 each; $18 for 4 issues.

Lilith Publications, 250 West 57th Street, #2432, New York, NY 10107

Email: LilithMag@aol.com

Long Shot

Powerful photographs, wonderful short fiction, and some of the best poetry in the land. $8 each; $22 for 4 issues.

Danny Shot, Long Shot Productions, PO Box 6238, Hoboken, NJ 07030

The Lumpen Times

The leading Chicago magazine, reporting on everything happening in the underground. $4 each; $25 for 11 issues.

The Lumpen Times, 2558 West Armitage Avenue, Chicago, IL 60647

Maximumrocknroll

The grandfather of all punk zines. $3 each; $18 for 6 issues.

Maximumrocknroll, PO Box 460760, San Francisco, CA 94146-0760

McJob

Tales of crappy jobs and incompetent bosses. $2.

Julee Peezlee, Dyslexic, PO Box 11794, Berkeley, CA 94712-2794

Mouth

The Voice of Disability Rights

A vital publication that empowers disabled people with news, analysis, and satire. $4 each; $32 for 6 issues.

Lucy Gwin, Free Hand Press, 61 Brighton Street, Rochester, NY 14607

Mudflap

Great comix, wonderful travel stories, and reports on all that's happening in San Francisco. $1 + 2 stamps.

Greta, Mudflap, PO Box 410894, San Francisco, CA 94141-0894

Murder Can Be Fun

Detailed research into mass murders, serial killers, and naughty little boys and girls. $2.

John Marr, PO Box 640111, San Francisco, CA 94164

Email: mcbfjohn@aol.com

No Longer a Fanzine
Long-running punk zine that includes political commentary along with interviews. $2.
Joseph Gervasi, 142 Frankford Avenue, Blackwood, NJ 08012

Obscure Publications
The zine about zines which features plenty of news and in-depth discussions about the latest trends. $1 plus a stamp. $5 for 5 issues.
Jim Romenesko, 45 S. Albert Street, Saint Paul, MN 55105
Email: obscure@primenet.com

Organ & Bongos
A fun, hip zine that covers the music and films of vintage cocktail culture. $3 each; $12 for 4 issues.
Russell Scheidelman, PO Box 20396, Seattle, WA 98102
URL: http://www.compumedia.com/~callisto/organ.htm/

Out West
The Newspaper That Roams
This publication uncovers the weirdest sights that the West can offer. $3.50 each; $11.95 for 4 issues.
Chuck Woodbury, Out West, 9792 Edmonds Way, Suite 265, Edmonds, WA 98020
Email: outwestcw@aol.com—URL: http://www.outwestnewspaper.com/

Paranoia
The Conspiracy Reader
Well-researched conspiracy theory presented in a very clear style. $5 each; $15 for 4 issues.
Paranoia, PO Box 1041, Providence, RI 02903
Email: alhidell@aol.com

Pasty
Personal discussions on everything from sex to pooping to working in a condom store. $2.
Sarah-Katherine, PO Box 040160, Brooklyn, NY 11204-0160

Pills-a-Go-Go
Journal of Pills
One of the most interesting zines, featuring news about the hottest new drugs, OTC medicines, and the latest FDA crackdowns. $2 each; $12 for 6 issues.
Pills-a-Go-Go:, 1202 East Pike Street, #849, Seattle, WA 98122-3934

Pinch Point
If you want brutal emotions and stinging satire, check this out. $2.
Afrin Argon, PO Box 128, North Lima, OH 44452

Preparation X
Sophisticated discussions about TV, malls, raves, junk food, and all forms of childhood experiences. $1.50.
Todd Morman, PO Box 33561, Raleigh, NC 27636
Email: tmorman@email.unc.edu

Princess
Well-written, witty, and very girly, this one covers fashion with the occasional tongue in cheek. $3.
Francesca E. Castagnoli, 175 Fifth Avenue, Suite #2416, New York, NY 10010
Email: Prinsss@aol.com

Psychotronic Video
The leading guide to obscure, trashy videos. $5 each; $25 for 1 year (6 issues).
Michael Weldon, Psychotronic, 3309 Rt. 97, Narrowsburg, NY 12764-6126

Punk Planet
A thick punk zine that covers the scene without taking itself too seriously. $2.
Julia Cole, PO Box 1711, Hoboken, NJ 07030-9998
Email: punkplanet@aol.com

Queer Zine Explosion
The complete guide to gay- and lesbian-oriented publications. 2 stamps; $2 for 4 issues.
Larry-bob, PO Box 590488, San Francisco, CA 94159-0488
Email: lroberts@bellahs.com

The Realist
Paul Krassner's long-running newsletter of political satire. $2 each; $12 for 6 issues.
Paul Krassner, The Realist, PO Box 1230, Venice, CA 90294

Religion of the Month Club
A zine about obsession—in all its bizarre forms. (No longer being published.) $3.
I.A. Media, PO Box 2430, Santa Clara, CA 95055-2430
Email: erp@netuser.com—URL: http://www.netuser.com/~erp/ROTMC/

Rock & Rap Confidential
The intelligent rock music newsletter. Price: on request; $27 for 6 issues.
Dave Marsh, Rock & Rap Confidential, PO Box 341305, Los Angeles, CA 90034
Email: rockrap@aol.com—URL: http://www.kaiwan.com/rockrap/

Rollerderby
Lisa Carver's and Dame Darcy's zine of punk rock, comics, childhood, and an obsession with Fabio. $3 each; $10 for 4 issues.
Lisa Carver, PO Box 18054, Denver, CO 80218

Schlock
The Journal of Low-Brow Cinema and Culture
Enthusiastic look at bad movies on video and late night TV. $2.
John Chilson, 3841 Fourth Avenue, #192, San Diego, CA 92103

Scram
A great zine that covers music, comics, and all forms of pop culture. $5 each; $16 for 4 issues.
Kim Cooper, PO Box 461626, Hollywood, CA 90046-1626
Email: scram@bubblegum.net

Sidney Suppey's Quarterly and Confused Pet Monthly
A long-running zine that was a zine before there was even a word for it. $2.
Candi Strecker, PO Box 515, Brisbane, CA 94005-0515
Email: strecker@sirius.com

Slug & Lettuce
The punk rock contact network with lots of personal ads and record reviews. 55¢.
Christine Boarts, PO Box 2067, Peter Stuyvesant Station, NY 10009-8914

Small Press Review
The main resource for reviews and information on small press literature. $25 for 12 issues.
Dustbooks, PO Box 100, Paradise, CA 95967

Snevil
An exciting publication that covered sex, drugs, and comic books. (No longer being published.) $4.
Peter Bernard, Cowpuppy, PO Box 20342, New York, NY 10009

Sony Free
A one-shot newspaper which explored the Sony-sponsored music festival. (No longer being published.)
Todd Morman, PO Box 33561, Raleigh, NC 27636

Stay Free
Sophisticated pop cultural analysis with a backbone of political awareness. $4.
Carrie McLaren, 341 Lafayette Street, #558, New York, NY 10012

Strange-Looking Exile
The Comix Zine For Queer Dudes and Babes
Robert Kirby's anthology of cutting-edge comics by gays and lesbians. (No longer being published.) $4.25.
Stacy Sheehan, Giant Ass Publishing, PO Box 214, New Haven, CT 06502
Email: giantass@aol.com

Temp Slave
The zine for exploited temp workers everywhere. $3 each; $10 for 4 issues.
Keffo, PO Box 8284, Madison, WI 53708-8284

Theoryslut
Thoughtful discussions about sociological theory that avoid the trappings of academia. $3.50.
Theoryslut, PO Box 426965, San Francisco, CA 94142
Email: strghtup@well.com

Twilight of the Idols
Twisted stories of religious blasphemy and recipes for destruction. (No longer being published.) $3.
John Marmysz, 3739 Balboa Street, #142, San Francisco, CA 94121
Email: geinster@aol.com—URL: http://users.aol.com/geinster/nilB.html

Twisted Image
Hilarious comics that explore the absurdities of punk rock and modern society. (No longer being published.) $20 for set.
Ace Backwords, 1630 University Avenue, #26, Berkeley, CA 94703

Verbivore
A well-edited zine that explores the absurdity of modern society. $3 each; $10 for 4 issues.
Jeremy Braddock, 532 LaGuardia Place, Suite 573, New York, NY 10012-1428
Email: braddock@dept.english.upenn.edu—URL: http://www.zine.net/verbivore/

Whorezine
Politics, humor, resources, and stories by and for sex workers. $4.
Whorezine, 2300 Market Street, #19, San Francisco, CA 94114

World War 3 Illustrated
Politically aware, cutting-edge comics. $4.
World War 3 Illustrated, PO Box 20271, Peter Stuyvesant, New York, NY 10009

You Sank My Battleship!
One of the better chroniclers of pop culture—vintage monster movies, '70s TV, and the band Splitsville. $1 each; $4 for 4 issues.
Jennifer Marsh, 822 Guilford Avenue, #141, Baltimore, MD 21202

acknowledgments

I want to thank all the zine publishers, writers, illustrators, and photographers who helped me get this book together. Without them, this book would never have existed. Every effort was made to contact the copyright holder and get the correct information. I apologize for any errors or oversights.

Tales from the Old-School Zine Years," by Candi Strecker, reprinted from *Sidney Suppey's Quarterly*, March '96, with permission from the author; "Larry-bob's Guide to Selling Out," by Larry-bob, reprinted from *Holy Tit-clamps*, #13, February '94, with permission from the author; "What I was Taught," by John Kehoe, reprinted from *Gulp*, #6, Summer '94, with permission from the author, cover for "Gulp," reprinted by permission from Andy Stevens; "The Real Freakies," by Jackie End, reprinted from *The Freakie Magnet*, Vol. 1, #2, Winter '94, with permission from the author, art for "The Real Freakies" © Ralston Purina; "Yorinate in Kup," by Fran Pelzman Liscio, reprinted from *Hip-Hop Housewife*, with permission from the author; "Les Pennick's Smart Computer Shopper Tips," by Ken Davis, reprinted from *Hitch*, #8, August '95, with permission from the author; "Plasma Donation: Lazy Man's Dream or Needle-Ridden Nightmare?" by Ryun Patterson, reprinted from *Hitch*, October '95, with permission from the author, illustrations for "Plasma Donation: Lazy Man's Dream," used by permission from Ryun Patterson; "Why," by Bob Flanagan, reprinted from *Chemical Imbalance*, Vol. 2, #3, with permission from the estate of Bob Flanagan; "The Unbearable Melancholy Saga of the Rainbow Man," by Sam Green, reprinted from *Verbivore*, #2, Summer '95, with permission from the author, photographs for "The Unbearable Melancholy Saga of the Rainbow Man" used by permission from Nick Gunderson; "The Bad Boys of the Vatican," by Jeff Schweers, reprinted from *DIS*, Vol.1, #2, 1991, with permission from the author, illustrations for "The Bad Boys of the Vatican" used by permission from Jeff Schweers; "Side Effects of Living: 25 Reasons to Drink," by Michael Gorgei, reprinted from *Pinch Point*, #10, with permission from the author; "Surviving the Low Life: Better Living Through Crank," by Jeff Koyen, reprinted from *Crank*, #3, with permission from the author; "I Was a Manic-Depressive, Dope-Shooting, Suicidal Homosexual," by LMNOP, reprinted from *babysue*, Vol. 4, #2, with permission from the author; "The Sleaziest Theater in America," by Jack Stevenson, reprinted from *Celluloid All*, #5, with permission from the author, photographs for "The Sleaziest Theater in America" used by permission from Jack Stevenson; "24 Hours in Hell's Pantry," by Sam Pratt, reprinted from *Ersatz Monthly*, Vol. 26, #5, with permission from the author; "Surveillance," by Gregory Hischak, reprinted from *Farm Pulp*, #22, Nov./Dec. '94, with permission from the author; "Going Out," by Straight Up, reprinted from *Theoryslut*, #1, with permission from the author, illustrations for "Going Out" used by permission from Lizzard Henry; "The Day Pop Culture Moved In," by Ariel Gore, reprinted from *Hip Mama*, #1, Winter '94, with permission from the author; "Mr. Booze," by Russell Scheidelman, reprinted from *Organ & Bongos*, #1, September '95, with permission from the author, illustration for "Mr. Booze" used by permission from Russell Scheidelman; "Thus Spake Cinderfella," by A. S. Hamrah, reprinted from *Hermenaut*, #7, with permission from the author; "The Skinny on Hello Kitty," by Phoebe Harding aka "Coochie Galore," reprinted from *You Sank My Battleship!*, #1, with permission from the author; "At Home in the Seventies," by Candi Strecker, reprinted from *It's a Wonderful Lifestyle*, #2, with permission from the author, illustrations for "At Home in the Seventies" used by permission from Candi Strecker; "Keep on Shtuppin'," by Ace Backwords, reprinted from *Twisted Image*, #43, October '92, with permission from the author; "Picking up (Jack) Chicks," by Dan Kelly, reprinted from *Schlock*, #6, with permission from the author, art for "Picking up (Jack) Chicks" © Jack T. Chick; "Foreskins Forever! Circumcision Is Mutilation," by J. P. Slee(z)e, reprinted from *Batteries Not Included*, Vol. 1, #6, July '94, with permission from the author; "Pussy Galore," by Sarah-Katherine Lewis, reprinted from *Pasty*, #1, with permission from the author; "Private Club," by Robert Kirby, story by Orland Outland, reprinted from *Strange-Looking Exile*, #5, Winter '94, with permission from the author; "True Confessions," by Bill Brent, reprinted from *Black Sheets*, #4, with permission from the author; "I Was a Phone Sex Girl," by Connie L., reprinted from *Snevil*, #1, 1992, with permission from the author; "Lappsapoppin': Selwyn Harris Lap Dances Around NYC," by Selwyn Harris, reprinted from *Happyland*, #4, with permission from the author; "Puzzling Through the Peep Show," by Sasha Cagen, reprinted from *Cupsize*, with permission from the author; "My So-Called Sex Life," by Sky Ryan, reprinted from *How Perfectly Goddamn Delightful It All Is Sure to Be*, with permission from the author; "Thrift Store Record Shopping," by Kim Cooper and Richard Hutt, reprinted from *Scram*, #4, with permission from the author; "Diary of a Mad Tracker," by Malcom Riviera, reprinted from *8-Track Mind*, #77, Summer '93, with permission from the author, photographs for "Diary of a Mad Tracker" used by permission from Malcolm Riviera; "Hey, Sony—What Makes Those CD's So Darn Popular?," by Negativland, reprinted from *Sony Free*, #1, with permission from the author; "My Little Piece of Kurt," by Megan Kelso, reprinted from *Girlfrenzy*, June '94, with permission from the author; "The Invisible Link," by Al Aronowitz, reprinted from *Long Shot*, #16, 1994, with permission from the author; "The *Lies* Key to U.S. Politics, Circa 1996," by Jon Worley, reprinted from *Lies*, #6, November '95, with permission from the author; "Murder by Charity," by Lucy Gwin, reprinted from *Mouth*, September '93, with permission from the author; "Get Fat, Don't Die," by Michael C. Botkin, reprinted from *Diseased Pariah News*, #1, 1990, with permission from the author; "Crime and the Drug War," by Kirby R. Cundiff, Ph.D., reprinted from *Claustrophobia*, Vol. 3, #8, August '94, with permission from the author; "Barter Faires: Why Use Money At All?," by Zachary Lyons, reprinted from *Boycott Quarterly*, Vol. 2, #3, Winter '95, with permission from the author, "The Day My Hair Fell Off," by Lisa Palac, reprinted from *Bust*, #3, Spring '94, with permission from the author, illustrations for "The Day My Hair Fell Off" used by permission from Shaolin; "Transgressive Hair: The Last Frontier," by Susan Schnur, reprinted from *Lilith*, Vol. 20, #1, Spring '95, with permission from *Lilith*, photograph for "Transgressive Hair: The Last Frontier" used by permission from Jennifer Miller; "A Lifetime of Support," by Donna Black, reprinted from *Hysteria*, #8, Spring '95, with permission of Hysteria Publications; "Ask the Gear Queen," by April Miller, reprinted from *Fat Girl*, #4, with permission from the author; "A Closet Affair," by Francesca Castagnoli, reprinted from *Princess*, #2, November '95, with permission from the author; "The Best of Roadside Journal," by Chuck Woodbury, reprinted from *Out West*, #21, Winter '93, with permission from the author; "How to Be Cheap (Japan Style)," by Matt Exile, reprinted from *Exile Osaka*, #2, with permission from the author; "Never Put Anything in Yer Ear Except Yer Elbow," by Marko Krabschaque, reprinted from *Grade D But Edible*, #57, with permission from the author; "The Adventures of Richard," by Greta S., reprinted from *Mudflap*, 1992, with permission from the author; "Stitch," by Aaron Cometbus, reprinted from *Cometbus*, #28, with permission from the author; "Who is Bozo Texino?," by Bill Daniel, reprinted from *Cometbus*, #27, with permission from the author, photographs for "Who is Bozo Texino?" used by permission from Bill Daniel; "I Am Hobart: Dishwasher as Man and Machine," by Randy Russell, reprinted from *American Job*, #3, November '94, with permission from the author; "Thank You for Calling Sega," by Brendan P. Bartholomew, reprinted from *Temp Slave*, #6, with permission from the author; "Weekend Warrior: Working Part-time as a Soldier," by John Marmysz, reprinted from *Twilight of the Idols*, #7, with permission from the author; "What's the Worst Job You Ever Had?" by David Greenberger and Friends, reprinted from *Duplex Planet*, #127, with permission from the author; "Tales from the Scrypt," by Kim Perkins, reprinted from *Probable Cause*, Vol. 2, #1, Winter '95, with permission from the author; "The Seth Friedman Method," by R. Seth Friedman, reprinted from *Food for Thought*, #2, July '91, with permission from the author; "I Live for Olives," by Jill Cornfield, reprinted from *Cooking on the Edge*, Nov/Dec. '95, with permission from the author; "Giving Thanks for What You Don't Have," by Dan Goldberg, reprinted from *Curmudgeon's Home Companion*, November '93, with permission from the author; "First Dinner Parties, or Entertaining Without a Net," by Catherine S. Vodrey, reprinted from *Convivium*, Sept./Oct. '93, with permission from the author; "Talking About Chickens," by Rick Platt, Michael J. Johnson, and Owen Straum, reprinted from *Religion of the Month Club*, #20, with permission from the publisher; "Toast Modernism," © Paul Lukas, reprinted from *Beer Frame*, #6, with permission from the author; "Places to Shoot, Things to Shoot," by Holister Kopp, reprinted from *Gun Fag Manifesto*, #1, March '94, with permission from the author; "Shopper's Guide to COCOTS," by Count Zero, reprinted from *2600*, Vol. 9, #3, Autumn '92, with permission from the publisher; "Japan's Speed Culture," by Jim Hogshire, reprinted from *Pills-a-Go-Go*, #18, Spring '93, with permission from the author; "Venom: Poison or Panacea?" by Michael Crosby, reprinted from *Eye*, #5, with permission from the author; "Choo Choo Crash Bang," by John Marr, reprinted from *Murder Can Be Fun*, #17, with permission from the author; "Tim's True Tales of Horror and Gore," by Tim Hartman, reprinted from *Hungry Freaks*, #2, with permission from the author.